# The New Poverty in Canada

Ethnic Groups and Ghetto Neighbourhoods

# DEDICATION

*To those who fight for the rights of those who cannot fight for their own rights.*

## Acknowledgement

Many people have contributed to the successful completion of this book. Particularly, we would like to appreciate the help and support of Nicholas Tavouchis, Douglas Rennie, and Daly de Gonge, who kindly reviewed different segments of the manuscript and made useful editorial suggestions. The comments of Wayne Taylor, Dan Albas, Dan Chekki, and Ram Tiwari were also very helpful.

We would also like to acknowledge the financial support for the project by the Prairie Center of Excellence for Research on Immigration and Integration.

Last, but not the least, we would like to thank Keith Thompson for his quick reaction and effective way of bringing the manuscript to print in such a short time.

# The New Poverty in Canada

## Ethnic Groups and Ghetto Neighbourhoods

Abdolmohammad Kazemipur
and Shiva S. Halli

*University of Manitoba*
*Winnipeg, Manitoba*

**TEP**

THOMPSON EDUCATIONAL PUBLISHING, INC.

Toronto

Website: www.thompsonbooks.com
Email: publisher@thompsonbooks.com
Tel: (416) 766-2763
Fax: (416) 766-0398
Copies of the book may be ordered from General Distribution Services.

**Canadian Cataloguing in Publication Data**

Halli, Shiva S., 1952-
   The new poverty in Canada : ethnic groups and ghetto neighbourhoods
Includes bibliographical references.
ISBN 1-55077-108-6
1. Poverty - Canada. 2. Urban poor - Canada. 3. Minorities - Canada - Economic conditions - 20th century. 4. Immigrants -Canada - Economic conditions - 20th century.
I. Kazemipur, A. (Abdolmohammmad). II title.
HC120.P6H28   2000     305.5'69'097109049     C99-932905-7

Text and cover design: Danielle Baum

We acknowledge the support of the Government of Canada through the Book Publishing Industry Development Program for our publishing activities.

Printed in Canada.

1 2 3 4 5    06 05 04 03 02 01 00

# TABLE OF CONTENTS

# CHAPTER ONE

# The New Poverty Strikes Canada

During the 1990s, a new surge of poverty struck the industrial nations in the Western Hemisphere, particularly in North America. Resulting from such developments as slower economic growth at both national and international levels, globalization, and erosion of the welfare state, this poverty surge also coincided with an unexpected hardening of racial and ethnic cleavages and an unprecedented rise in the importance of small-scale communities. The simultaneous strike of these three forces created new configurations of poverty (Lawson and Wilson, 1995): a distinguishable ethnic and racial colour and a visible neighbourhood dimension. These configurations made the poverty of the 1990s a *new poverty*, distinct from that of the pre-1960s.

## The Rise of Poverty in the 1990s

While common to almost all industrial countries in the Western Hemisphere, the *new poverty* turned out to be more visible in North America (McFate, 1995). During the 1980s and the 1990s, the poverty rate of European countries remained mostly single digit, in clear contrast to the double-digit rates in North America (Danziger and Weinberg, 1994). Let's take Canada as an example. While in the 1980s, except for the recession years of 1983 and 1984, the poverty rate of Canadian families had remained relatively stable and even declined towards the end of the decade (12.1% in 1990, compared to 13.2% in 1980) (National Council of Welfare, 1992:11), this rate rose to 15.8% in 1991 and 16.3% in 1996.[1] In the United States, likewise, the poverty rate was higher in 1993 than in 1973 (Danziger and Weinberg, 1994:18). These poverty rates were high, not only relative to what they had been in the early 1970s, but also relative to what analysts expected and to what they were in other countries with similar standards of living (Danziger and Weinberg, 1994). The persistence of these high

---

1. Calculated by authors, using Census Data 1991 and 1996 CD-ROMs and Statistics Canada Low Income Cut-Offs.

poverty rates indicates that they are more than passing fluctuations attributable to temporary economic recessions and business cycles. Instead, they are here to stay.

There are other developments that may elevate the likelihood that the poverty rates of Canada and the United States will remain high, at least for a while: the declining income of the middle classes, and the rising concentration of wealth of the upper classes. In Canada, the distribution of income among five quintiles shows a recent decline, however small, in the income share of family units in the second and third quintiles (Gillespie, 1997:54). The process is intensified by the heavy tax burden imposed upon middle-class families in Canada. A similar trend in the United States raised the Gini Coefficient[2] to 0.403 in 1992, from 0.357 in 1975 (Danziger and Weinberg, 1994:23). This development puts many lower middle-class families on the verge of poverty.

Along with the declining income of the middle classes, there has been an increasing concentration of wealth and income within a narrow segment of the upper classes in both countries. Richardson (1996 [1992]:202), for instance, argues that "in 1978 the 17 largest enterprises controlled 63.6 percent of the assets of *Financial Post*'s largest Canadian corporations. By 1987, 74.5 percent of the assets of the 186 largest Canadian non-financial corporations were controlled by just 17 dominant enterprises." Similarly, in the United States, the share of the top quintile rose to 44.6% of total income in 1992, compared to 41.1% in 1972. The share of the top 5%, too, increased from 15.5 to 17.6% in the same period. This trend indicates that there is no room in the ranks of the higher classes for new companies. The middle-class families who drop out of the middle-income layers have only one way to go: down. This has one inevitable consequence: an increase in the population of the lower classes, whose income is the most likely to fall below the poverty line.

The new wave of poverty is different from the earlier ones, not only in size but also in the composition of its victims. The poverty rates of different groups in Canada show that, in 1996, female-headed, lone-parent families with children, women, unattached individuals, common-law families, young adults 18-24 years, and the elderly were over-represented among the poor.[3] A more or less similar pattern was also found in the United States (McFate, 1995). According to McFate (1995), certain social and economic developments catalyzed the emergence of this particular poverty pattern. The high poverty rate of women and single mothers (referred to in the poverty literature as the *feminization* of poverty), for instance, was aggravated by both the high divorce rate, which deprived many families of dual

---

2. Gini Coefficient is used as an indicator of income inequality. It varies from 0 to 1, with 0 indicating a total absence of inequality and 1 indicating the existence of full inequality.

3. Based on Statistics Canada 1996 Summary Tables, Statistics Canada web site.

incomes, as well as the concentration of female workers in low-paying, part-time jobs. The poverty of young adults was intensified by the slower economic growth of the 1980s and the 1990s, which led to an increase in unemployment. The poverty of the elderly is related, to some extent, to a demographic trend in industrial countries: an increasing percentage of the population is now living beyond their "earning years," leaving more citizens dependent on government support for longer periods. For this support, they are depending on a non-elderly population that has not been increasing in number as rapidly as they have. In the case of the elderly, it now seems as if the industrial nations have become captives of their past success.

Aside from these catalysts, however, there existed some real causes for this unexpected rise of poverty, one of which was the slower economic growth, both globally and locally. Globally, the rate of economic growth did noticeably drop, from 5.2% in the 1960s to 3.4% in the 1970s, 2.9% in the 1980s, and 0.6% for the early years of 1990s (Krahn, 1995:2.24). This trend was also reflected locally. In Canada, for example, an examination of three measures of economic growth—GNP, consumption expenditure, and personal disposable income—shows "a rapid increase over the period from 1960 to the mid-1970s, a slower and more erratic increase from the mid-1970s to the late 1980s, and stagnation or even decline since then" (Robson and Scarth, 1997:14). A slower-growing economy means a smaller economic surplus to be distributed among the population, a lower level of well-being, and hence a greater likelihood that lower-class families will fall victim to poverty.

Globalization was another factor that contributed to the rise of the new poverty. Resulting from conspicuous improvements in transportation, communication and information technologies, globalization significantly lessened the importance of geographical distance (Marchak, 1991), and helped capital and labour flow more easily and quickly all across the world. It provided a favourable ground for economic activities to be organized on a global, rather than local and national, scale. As a result, many economic activities, especially in the manufacturing sector, moved from industrial countries to developing ones in search of cheaper labour and less regulated working environments. Such relocations left behind pools of unemployed, who were the first victims to poverty-generating forces.

In addition to slower economic growth and globalization, and partly resulting from them, the gradual demise of the welfare state also had an aggravating effect on poverty. Welfare states were born in the industrial nations, out of the necessity to elevate the purchasing power of domestic populations in the aftermath of the 1929 Great Depression. The industrial nations erected various protective systems to help their domestic populations maintain a minimum level of income, that is, a minimum level of demand for commodities in the market (Teeple, 1995). The globalized capital was no longer concerned merely about the domestic market, as it had an enlarged market, namely, the whole world population. Hence, there was no need to preserve the purchasing power of domestic populations.[4] The result: the shrinkage of welfare systems and the gradual removal of the protective wall against poverty for vulnerable groups.

## Hardening of Racial and Ethnic Cleavages

Along with the increase in the level of poverty, the racial and ethnic cleavages hardened across the industrial world (Lawson and Wilson, 1995). Some even considered this development to be a result of the increased poverty, arguing that, in an age of shrinking resources, ascribed characteristics such as race, ethnicity, language, and religion might play important roles in the process of resource allocation (Hettne, 1995). The fact that poverty has hit certain racial and/or ethnic minorities harder corroborates that this possibility is not far from reality (hence, the concept of the *racialization* of poverty). In the United States, for instance, while poverty has affected all economically marginal groups, Lawson and Wilson (1995:693) argue "the urban black poor have been particularly devastated." They contend that a similar linkage between race or minority status and social exclusion and deprivation has also become increasingly evident in Western Europe, "due to the upsurge of xenophobia and racism since the late 1980s."

In Canada, poverty researchers have vastly studied the *feminization* of poverty (see, for instance, Duffy and Mandell, 1996 [1994]; Duffy et al., 1988; Duffy and Pupo, 1992; Goldberg, 1990), but largely ignored the *racialization* (or, in the case of Canada, *ethnicization*) of poverty. The studies closest to this issue are those on the situation of the Aboriginal and visible minorities in the Canadian economy. Although these studies were successful enough to lead to the adoption of the Employment Equity program, they were geared towards the middle-class, rather than the poor members' of these groups. The lower class (or in some cases, the "underclass") members of such groups were immensely neglected. Along similar lines, the possible linkage between immigration status and poverty went virtually unexplored.

## Rising Importance of Community Life

The surge of poverty and the hardening of ethnic and racial cleavages were contemporaneous with the rising importance of small-scale communities. This was far from an accidental turn of events. Mahon (1991) believes that, as a result of the gradual erosion of the nation-state, two other agents of action have emerged, one above nation-state, the other below it. Transnational corporations, international organizations, and special interest groups were examples of the former (Morss, 1991), local and regional units, of the latter. Barber (1996 [1992]) calls these players

---

4. For some excellent analyses of the effects of globalization on the welfare state, see Teeple (1995) and Olsen (1996).

the *McWorld* forces, which "demand integration and uniformity," and the *Jihad* forces, which are for "retribalization of large swaths of humankind." Given the declining role of the nation-state, these two groups of players or forces had to interact with one another directly.

Literature reflects this development greatly. In *The Spirit of Community*, Etzioni (1993), for instance, argues that the whole social and political map of the United States needs to be re-drawn with community at the centre. He argues that, in recent years, Americans have developed "a tendency to claim rights for themselves and to leave responsibilities to government" (p.4); and, in an effort to propose an alternative to this imbalance, he and a dozen other social thinkers formed a new movement they called "communitariansim" and launched a publication entitled *The Responsive Community: Rights and Responsibilities*. In addition to this, community is also approached as an economic entity, reflected in the a fast growing literature on Community Economic Development (CED). CED is, according to Shragge (1993:i), "a relatively new form of community intervention which has become so popular an approach, because it appears to reconcile both business and community interests." The underlying philosophy of CED strategy is that "the concrete needs of the local community must shape local practice" (Shragge, 1993:i-ii).

One problem, however, with all these communitarian approaches is that there is little agreement on what they mean by *community*. According to Sampson (1997), although the oldest known form of community was neighbourhood, that is, a geographic locale, the word is now increasingly used to refer to common membership in some association or group and shared values and deep commitments. With the expansion of cyberspace, "virtual community" is also added to the list. While all sorts of communities exert some influence on social life, local community based on shared space, that is, neighbourhood, remains a particularly important arena "for the realization of common values and the maintenance of effective social controls" (Sampson, 1997:2). This importance has led to the resurgence of research interest in the influences of neighbourhood (Brooks-Gunn et al., 1997).

This new interest is best reflected in the studies in the area of social geography. With an interest in "the spatial distribution of the social classes," this sub-discipline has been a vivid and fast growing area of research over the last few years (McDowell, 1997:xi). In this line of study, the reciprocal relationship between the constitution of places and people is closely examined (McDowell, 1997:xi). As an example, some social geographic studies have shown that West Hollywood has become an area of "alternative lifestyle," particularly for those associated with the music industry; relatively affluent gays and lesbians, for example, constitute about 30-40% of West Hollywood's population, giving rise to a distinct gay identity in this neighbourhood (Forest, 1995). This underscores the relationship between the social composition of neighbourhoods and the cultural identities they nurture. There is little doubt that the identity such a neighbourhood nurtures would be radically different if poor heterosexuals, rather than affluent homosexuals, constituted the majority of its population. The issue of the linkage between a neighbourhood's composition and its dominant sub-culture, indeed, has been the canon of a recently emerged body of literature on neighbourhood poverty and its racial and/or ethnic dimension.

## Ethnic Minorities in Poor Neighbourhoods

The interaction of the three aforementioned forces–the rise of poverty, the hardening of racial and ethnic cleavages, and the rise in the influence of neighbourhoods–gave the *new poverty* another unique feature: poverty has become spatially concentrated in certain neighbourhoods, known as "ghettos," "inner city," and "poverty zones;" and they have become the habitats mostly of minority groups. The minorities over-represented in poor neighbourhoods vary from one society to another: a domestic racial minority, the Blacks, in the United States (Jargowsky and Bane, 1991), and certain groups of immigrants in Europe (Brooks-Gunn et al., 1997; Musterd and Ostendorf, 1997; Lawson and Wilson, 1995).

One serious consequence of the heavy concentration of poor in certain areas of a city–that is, a high level of neighbourhood poverty–is the massive breakdown of social institutions in such areas (Massey and Eggers, 1990). Another is the severity of the problems of joblessness, family disruption, teenage pregnancy, failing schools, crime, and drug abuse (Massey and Denton, 1993). The prevalence of such social ills in a neighbourhood can, in turn, have serious consequences for the socialization of the younger generation (Lawson and Wilson, 1997). This often occurs through a process called *transmission by percept*, whereby a person's exposure to certain attitudes and actions is so frequent that these become a part of his or her own outlook (Wilson, 1996). In this manner, individual skills, habits, and styles are often shaped by the frequency at which they are found within the community. The visible presence of minorities in such neighbourhoods can increasingly stigmatize them, leading to their social exclusion from the mainstream society.

Such social disparity can provide a favourable ground for growth of racist and anti-immigrant sentiments. The division of public opinion along racial lines in the aftermath of the O.J. Simpson trial in the United States and the antagonistic views of Quebec separatists in Canada towards other ethnic groups after their failure in the 1995 referendum were manifestations of such a development in North America. Similar events have also occurred in Europe: attacks on Algerians and Black Africans in several French cities, riots in black neighbourhoods in Britain, onslaughts on African immigrants in several Italian cities, tensions between Christians and Muslims as well as between racial minorities and whites in several Dutch cities, and so on (Wilson, 1996). Such events were mostly informed by an "upsurge of xenophobia and racism since the late 1980s" (Lawson and Wilson, 1995:693), which itself resulted from the fact that, as economic conditions worsened, many in the majority population come to view the growth of minorities as part of the problem (Wilson, 1996).

For social scientists, the aforementioned studies opened a new line of research with a heavy focus on neighbourhood poverty. Some examined the effects of *neighbourhood poverty*, such as the poor quality of civil services or high crime rates (e.g., Massey et al., 1991; Crane, 1991; Mayer, 1991). Others focused on causative factors, such as migration (Fitchen, 1995; Nord, Luloff and Jensen, 1995), housing (Wilson, 1995), employment (Iceland, 1995), public housing projects (Massey and Kanaiapuni, 1993), and urban housing markets (Massey et al., 1994).

The spatial concentration of poverty, somewhat surprisingly, has not been of particular interest to Canadian researchers. In contrast to the vast number of studies on this issue in the United States and Europe, there is no comprehensive exploration of the magnitude and seriousness of the *spatial concentration of poverty* (SCOP) in Canada. There are some journalistic writings on the issue but they lack a sharp focus on SCOP, addressing the problem of general poverty or the underclass (see, for instance, Welsh, 1994; Goar, 1993; Ruttan, 1992; Cheney, 1988). The few scholarly works on SCOP, on the other hand, do not provide a comprehensive picture that allows a comparative vision; some have approached the issue too broadly, making general international comparisons (see Hajnal, 1995); others, too narrowly, limiting themselves to few cities (see Ley and Smith, 1997). The studies equipped with the right scope lack the proper focus, as they tend to discuss spatial concentration of poverty in the broader context of inequality (see MacLachlan and Sawada, 1997). All in all, compared to the United States, the spatial concentration of poverty in Canada has gone virtually unnoticed.

## The Aims and Organization of the Book

Building upon the previous research on SCOP, the present study has two major aims: to provide a comprehensive picture of Canadian cities with regard to the *spatial concentration of poverty* (that is, *neighbourhood poverty*), and to examine whether or not there is an ethnic dimension associated with it. Neighbourhood, poverty and ethnicity, therefore, constitute the conceptual building blocks of this book.

These conceptual building blocks give the study a multidisciplinary nature; neighbourhood has been of special interest to geographers; poverty has concerned mainly economists; ethnicity has received the attention of sociologists. This multidisciplinary nature acts as an assurance of authenticity, because it is now relatively established that, in isolation from each other, the social sciences cannot succeed. The conventional distinctions among the social sciences are now increasingly seen as outdated, for some, unproductive legacies of the nineteenth century (Wallerstein, 1987). Lively debates and significant findings are increasingly found in the boundary areas of different disciplines. The subject matter of the following chapters reflect this multi-dimensional nature.

Chapter Two, "Neighbourhood Poverty: The Magnitude," begins with a review of the literature on poverty. It provides a detailed discussion of the debate on the definition of poverty, particularly the *relative* versus the *absolute* approaches. This is followed by a discussion of the major theories of poverty, along with the studies on the groups most severely affected by the recent rise of poverty in the 1990s, and their implications for public policy.

The chapter then focuses on neighbourhood poverty (or spatial concentration of poverty). The aims of this section of Chapter Two are two-fold. The first aim is to provide a conceptual backdrop for neighbourhood poverty, its importance, and its potential consequences for those most severely affected by it. It is particularly discussed that living in a poor neighbourhood can lead to isolation from the mainstream culture, development of a culture of poverty, and the suppression of the desire for change through certain psychological processes. The second aim is to provide a comparative picture of the magnitude of neighbourhood poverty in Canadian cities. In order to approach this goal, two statistical measures of neighbourhood poverty are suggested and applied. One measure looks at the groupings of neighbourhoods into five poverty categories; the other looks at the distribution of population in these categories.

The focus of the book, however, is to examine how different groups are represented in poor neighbourhoods. Such representation tends to result from two factors: the group's initial level of concentration in urban space and its level of poverty. The first factor is address in Chapter Three, the second in Chapter Four.

Chapter Three, "Neighbourhood: The Ethnic Dimension" begins by offering a conceptual framework to explain the factors behind the rise of ethnic sentiments in the last decade or so. While acknowledging the newness of the phenomenon and the fact that there is as yet no comprehensive and adequate theory available to explain why such an unprecedented rise of ethnicity has occurred, the chapter highlights some of the possible reasons that may have contributed to this. The chapter then focuses on the spatial concentration of ethnic groups in Canadian urban neighbourhoods. First, the literature on spatial trends is discussed; then, the empirical measures employed in previous studies are introduced; and finally, a comparative picture of the spatial concentration and/or segregation of various ethnic groups in different Canadian cities is presented and discussed.

The second factor is addressed in Chapter Four, "Poverty: The Ethnic Dimension." The chapter begins with a descriptive picture of the poverty of ethnic groups. Through an examination of the level of poverty for members of different ethnic groups living in Canadian cities, the point is made that the problem of poverty seems to be more acute for those groups consisting of recent immigrants to Canada from developing countries. This raises the conceptual possibility that the poverty experience of such groups may have to do with problems associated with their immigration status: unfamiliarity with the language of the host country, the mismatch of occupational skills and job market demands, possible discriminatory practices, and so on. The chapter, therefore, includes the immigration status and its associated variables as integral parts of the analysis of the poverty of ethnic groups.

Based on the poverty literature, and as an effort to understand and explain the determinants of ethnic groups' poverty, three possible explanations are offered in Chapter Four: *human capital* factors, *structural* factors, and *assimilation and/or integration* factors. The first looks at variables such as education, age, and migration. The second involves the sector of the economy in which a person works, along with the full-time or part-time nature of the job. The third takes into account variables associated mainly with immigrants, such as language skills, year of immigration, and age at the time of arrival. A regression model is then developed to test the validity of the alternative explanations. Given that being an immigrant appears to contribute to the likelihood of one's living in poverty, distinct logistic regression models are developed for the whole population and its immigrant and non-immigrant sub-populations.

By detailed examinations of the neighbourhood dimension of poverty, the ethnic dimension of neighbourhood, and the ethnic dimension of poverty, Chapters Two through Four set the stage for a simultaneous examination of these three dimensions: *neighbourhood, poverty*, and *ethnicity*. Chapter Five, "Neighbourhood Poverty: The Ethnic Dimension," attempts to examine the issue in an integrated fashion. The chapter begins with an account of the recent attention given to neighbourhood poverty, followed by a discussion of the major hypotheses put forth to explain the magnitude of the neighbourhood poverty of ethnic groups. Two hypotheses are particularly singled out: the *mismatch hypothesis* and the *segregation hypothesis*. Given the lack of any previous study of this issue in Canada, it is particularly important to test these hypotheses within the Canadian context. Still, an additional effort is made to improve these hypotheses by introducing the notion of the *culture of poverty* as an integrated part of the conceptual model. In the expanded conceptual framework, it is hypothesized that the over-representation of an ethnic group in extremely poor neighbourhoods may lead to their subscription to the culture of poverty. A series of multiple regression models are developed to empirically test the discussed hypotheses.

It may be helpful here to add a general point about the nature of Chapters Two through Five. Chapters Two and Three provide the descriptive picture of the two major components of this study; that is, neighbourhood poverty and ethnic spatial concentration and/or segregation. The next two chapters involve the analytic and inferential analysis of the ethnic groups' poverty and their neighbourhood poverty. The theoretical discussions in the first two chapters are meant only to provide the reader with a conceptual backdrop for the issues under study. The theoretical discussions in the latter two chapters, however, are conceptual frameworks within which the issues under study can be explained and analyzed. The research hypotheses, therefore, appear only in Chapters Four and Five.

Chapter Six, "Conclusion, Implications, and Limitations of the Study," provides a summary of the findings, along with their policy implications. After a discussion of the data limitations a study of this nature encounters, some suggestions for data generation practices are made. Also, the underlying assumptions of the study are discussed, and some new directions for further research are offered.

# CHAPTER TWO

# Neighbourhood Poverty: The Magnitude

The poverty surge in Western industrial nations in the 1990s has revived an interest in poverty research, after a decade of total negligence of the issue (Burton, 1992). The previous wave of poverty research, which produced some very lively accounts of poverty in the late 1960s and early 1970s (see, for instance, Reid, 1972; Deiter, 1970; Sheffe, 1970; Harp and Hofley, 1971; Adams et al., 1971; Mann, 1970; Johnson, 1974; Lederer, 1972), came to an abrupt halt, partly as a result of some relative successes in anti-poverty struggle (Danziger et al., 1994). In the early 1990s, however, writing on poverty-related issues regained prominence (Burton, 1992).

While this new surge of poverty was common to most Western industrial nations, it was more severe in North America than in Western Europe (McFate, Smeeding, and Rainwater, 1995). The similar poverty trends of Canada and the United States, along with other historical commonalities, has made the Canadian poverty debate in many ways similar to its American counterpart (on Canada, see, for example, Chekki, 1995; Sarlo, 1992, 1994; Canadian Institute of Child Health, 1994; Bolaria and Wotherspoon, 1995; and on the U.S., Burton, 1992; Danziger et al., 1994; Wilson, 1987, 1996; McFate, Lawson, and Wilson, 1995). Nevertheless, neither the diversity nor the intensity of discussion in Canada has been as great as in the United States. This could partly result from a particular image in the minds of many Canadians of Canada as a "classless" society; for them, poverty has been invisible (Hofley, 1971). This, in turn, results from the fact that, according to Hofley (1971:104), "the vast majority of persons with whom they interact are, just as they themselves are, members of the middle class." The dominance of such a perception of social reality can seriously hinder the giving of any considerable attention to people of lower classes as well as to the poor. Despite this, however, the debate on poverty in Canada is intensifying.

In what follows, a review of the major themes of concern in the recent poverty debate both in Canada and the United States is presented. The debates are mainly clustered around such issues as the definition of poverty, its causes, the groups more vulnerable to it, and the related public policies. The literature on neighbourhood poverty is then discussed at length.

## A Review of Poverty Literature

### *The Definition of Poverty*

While no one seems to disagree with the commonsensical definition of *poverty* as the state of lacking adequate means to satisfy "basic needs," the issue of how to decide what constitutes basic needs has stimulated a great deal of disagreement. The primary efforts to define poverty were based on the implicit assumption that basic needs, by definition, were impervious to social and cultural contexts. Drawing on such an assumption, then, the poverty line was formulated as the financial resources an individual or a family needs in order to purchase the basic necessities of life or to survive at a subsistence level. It soon became evident, however, that poverty is a relative, and not universal, experience; since there are different standards of living, there are also different standards for poverty. This realization forced researchers and policy makers to define poverty in relation to particular groups. Despite this modification, the initial perception remained, still appealing to some. In poverty literature, this conceptual duality has been referred to in terms such as *subsistence criteria* versus *relative deprivation* (Whyte, 1971), *basic needs* versus *relative* approach (Sarlo, 1992, 1994), *economic* versus *socio-cultural* (Oster et al., 1978), *physical* versus *social* (Ross et al., 1994), and more commonly, *absolute* versus *relative* definition.

The implication of the two concepts and definitions of poverty, i.e., *absolute* versus *relative*, is profound. For example, those who adhere to the absolute definition have excitedly reported that, in the early 1990s, Canada's "real poverty rate" was less than 4%, and not the 12.1% official rate (see, for instance, Sarlo, 1994). Others, according to Chekki (1995:250), have "chided Canada for lack of progress on reducing poverty." This has encouraged a few other, less common, measures of poverty, each adopting a variation of the two major approaches mentioned earlier.[5]

Despite the multiplicity of poverty measures suggested, most discussions of poverty in Canada during the last 25 years have relied on a measure of poverty suggested by Statistics Canada–Low Income Cut-Offs (LICO). According to Krahn (1995:2.18), the data obtained from the annual Survey of Consumer Finances indicate that the average Canadian family spends about 36% of (pre-tax) income on the basic necessities (food, shelter,

---

5. Some of the suggested measures of poverty are: Statistics Canada Low Income Cut-Offs, Canadian Council on Social Development Income Lines, Senate Committee Poverty Lines, Metropolitan Toronto Social Planning Council Budget Guides, Montreal Diet Dispensary Guidelines, Fraser Institute Poverty Lines, Provincial Social Assistance Rates, and Public Opinion-based poverty lines. For a detailed discussion of these measures, see Ross (1994:13-25).

and clothing). To establish the LICO line, Statistics Canada adds 20% to this figure. Hence, any family spending more than 56% of gross income on the basic necessities is considered poor. The low-income lines are then calculated for communities and for families of various sizes within those communities. Table 2-1 contains the poverty lines for families and communities of different sizes.

The Statistics Canada's LICOs have recently come under fierce attack by Fraser Institute researchers. They argue that a relative definition of poverty such as the Statistics Canada's LICOs gives a false perception of the poverty status in society, because it looks at the bottom end of the income scale as the poverty area, and there will always be a bottom end in this scale. This means that, no matter what policies are adopted, there will always remain a certain level of poverty in Canada due to the deficiencies of the measure used (Sarlo, 1992, 1994). They have also become cynical of the poverty researchers, claiming that they prefer LICOs, partly because it will keep alive their subject of interest, poverty. For them, the Fraser Institute researchers contend, poverty research is viewed as a business rather than a sincere effort to deal with a social problem.

TABLE 2-1

THE LOW-INCOME CUT-OFFS FOR FAMILIES AND UNATTACHED INDIVIDUALS, **1991**

| Family Size | Size of Area of Residence | | | | |
|---|---|---|---|---|---|
| | 500,000 or more | 100,000 to 499,999 | 30,000 to 99,999 | Small Urban Areas | Rural Areas (Farm and non-Farm) |
| | 1990 Dollars | | | | |
| 1 | 14,155 | 12,433 | 12,146 | 11,072 | 9,637 |
| 2 | 19,187 | 16,854 | 16,464 | 15,008 | 13,064 |
| 3 | 24,389 | 21,662 | 20,926 | 19,076 | 16,605 |
| 4 | 28,081 | 24,662 | 24,094 | 21,964 | 19,117 |
| 5 | 30,680 | 26,946 | 26,324 | 23,997 | 20,887 |
| 6 | 33,303 | 29,248 | 28,573 | 26,047 | 22,672 |
| 7 or more | 35,818 | 31,460 | 30,734 | 28,017 | 24,385 |

Source: Statistics Canada, Census Data CD-ROM on Families, 1991

Instead of the relative LICOs, the Fraser Institute has suggested an alternative measure based on an absolute definition of poverty. To formulate this definition, they have first listed the "basic needs" of Canadians in detail and then estimated the costs of satisfying those needs in cities and for families of different sizes. This has resulted in a different set of poverty lines, far lower than LICOs, based on which they have argued that the problem of poverty in Canada is far less serious than is often thought. Despite this proposal, LICOs are still vastly used as poverty indicators (see Sarlo, 1992, 1994).

While the LICOs are commonly considered to be the poverty line, the irony is that Statistics Canada has never taken them as such. In a recent article, the chief statistician of Canada, Ivan P. Fellegi, has commented on the poverty line and LICO. His observations are worth citing at length.

> [T]here is still no internationally accepted definition of poverty.... The lack of an internationally accepted definition also reflects indecision as to whether an international standard definition should allow comparisons of well-being across countries compared to some international norm, or whether poverty lines should be established by reference to the norms within each country.... Both the relative income and the absolute income approaches involve judgmental and hence ultimately arbitrary choices. In the case of the relative approach, the fundamental decision is what fraction of the overall average or median income constitutes poverty. Is it one half, one third, or some other proportion? In the case of the absolute approach, the number of individual judgements required to arrive at a poverty line is far larger. Calculating the minimum income that is needed to purchase the "necessities" of life first requires deciding on what constitutes a "necessity" in food, in clothing, in shelter and in a multitude of other purchases from transportation to reading material.... [P]overty is intrinsically a question of social consensus, at a point in time and in the context of a given country.... It is through the political process that democratic societies achieve social consensus in domains that are intrinsically judgmental.... In Canada the political powers have not expressed their views as yet: neither the provincial nor the federal governments have set official poverty lines.... Statistics Canada does not and cannot measure the level of "poverty" in Canada.... [T]he Low Income Cut-Offs ... identifies those who are substantially worse off than the average. Of course, being significantly worse off than the average does not necessarily mean that one is poor (Fellegi, 1996:1-4).

Even if there were agreement among poverty researchers as to which measure to use, there is still a further complication. Since both of the above measures rely on income to decide the purchasing power of a family, a disagreement arises, according to Ruggles (1990), over which income to use: pre-tax or post-tax, with government transfers or without it, documented or non-documented income. Also, there is uncertainty as to how to account for non-cash income in the form of food, inexpensive housing, free health services, and child-care, which otherwise would have been a financial burden; and, how to account for wealth, along with income. A radically different view even suggested the dropping of "income" as a basis of comparison and the use of "consumption," instead. The latter group raised the problem of how to define the poverty status of two families with the same decent income, one generous in spending, the other conservative; should both families be considered non-poor, even if the members of one are starving? The seriousness of such a question has opened the gate for an entirely different approach in which the consumption pattern, rather than income level, is considered as the indicator of a family's well-being (see Mayer, 1995).

There is no prospect of a settlement of these disagreements. The main reason for this situation is the fact that the adoption of each one of the suggested measures involves what Fellegi called "judgmental choices." One such "judgmental choice" is that there is no universal definition of "basic needs." Another is that a sophisticated measure will be of little use if there is no reliable way to gather data on it. Such "judgmental choices" have resulted in the ongoing, wide use of the relative measures of poverty, both in Canada and the United States.

## *The Cause(s) of Poverty*

A wider disagreement exists over what causes poverty. The numerous accounts of poverty generation mechanisms cluster around three sets of factors: *individual, structural,* and *cultural.* The emphasis on the individual factor is perhaps the oldest explanation; it is also the most appealing in North America, due to the preponderance of an individualistic orientation (Tepperman, 1994). The structural and cultural explanations of poverty, on the other hand, deal with larger trends in society, rather than with individuals. The two, however, have long been viewed as being opposed to each other (Greenstone, 1991).

Despite its longer history, the individualistic explanation of poverty found its most systematic expression in the ideas of American psychologist David McClelland (McClelland, 1972; McClelland and Winter, 1969). In an effort to understand the backwardness of Third World countries, he raises the point that the factor missing in these countries is a particular type of personal orientation, or a personality component. He calls this missing component the "Need of Achievement" (NA): a strong and serious eagerness towards accomplishment, innovation, risk taking, entrepreneur ship, and long-term planning. The "NA viruses," according to McClelland (1972), need to be diffused in a society before it can step out of the poverty trap. Although in its original formulation the NA theory addressed the poverty of nations, it was later used as an explanation of individual poverty as well.

Stemming from a Marxist origin, the structural view puts more emphasis on socio-economic structure as the cause of poverty. The poor exist, according to this view, because of the uneven distribution of wealth and power inherent in class-based societies. In the capitalist system, for example, work is organized so that the economic surplus produced by the workers ends up in the hands of the bourgeois class. As a result, in a capitalist system, two inevitable trends coincide: "the expansion of existing wealth" with "degradation of the labourer, and a most straitened exhaustion of his vital powers" (Marx, 1973 [1939]:750). The inevitable outcome of this process is the widening gap between capitalists and the working class, leaving the former with enormous wealth and the latter with devastating poverty. Faced with the inadequacy of the orthodox formulation of this view, the neo-Marxist thinkers expanded it with the "split labour market theory" (Satzewich, 1998). This theory holds that the economy is structurally divided into two sections, one with a tendency to grow, the other to sink; those employed in the latter are destined to poverty. Despite their slight differences, both versions of the structural view contend that poverty has its origin somewhere beyond the personality or lifestyle of the individual; it is caused by macroeconomic trends in society.

The cultural perspective, by contrast, looks for the source of poverty in cultural habits and lifestyles, such as a strong belief in fatalism, helplessness, dependence and inferiority, weak ego, and a strong present-time orientation. The source of the problem is, as proponents of this view emphasize, "a culture that irrationally sanctions dysfunctional conduct" (Greenstone, 1991:399). In many respects, this view bears some resemblance to the individualistic approach; the difference is in the scale: one attributes poverty to an individual lifestyle, the other to a collective culture.

The cultural view has been an extension of the notion of *culture of poverty* suggested by Oscar Lewis (1966). The extension, however, diverges markedly from the way the theory was originally formulated, as this theory has been often misconceived and misrepresented. In Lewis's ideas, conservatives found a rationale for blaming the poor for their poverty. Marxists, on the other hand, criticized Lewis for overlooking the economic and class factors. When one compares these interpretations with what Lewis actually said, one finds them to be pretty misleading.

In a short article written in 1966, Lewis (1966) raises a number of interesting points that both his critics and his supporters seem to have disregarded. First, he rejects the notion that culture of poverty is "just a matter of deprivation or disorganization, a term signifying the absence of something"; it is, rather, "a culture in the traditional anthropological sense in that it provides human beings with a design for living, with a ready-made set of solutions for human problems, and so serves a significant adaptive function" (Lewis, 1966:222). This point alone invalidates many of the critiques of the notion of culture of poverty made by Marxists. If a culture of poverty emerges among the poor as a strategy to cope with their poverty, it cannot be, as Marxists tend to claim, the cause of poverty. Poverty precedes the culture of poverty; therefore, the latter cannot have a role in the genesis of the former.

Second, a culture of poverty does not develop among all the poor. Lewis stresses that "there are numerous examples of poor people whose way of life I would not characterize as belonging to this subculture": Jews in Eastern Europe, the poor in post-revolutionary Cuba, the Algerian poor, and about 80% of the American poor (1966:226). So, although the culture of poverty accompanies poverty, according to Lewis this is far from a universal and inevitable accompaniment.

Third, once the culture of poverty is formed, Lewis (1966:224) argues, "it tends to perpetuate itself." In this respect, the culture of poverty is like general culture: it takes on a life of its own, resists change, and reinforces the socio-economic circumstances it corresponds with in many ways, including socialization. As Lewis points out, "by the time slum children are six or seven they have usually absorbed the basic attitudes and values of their subculture. Thereafter they are psychologically unready to take full advantages of changing conditions or improving opportunities that may develop in lifetime." This means that the culture of poverty more heavily affects the second generation of the poor. For them, it is no longer a coping strategy; it is, rather, a way of life.[6]

The crux of misunderstanding about the culture of poverty is, we believe, the confusion between the *creation* and *perpetuation* of poverty. While the former can be, as Marxists argue, a function of socio-economic structure, the latter arises from the culture of poverty itself. The change of conditions may remove the poverty but does not necessarily eradicate the culture of poverty, after it has found "a life of its own." It may take at least one generation for a new culture to come about. One can find many examples of this: the perseverance of the original culture among the first generation of immigrants, the persistence of cultural habits among the settled nomads, and so on. We can, therefore, safely argue that Oscar Lewis's thesis is addressing the inter-generational perpetuation of poverty through the culture of poverty, rather than the initial generation of poverty. Besides, the relationship between poverty and the culture of poverty does not need to be rigid and one-way. Simpson and Yinger (1972:176), for example, have admirably linked the two, by suggesting that "low opportunity leads to low motivation and skill which, when widely shared, leads to values adapted to poverty that prevent recognition or pursuit of available opportunities."

The different views on the causes of poverty can be empirically examined against the distribution of poverty among various segments of a population. If the source of the problem is individual lifestyle, we should not normally expect to see distinguished patterns of poverty for different groups; the individual factor creates an all-inclusive randomness. If the problem is caused by cultural orientation, we should see some patterned variations of poverty along cultural lines. For the structural factor to be valid, we need to spot different levels of poverty among those with different economic statuses. For these reasons, the discussion on causes of poverty often leads to an examination of the groups more severely affected by poverty, that is, the vulnerable groups.

6. Interesting enough, about a decade ago, Tatyana Zaslavskaya, a Russian Marxist sociologist who became the head of the first poll institute in Russia at the time of Michael Gorbachev, suggested a very "Lewisian" type of analysis, referring to the major impediments to Gorbachev's reforms. She pointed out that Gorbachev was facing resistance to reforms among three layers of society; one, the top leadership in the Communist Party and politburo, second, the middle-rank managers, and third, the rank-and-file people. With regard to the last groups, Zaslavskaya mentioned that during the 70 years of a corrupted communist regime, the Russians had developed a particular lifestyle and culture in order to survive, both economically and psychologically. The result of this culture is a specific type of personality she had called "Homo-Sovieticus." While people support the reforms and like to see communist regime gone, Zaslavskaya argued, their culture does resist the reforms.

## *Vulnerable Groups*

A great deal of recent research has been concentrated on identifying the vulnerable groups in the face of poverty. Some of the groups most severely hit by poverty consist of females (with or without children), young adults of 18-24 years, children, and the elderly. Using 1996 census data, Table 2-2 provides the poverty rates of these and many other categories of people in Canada. The rates included are arranged in declining order, with the overall poverty rate of Canadian families at the top (16.3%) for comparative purposes.

One of the most vulnerable groups in Canada is the young adults, with a poverty rate of more than 1.5 times the national rate. A similar situation exists for young adults in other industrial countries, such as the United States, Britain, Germany, Netherlands, and Sweden; the vulnerability of this group increased in the 1980s because they tended to have both higher rates of unemployment and lower wages (McFate et al., 1995). In the United States, which is regarded as having the most dynamic economy of all, according to Rifkin (1995:167), out of 1.8 million workers who lost their jobs between 1989 and 1993, only a third were able to find new jobs and then only at a 20 percent drop in pay. This corroborates that the poverty of young adults who are about to enter the job market is directly affected by larger economic trends.

Women are another vulnerable group. In Canada, their poverty rate has been close to three times the national rate (45.3% as opposed to 16.3%). The term *feminization* of poverty is now commonly used to refer to the fact that women, and especially those who head families with young children, are increasingly over-represented among the poor (see, among others, Duffy and Mandell, 1996 [1994]; Duffy et al., 1988; Duffy and Pupo, 1992; Goldberg, 1990). One reason for this is that these women must divide their time between the paid workforce and child-rearing (McFate et al., 1995:47).

TABLE 2-2

THE POVERTY RATE BY TYPE OF FAMILY, 1996

| Type of Economic Families | Poverty Rate |
|---|---|
| **Total – Economic families** | **16.3** |
| Female reference person families with never-married children only | 48.0 |
| Female | 45.3 |
| Total – Unattached individuals | 42.2 |
| Non-husband-wife families | 39.5 |
| Male | 38.7 |
| 18 – 24 years | 26.0 |
| Under 6 years | 25.8 |
| Male reference person families with never-married children only | 23.9 |
| Under 15 years | 23.4 |
| 6 – 9 years | 23.4 |
| 10 – 14 years | 20.7 |
| 70 years and over | 20.5 |
| 25 – 34 years | 20.3 |
| 15 – 17 years | 19.6 |
| 55 – 64 years | 18.0 |
| 65 – 69 years | 16.9 |
| 35 – 44 years | 16.6 |
| 45 – 54 years | 14.0 |
| Married couples with never-married children only | 12.6 |
| Husband-wife families | 11.7 |

Hardships are compounded when lone-parent women are also young adults. In such situations, women are triply jeopardized: because of their domestic roles, because of the discrimination they may face in the job market, and because of their unstable economic situation as young adults. A lack of adequate education exponentially aggravates their difficulties.

Children have been another target of poverty. The proportion of children under 18 who live in poverty rose from 14.9% in 1980 to 18.2% in 1992 (Bolaria and Wotherspoon, 1995:503). In 1996, children under 9 had poverty rates at least 1.5 times the national rate. This increase has been, at least partly, a consequence of the feminization of poverty. Moreover, high divorce rates in Canada, and the fact that the custody of children in most cases is awarded to the mother, also contribute to high levels of child poverty. In this connection, it is known but not accurately documented that many fathers fail to honour child support agreements after divorce. This results in serious problems for children, including poor housing conditions, inadequate clothing, and malnutrition. During the 1990s, the extent of malnutrition among children in particular has been the subject of reports by both governmental bodies and Non-Governmental Organizations (NGOs) (see Canadian Institute of Child Health, 1994).

The elderly are also at high risk of poverty. Considerable cutbacks in welfare budgets, along with their limited access to jobs and even more limited capacity to adjust themselves to the job market, keep these individuals on the brink of poverty. An underlying demographic transformation in Canada aggravates this situation: a large, aged population must rely on the smaller, young, but unemployed segment of the population. This raises serious doubts concerning the effective continuation of the welfare system. Without major innovations in public policy, the elders are going to be among the groups most severely affected by poverty.

There is another likely vulnerable group that has gone almost entirely unnoticed in the Canadian poverty debate: members of visible minority ethnic groups. This negligence is quite surprising, given the recent rise of ethnic dynamics and the consequent attention to this issue in almost all industrial nations, and the visibility of these groups in the Canadian population (9.3% and 11.2% of the Canadian population in 1991 and 1996, respectively).

It seems that poverty researchers in Canada have not yet caught up with the recent rise in the importance of ethnicity in the poverty debate. This is one, but not the only, source of discrepancy between the realities of poverty and public policy in Canada. Such disparities have stimulated a great deal of discussion about the relevance of public policies designed to address poverty.

## *Poverty and Public Policy*

The recent rise of poverty in the 1990s coincided with a period of crisis in the welfare system. As a central component of public policy, the welfare system owed its post-World War II expansion to the wide acceptance of certain assumptions, which were challenged in the late 1970s and 1980s (McFate, 1995). One assumption was that the high economic growth of the post-war period would continue. Another was that ongoing economic growth would provide a surplus, which would be redistributed. It was also believed that the economy would create enough jobs to make full employment possible. Steady growth, constant income redistribution, and full employment, however, all came to an end in the early 1970s, making welfare system increasingly non-sustainable.

That, however, was not the only source of trouble for the welfare system; it also suffered because of an underlying demographic change. Like many other developed countries, Canada had to recognize that an increasing percentage of its population live long beyond their earning years, leaving more elderly citizens dependent on government support for longer periods. For this support they are reliant on a non-elderly population that has not been increasing as rapidly as their own segment (McFate, 1995:2). This demographic development posed serious challenges to the normal functioning of the welfare system because the welfare states were dependent on the income they would garner from the non-elderly population (in the form of taxes, pension plans, and so on.) to support the elderly; as a result, resources available to the welfare system shrank dramatically (see Li, 1996).

Despite many adjustments, the welfare programs proved incapable of coping with the multitude of problems that surfaced in the 1970s and 1980s. With regard to poverty, the policies were so inadequate that, in many cases, more people were pushed into poverty than were lifted out of it. Heavy income taxes for those who were marginally beyond the tax exemption threshold, for instance, added to the number of poor in some industrial countries (McFate et al., 1995). The mismatch between policies and the corresponding realities made the 1990s a time for a wholesale re-examination of social policies (Kieranes, 1996:vii). In the case of poverty, the main questions have revolved around the role of the welfare system in ameliorating or decreasing the poverty levels and the kinds of solutions available.

One interpretation of the relationship between poverty and public policy revolves around the idea that the increasing support provided by the welfare state, in the form of cash assistance, disability insurance, food stamps, medical insurance, and housing subsidies, changed the situation for the poor so that they no longer have to work in order to survive (Peterson, 1991). This line of reasoning is more or less adopted by Murray (1984), Mead (1986), Glazer (1988), Lenkowsky (1986), and Anderson (1978). They believe that, once having fallen victim to poverty, the poor tend to remain poor because of the generosity of the welfare system. For them, the remedy is a reform in public policy.

An opposing view, more informed by the structural explanation of poverty, holds that poverty is generated by the negative impacts of macroeconomic trends; a reform in public policy, therefore, is needed in order to compensate for the undesirable impacts of these trends on the lives of vulnerable groups. Such a reform needs to be directed towards providing better employment, in terms of either stability and availability (Rifkin, 1995) or payment (Blank, 1994).

The public policies designed to deal with poverty were further challenged by the emergence of some new forms of poverty during the 1980s. Overall poverty was no longer the only concern. The severity and persistence of poverty began emerging as other concerns. Also, very recently, the study of *neighbourhood poverty* or *spatial concentration of poverty* (SCOP) has attracted some attention. Unlike the previous studies that focused on the poverty of individuals and families, the SCOP research concerns itself with the poverty of neighbourhoods. In other words, while the poverty analysts have focused on human entities, the SCOP analysts have adopted geographical units as their units of analysis.

## *Neighbourhood Poverty: The Neglected Dimension*

In the SCOP literature, poverty is defined rather unconventionally. Conventional poverty analysts have defined as poor an individual or a family that cannot afford the basic necessities of life, or that spends more than a certain proportion of income on such necessities. The SCOP researchers, however, have defined as poor a neighbourhood with more than 20% of its population being poor (Wilson, 1987:46).

The neighbourhood poverty rate has the same conceptual properties as the national poverty rate. Like the national poverty rate, which states the number of poor individuals and/or families as a proportion of the total population of a country, the neighbourhood poverty rate reveals what proportion of the population of a neighbourhood is poor. The national rates allow for international comparison; the neighbourhood rates for inter-neighbourhood comparison. Both measures, indeed, tell us about the overall well-being of a community, be it a nation or a neighbourhood.

The SCOP researchers have not been primarily concerned with the definition of poverty per se. Rather, they have been more interested in the comparative study of neighbourhoods of different poverty levels. They are particularly interested in examining the social fabric of neighbourhoods with high poverty rates. However, they cannot be quite indifferent to, and their studies cannot be independent from, the way poverty is defined. Were some other income thresholds chosen to determine the poverty line, the poverty rates of a certain society would be over- or under-estimated, and so would the poverty rates of neighbourhoods. Nevertheless, the choice of thresholds would not seriously affect a comparative account of neighbourhoods. Moreover, the SCOP analysts face a practical limitation in their studies; neighbourhood poverty rates are available through census data, which are based on the official definition of poverty. The SCOP researchers, therefore, have to rely on the official poverty definitions and thresholds.

Despite some scattered previous works, the systematic study of SCOP began in the United States with publication of Wilson's (1987) *The Truly Disadvantaged.* Studying Chicago's neighbourhoods, Wilson argues that since the early 1970s there has been a visible increase in the number of extremely poor neighbourhoods–those with poverty rates of 40% and higher. He calls such areas, mostly located in inner city Chicago, "ghetto neighbourhoods," or later, "ghetto poverty tracts" (Wilson, 1996:6).

The sharp rise of poverty, Wilson argues, noticeably deteriorated social and economic conditions of "ghetto neighbourhoods." This deterioration is well reflected in the statement of one observer of such neighbourhoods in Chicago: "When I walked down Sixty-third Street when I was young, everything that you wanted was there. But now, coming back as an adult with my child, those resources are just gone, completely" (Wilson, 1996:5). Another elderly woman who lived in a similar neighbourhood for more than 40 years makes similar comments.

> I've been here since March 21, 1953. When I moved in, the
> neighbourhood was intact. It was intact with homes, beautiful homes,
> mini mansions, with stores, laundromats, with cleaners.... We had
> drugstores. We had doctors' offices in the neighbourhood. We had the
> middle class and upper middle class. It has gone from affluent to where
> it is today. And I would like to see it come back, that we can have some
> of things we had.... I would like to see some of the things come back so
> I can enjoy them like we did when we first came in (Wilson, 1996:3).

Resulting from the exodus of middle- and working-class families, the
high poverty of such "ghetto poverty tracts" led to the extreme "social
isolation" of the dwellers, mainly Blacks.

> Lower-class, working-class, and middle-class black families all lived
> more or less in the same communities ... sent their children to the same
> schools, availed themselves of the same recreational facilities, and
> shopped at the same stores. Whereas today's black middle-class
> professionals no longer tend to live in ghetto neighbourhoods and have
> moved increasingly into mainstream occupations outside the black
> community, the black middle-class professionals of the 1940s and 1950s
> (doctors, teachers, lawyers, social workers, ministers) lived in higher-
> income neighbourhoods of the ghetto and serviced the black
> community. Accompanying the black middle-class exodus has been a
> growing movement of stable working-class blacks from ghetto
> neighbourhoods to higher-income neighbourhoods in other parts of
> the city and to suburbs. In the earlier years, the black middle and
> working classes were confined by restrictive covenants to communities
> also inhabited by the lower class; their very presence provided stability
> to inner-city neighbourhoods and reinforced and perpetuated
> mainstream patterns of norms and behaviour (Wilson, 1987:76).

The outcome of this development for Blacks in ghettos was, Wilson
argues, the removal of a "social buffer" that had kept them attached to the
mainstream population. With the removal of this social buffer, which
"provided stability to inner city neighbourhoods and reinforced and
perpetuated mainstream patterns of norms and behavior" (Wilson,
1987:76), the dwellers began developing their own distinct norms and
patterns of behaviour.

> This argument is based on the assumption that even if the truly
> disadvantaged segments of an inner-city area experience a significant
> increase in long-term spells of joblessness, the basic institutions in that
> area (churches, schools, stores, recreational facilities, etc.) would remain
> viable if much of the base of their support comes from the more
> economically stable and secure families. Moreover, the very presence
> of these families during such periods provides mainstream role models
> that help keep alive the perception that education is meaningful, that
> steady employment is a viable alternative to welfare, and the family
> stability is the norm, not the exception (Wilson, 1987:56).

The immediate factors behind this whole development, according to
Wilson (1987), are the outmigration of non-poor whites and the rise in the
number of residents in concentrated poverty areas who have become poor.
In a later work, he added a third factor: the movement of poor people into
poor neighbourhoods (Wilson, 1996). Despite the over-representation of

American Blacks in "ghetto poverty tracts," Wilson found that the whole process stemmed from a race-neutral trend in the economy, i.e., the decline of the manufacturing sector in favour of a fast growing service sector. In his *When Work Disappears*, Wilson (1996) more strongly relates the problem to structural changes in the economy and the job market, which resulted in higher unemployment rates for Blacks in large American manufacturing-based cities, such as Chicago and Detroit. The solution, according to Wilson, is a race-neutral public policy, rather than a race-specific one.

The SCOP research in the United States was furthered by Massey et al. (1987), Massey and Eggers (1990), and, most significantly, by Massey and Denton (1993). The last concentrated on the variables that Wilson had regarded as unimportant. For example, they argue that the experience of SCOP by racial minorities is directly related to race-specific factors, such as their residential segregation. In *American Apartheid*, Massey and Denton (1993) show the different levels of neighbourhood poverty for racial groups with different degrees of residential segregation. They also raise the point that, as a result of the extreme segregation and high rates of poverty concentration of Blacks, the culture of poverty has developed among them, a point Wilson tried to reject in his works.

These works triggered a range of studies of SCOP in American cities. Some studies show the relationship between the poverty of neighbourhoods and the quality of civil services or crime rates within them (Massey et al., 1991; Massey et al., 1987). Crane (1991), assessing neighbourhood effects on teenage child-bearing and school dropout rates, shows that living in a community or attending a school with a disproportionate number of poor people or minorities increases the chance that an adolescent will drop out or have a child out of wedlock. Mayer (1991) illustrates that such a finding holds even after the person's family background is taken into account.

Other studies examined the causes, rather than the effects, of the high rates of neighbourhood poverty. The factors highlighted in such studies constitute a wide range of variables, such as migration (Fitchen, 1995; Nord, Luloff and Jensen, 1995), housing (Wilson, 1995), public housing projects (Massey and Kanaiapuni, 1993), the urban housing market (Massey et al., 1994), and employment (Iceland, 1995). In general, however, these factors are more or less reflections of the broader economic reorganization that Wilson had previously underscored.

The rise of research on SCOP in the United States has sparked a similar interest among European researchers. The findings of European studies are mixed: no European city has experienced the level of concentrated poverty and racial and ethnic segregation typical of American metropolises; however, the process of social polarization in the cities seems to have begun (Lawson and Wilson, 1995). In terms of the over-represented groups in ghetto neighbourhoods, immigrants and certain ethnic groups seem to be the European counterpart of the American Blacks (Silver, 1993; Roelandt and Veenman, 1992; Van Kempen, 1994).

The research on SCOP in Canada has been, surprisingly enough, very little, and it has come very late. The reasons for this negligence are not clear. One possibility is that it is due to the gratification resulting from the United Nations' (UN) ranking of Canada as the most desirable country in which to live, in terms of the Human Development Index. Recent evaluations by the UN, however, ranked Canada tenth, after poverty was taken into account. Moreover, those few concerned with poverty were more interested in the poverty of women and children. Lack of a spatial vision among poverty researchers may have seriously hampered SCOP research in Canada. Indeed, most of the studies of SCOP in Canada have been done by geographers rather than by sociologists or economists who are traditionally more concerned with poverty. Another reason may be the fact that, in comparison to the United States, Canadian cities are fewer and smaller. This limitation normally hinders the presentation of a lively comparative picture of SCOP on a societal scale. Also, the findings of conventional poverty research (on individuals and/or families) could be more easily and quickly translated into public policies through monetary measures. This might have led to a lesser degree of enthusiasm for SCOP research among the policy makers; hence, the possibility of less financial support. Lastly, in the United States, the SCOP research was strongly boosted after the Los Angeles riots of 1992 (Burton, 1992:14). These riots highlighted some of the potential dangers associated with extremely poor neighbourhoods. The lack of such violent and radical incidents in Canada has definitely contributed towards the neglect of SCOP by researchers in Canada.

The first attempt towards studying SCOP in Canada was made in the mid-1990s by Hajnal (1995) and was basically a comparison of Canada and the United States. The major finding of this study was that, despite the fewer number of people living in ghetto neighbourhoods in Canada, this number constitutes a higher proportion of the population as compared to the United States. Besides its descriptive nature, this study was limited because of its use of 1986 data, which did not cover the period in which the most visible increase in poverty occurred. It also fell short by inadequately illustrating the important dimension of SCOP, that is, its ethnic and/or racial feature.

In a more comprehensive study, MacLachlan and Sawada (1997) examined the income inequality and social polarization in Canadian metropolitan areas. While this study had a better coverage of the Canadian cities and a better methodology, it was more concerned with inequality than poverty. The study, however, was a big step forward in terms of linking the spatial trends in cities with larger structural changes in the economy and in society.

In more focused efforts, Ley and Smith (1997) and Murdie (1998) examined the spatial concentration of poverty in three Canadian CMAs. Examining the patterns of SCOP in Montreal, Vancouver, and Toronto,

Ley and Smith found the greatest incidence of deep poverty in the first city, a more conventional American model of inner-city ghettos in the second, and a suburbanization of SCOP in the third. In his study of Toronto, Murdie broadened the perspective by introducing the notions of *inner suburb* and *outer suburb*; the former comprise the constituent municipalities of Metropolitan Toronto outside the city of Toronto built between the end of World War II and the early 1970s, and the latter, the rapidly growing suburban municipalities beyond Metropolitan Toronto but within the Toronto CMA. He illustrates that it is the inner suburbs that have experienced increased incidence of low-income households, low educational achievement, lower levels of occupational status, and higher unemployment. Despite their limited scope, these studies have been very helpful in terms of showing the difference between Canada and the United States.

Most recently, Kazemipur and Halli (1997) made an effort to investigate the representation of immigrants in the high SCOP areas. They found a moderate positive correlation between the poverty level of a neighbourhood and the proportion of its population who were immigrants. The magnitude of correlations was highest for visible minority immigrants, such as the Vietnamese, Spanish, Chinese, and Blacks; the only other groups with an equally high correlation coefficient were the Aboriginals and the Polish. Interestingly, the correlations for those of European ethnic origins, such as the German, British, Dutch, Swedish, Finnish, and Jewish, were not low but negative.

Of all the above studies, none has an inter-urban perspective, nor has any adequately addressed the ethnic and/or racial dimension of spatially concentrated poverty. Also missing is a comprehensive conceptual framework within which one can situate and understand the conceptual significance of the spatial concentration of poverty. It is to this that we now turn.

## Why Spatial Concentration of Poverty? A Conceptual Backdrop

Since the foundation of sociology during the latter half of the nineteenth century, sociologists have been searching for the robust variables that shape life chances as well as social behaviour. *Social class* was one such variable, as was *race and ethnicity*. Later, the feminist movement of 1960s singled out *gender*. This means that knowing one's social class, gender, and racial and/or ethnic origin provides sociologists with valuable clues as to one's past, present, and future station in life. Of course, the relative significance of each of the three variables may vary from society to society; but, in any case, they remain the most influential ones.

The SCOP research points out that a fourth variable, *neighbourhood,* can be added to the list of the variables, with its long-lasting effects on life chances. This is to say that the choice of neighbourhood strongly conditions the social progress of its inhabitants. It is true that such a choice is itself influenced by other factors, such as income, race, and ethnicity; but, regardless of its source, neighbourhood begins shaping life chances in ways different from income, race, and ethnicity. The level of spatial concentration of poverty in the neighbourhood in which one lives, therefore, can further limit or expand one's life chances.

There are three ways through which the spatial concentration of poverty may contribute to shaping life chances. Social isolation and culture of poverty, mentioned earlier, are two of these ways; *transition from subjective poverty to objective poverty* is a third way. In what follows, after a brief touch on the first two, the third one will be discussed in more detail.

## *Social Isolation*

The fact that a poor family lives in a neighbourhood with a high level of poverty means that they live in proximity to other poor families. In extreme cases, the possibility of contact between poor and non-poor families is minimal. Also, such a concentration may undermine the public facilities available in the neighbourhood, such as schools, hospitals, recreational facilities, and churches. The inhabitants of poor neighbourhoods thus begin to build up their own impoverished institutional world, separate from the rest of society. Geographical isolation, as a result, leads to social isolation.

As mentioned earlier, Wilson (1987) was the first to highlight the seriousness of social isolation. He noted that the social isolation of Black Americans has deprived them of contact with the larger society. The lack of such contacts is later translated into the loss of positive role models, the declining desirability of education, the preference of welfare over employment, and detachment from the notion of the stable family (Wilson, 1987). In other words, in the high SCOP neighbourhoods, the fundamental components of the general culture are most likely missing.

## *Culture of Poverty*

Culture, in general, may be defined as the sharing of modes of behaviour and outlook within a community. The study of culture involves "an analysis of how culture is transmitted from generation to generation and the way in which it is sustained through social interaction in the community" (Wilson, 1996:66). In other words, culture has both a spatial and a temporal dimension: it is shared by members of a certain community, and it is carried over through generations. Some have suggested that culture is a "common stock of knowledge," which provides solutions, already made and tested by others, for the routine problems and issues in the lives of the individuals involved. Through this function, culture saves individuals from falling into the hands of the "tyranny of freedom" (Himelfarb and Richardson, 1991).

Culture mediates our adaptation to the environment in which we live, be it physical or social. This explains the diversity of cultures: different environments require different coping strategies. It also explains the emergence of subcultures among those who share a similar status in one or another aspect of their social lives. Culture, therefore, involves rational decisions, made over a period of time and in response to persistent conditions.

The culture of poverty is a clear example of a subculture. As Oscar Lewis (1966:222) argues, it serves "a significant adaptive function," allowing poor people to cope with feelings of hopelessness and despair that arise because their chances for socio-economic success are remote (Massey and Denton, 1993). Because of the interplay between the culture of poverty and the high chance of failure among certain groups, according to Simpson and Yinger (1972:175), "a complex value system" has developed as a method of dealing with "the realistic chances for failure and frustration." Such a culture persists as long as the corresponding poverty conditions exist, and remains distinct from the general culture as long as the corresponding conditions remain distinct. The distance between the general culture and the subculture, developed among those isolated socially and/or physically, is succinctly captured in a quotation cited by Simpson and Yinger (1972:173).

> In the customs governing sex behavior, the isolation of Negroes from the general culture is easily observable. It is one thing to know what the accepted standards are and then to violate them ... but it is quite another thing to have no conception of such standards. In a group of ten boys in Chicago ... the investigator found an almost complete absence of inhibition in their reporting of sex relations.... They reported their sex behavior, which a middle-class schoolteacher would condemn as immoral, as freely and unemotionally as they did their employment records or their love of swimming.... [T]heir sex behavior would indicate that they were thoroughly isolated from accepted middle-class standards.

Relying on the notion of the *culture of poverty*, Massey and Denton (1993) use the inner-city Black ghettos in American cities as an example of how SCOP leads to the formation of a different lifestyle. By concentrating poverty, they argue, "segregation simultaneously concentrates male joblessness, teenage motherhood, single parenthood, alcoholism, and drug abuse, thus creating an entirely black social world." Through gradual distancing from the middle-class culture, the ghetto culture represents features quite at odds with the normative culture of the wider society.

> Ghetto blacks ... face very different neighbourhood conditions.... A large share live in a geographically isolated and racially homogeneous neighbourhoods where poverty is endemic, joblessness is rife, schools are poor, and even high school graduates are unlikely to speak standard English with any facility. Employment opportunities are limited, and given the social isolation enforced by segregation, black men are not well connected to employers in the larger economy. As a result, young men coming of age in ghetto areas are relatively unlikely to find jobs capable of supporting a wife and children, and black women, facing a dearth of potential husbands and an absence of educational institutions capable of preparing them for gainful employment, cannot realistically

hope to conform to societal ideals and childbearing (Massey and Denton, 1993:166).

However, a culture of poverty does not merely develop as a reaction to the distinct living conditions in ghetto neighbourhoods; it can also develop through a process called *transmission by percept*, whereby a person's exposure to certain attitudes and actions is so frequent that they become a part of his or her own outlook. In this manner, individual skills, habits, and styles are often shaped by the frequency at which they are found in the community. A jobless family living in a neighbourhood with a relatively high rate of employment, for example, is different from a similar one living in a ghetto neighbourhood with its high rate of unemployment; the latter is affected not only by the same constraints as those of the former, but also by the behaviour and outlook of other jobless families in the neighbourhood (Wilson, 1996). Through this mechanism, the culture of poverty, therefore, finds in ghetto neighbourhoods a more favourable ground in which to germinate.

## *Objective vs. Subjective Poverty*

A common theme in both *social isolation* and *culture of poverty* theses is that those experiencing high SCOP conditions do not show a great desire for changing their living situation. A relevant question is on how these external conditions are internalized. What psychological process do people in ghetto neighbourhoods go through so that their living conditions mirror their mental make-up? This is not a question with which the proponents of either of the above theses were concerned.

In addressing these questions, we found Tocqueville's approach, as presented in *The Old Regime and the French Revolution* (1955 [1856]), useful. The book—an effort to understand the "background and nature of the revolution"—is most unconventional in its analysis of the relationship between socio-economic conditions and people's desire for change. Specifically, Tocqueville confutes the prevailing perception that, when socio-economic conditions deteriorate and become unbearable, the masses revolt. This view, Tocqueville holds, does not apply to the French Revolution.

In opposition, Tocqueville (1955 [1856]) argues, the economic situation of France had drastically improved in the last two decades before the revolution; there was a "spectacular increase in the wealth of individuals" (p.173). Also, "living conditions improved throughout the land" in the same period (p.174). Along with these changes in the economy, there also was a change in the mentality of the rulers. They began showing "a genuine respect for civic freedom and the rights of individuals," as well as "a real concern for the hardship of the poor" (p.172). The irony was that "the chief centers of the revolutionary movement" were "those parts of France in which the improvements in the standard of living was most pronounced" (p.175). How can this paradox be explained?

For Tocqueville, the answer lies in the "changed perception" of people. He argues that the reforms of the prior two decades not only improved the actual living conditions of the people, but also affected how they perceived their reality. The severe conditions that people had tolerated simply because they were thought to be inevitable and unchangeable were now gone. The seemingly inevitable was now proved to have been quite avoidable. This brought about a change in people's perception and tolerance of suffering: "Patiently endured so long as it seemed beyond redress, a grievance comes to appear intolerable once the possibility of removing it crosses men's minds" (Tocqueville, 1955 [1856]:177).

This "altered perception" awakened a desire for change–now that some sufferings have been eradicated, why not remove all of them? The revolution, as a result, unfolded. The source of the changed perceptions was in the subjective arena, rather than in the material or objective conditions. Any factor that hinders the emergence of such a subjective element will, therefore, hamper the motivation for change.

Tocqueville's theory of revolution has some far-reaching implications for the issue of change, social or individual. Building upon this theory, one can argue that it is the change in mentality, rather than material conditions, that triggers the process of change. The objective conditions, no matter how severe they may be, do not arouse a desire to change if the subjective element is absent. This schemata strongly applies to poverty as well.

In what may look like a reflection of Tocqueville's theory, Whyte (1971) introduces two definitions of poverty: *objective poverty* and *subjective poverty*. He suggests that an individual who is unable to satisfy his or her minimal needs for food, clothing, and shelter, and is unable to fulfil a normal occupational role to provide for these needs, is said to experience objective poverty; those who sense their deprivation manifest subjective poverty. While the former results from the economic status of the individual, the latter grows out of "a comparison of what an individual has with what he would like to have" (p.79). The two have distinct lives of their own, and due to this distinction, "objective poverty can exist without being experienced subjectively" (p.80).

This possibility provides a ground to link Whyte's conceptualization of poverty with Tocqueville's theory of revolution. One can say that a poor individual may make an effort to break out of the poverty trap only if he or she experiences poverty subjectively. Such an experience provides the necessary contrast between what "is" and what "ought to be." The discrepancy between the two triggers the effort to overcome poverty.

How can the above theoretical orientation help us to understand the spatial concentration of poverty, social isolation, and the culture of poverty outlined earlier? The concentration of poor in certain neighbourhoods means that their contacts are confined mostly to other poor; hence, their lack of awareness of the lifestyles and life approaches of the non-poor, and a lack of awareness of their own existential situation in contrast to the non-poor. This lack of knowledge of other possible alternatives leads them to believe that their situation is inevitable and unavoidable, the only one they can have. In other words, they do not shift from objective to subjective poverty. The poor who are spatially concentrated are more likely to consider their situation as, to use Tocqueville's phrase, "beyond redress."

A hypothetical example may help at this point. As always, the extreme cases are more telling. A comparison can be made between two poor families, one living in a rich neighbourhood and the other in a poor one. The first family not only has the chance to use the same facilities and enjoy similar social advantages, such as more security, but they are also in constant contact with non-poor families and are therefore aware of their lifestyle. This contrast with their own lifestyle makes them aware of their poverty and can potentially mobilize them to do something about it. Such a motivating experience is missing for the second family, living in a poor neighbourhood. While poverty can easily be seen as pathological and problematic for the first family, it will most likely remain as normal and unavoidable for the second. The transition from objective to subjective poverty is more likely to take place for the former, rather than the latter. As Whyte (1971:81) points out, "poverty will be phenomenologically different, and hence it will have a different meaning in a community in which everyone is poor as contrasted to one in which there is a wide range of economic difference."

In sum, the spatial concentration of poverty is not merely about the geographical distribution of a group of people in urban space. It can also lead to social and psychological processes with far-reaching consequences for the living conditions of the poor. If identified and measured properly, then, the spatial concentration of poverty and its consequences can be dealt with more effectively. The measurement of SCOP, therefore, merits some discussion.

## Measurement of the Spatial Concentration of Poverty: A Methodological Account

The *spatial concentration of poverty* (or *neighbourhood poverty*) can be examined in a number of ways. While referring to one phenomenon in general, each of these ways highlights a certain aspect of SCOP. In this section, two measures are introduced. The first looks at the distribution of census tracts in each city by their poverty rates. The second focuses on the distribution of population in census tracts with different poverty rates.

### *Census Tracts and SCOP*

To further Wilson's definition of *ghetto neighbourhoods* as "census tracts with a poverty rate of at least 40 percent," (Wilson, 1987; 1996) the SCOP researchers have proposed some detailed categorization: "poverty areas" for the census tracts with a 20-30% poverty rate, and "high to extreme poverty areas" for those with 30-40%. The use of this categorization reveals the general structure of each city in terms of the spatial concentration of poverty. It also shows the extent of inequality or homogeneity in each city, as far as neighbourhood poverty is concerned.

## *People and SCOP*

The main purpose of studying the spatial concentration of poverty is, of course, to examine how many people or what proportions of population live in high SCOP neighbourhoods. To address this, we can calculate the number of people who live in census tracts with different levels of poverty, both in absolute terms and relative to city population.

There is, however, a potential source of confusion here. Knowing that the census authorities have defined census tracts in such a way that each contains a population of about four thousand, one may ask if the second measure is not simply an extension of the first. In other words, could we not calculate the population of those in high SCOP areas simply by multiplying the number of census tracts by 4,000? The answer is no; and the reason is the different size of census tracts' populations within and among cities. Table 2-3 shows that the average population of census tracts varies from 5,738 in Vancouver to 2,906 in Saint John. This wide range indicates that a city may have more census tracts with a high SCOP, but it does not necessarily follow that it contains more people living in high SCOP zones. Due to this difference, it seems worthwhile to report the population index of SCOP in addition to census tracts structure.

TABLE 2-3

THE AVERAGE POPULATION OF CENSUS TRACTS BY CITY, **1991**

| City | Average population of census tracts | City | Average population of census tracts |
|---|---|---|---|
| Vancouver | 5378 | Peterborough | 4263 |
| Calgary | 4928 | Sudbury | 4260 |
| Oshawa | 4900 | Quebec | 4249 |
| Toronto | 4835 | Montreal | 4246 |
| Moncton | 4631 | Winnipeg | 4209 |
| Guelph | 4629 | Thunder Bay | 4148 |
| Brantford | 4624 | Trois-Rivières | 4009 |
| Chicoutimi-Jonquière | 4598 | Kingston | 3992 |
| Edmonton | 4515 | Matsqui | 3916 |
| Sherbrooke | 4490 | Regina | 3912 |
| Windsor | 4442 | Sault Ste. Marie | 3864 |
| Victoria | 4429 | Hamilton | 3701 |
| Ottawa-Hull | 4427 | Sarnia-Clearwater | 3661 |
| Kitchener | 4400 | Red Deer | 3633 |
| St. Catharines-Niagara | 4392 | North Bay | 3164 |
| Saskatoon | 4375 | Kamloops | 3084 |
| London | 4335 | Lethbridge | 3047 |
| Kelowna | 4302 | Prince George | 3028 |
| St. John's | 4296 | Saint John | 2906 |
| Halifax | 4273 | | |

## Sources of Data

In this study, the 1986 and 1991 census tract data have been used. These data sets include information on a wide range of variables but only in aggregate form, due to the confidentiality principle. The aggregate nature of data superimposes some limitations, the most serious of which is the impossibility of acquiring a profile of the socio-economic specifications of those who live in each neighbourhood. This shortcoming becomes more problematic in the inferential analyses concerned with the relationships between the individual and residential characteristics.

Some researchers in the United States have managed to avoid this problem through some custom data, including both the individual and census tract variables. By the insertion of some random errors in the data, it has become anonymous; hence, the problem of confidentiality has been taken care of. Such a database is not yet available in Canada, due to the lesser demand for it, as well as the more stringent restrictions set by Statistics Canada.

## Spatial Concentration of Poverty in Canadian Cities: Findings

### *Canadian Cities, SCOP, Census Tracts*

One way to explore the overall magnitude of the SCOP problem in Canada is to look at the distribution of neighbourhoods in different levels of poverty in a national scale. To acquire a general picture of the whole country, the proportions of census tracts in each poverty category and for all Canadian cities have been averaged and illustrated in Figure 2-1. The figure shows the overall changes in the distribution of census tracts during the period between the two census years of 1986 and 1991.

As Figure 2-1 illustrates, the proportions of census tracts in two extreme categories, less than 10% and more than 40% poverty rates, have increased between 1986 and 1991. On the other hand, the proportions of all the middle categories, that is, the census tracts with a poverty rate of 10-40%, have decreased. This combination suggests that, in terms of geographical appearance, Canadian cities are moving towards some sort of polarization. If this trend manifests in every city and continues in the future, we should expect to see more and more very rich and very poor neighbourhoods, side by side.

The trend observed above, however, does not reflect each city's unique appearance in this regard. A partial set of information on the distribution of census tracts in each city as well as the corresponding changes between 1986 and 1991 is represented in Figures 2-2 and 2-3.

A cursory look at the two Figures shows that the spatial concentration of poverty is far from being a universal problem. In general, the problem seems to be associated mostly with larger cities, such as Montreal, Quebec

City, Winnipeg, Regina, Saskatoon, Vancouver, and, to a lesser degree, Calgary and Edmonton. Out of these, Montreal and Winnipeg have the most severe situations as far as the proportion of census tracts in the "40% and more" category is concerned. A striking feature is that these two are the only cities for which the percentage of census tracts in this category has increased in the period between 1986 and 1991. They are also more or less over-represented in the second-worst category, the proportion of census tracts with a 30-40% poverty rate.

FIGURE **2-1**
THE AVERAGE PROPORTION OF CENSUS TRACTS IN DIFFERENT POVERTY AREAS, **1986-1991**

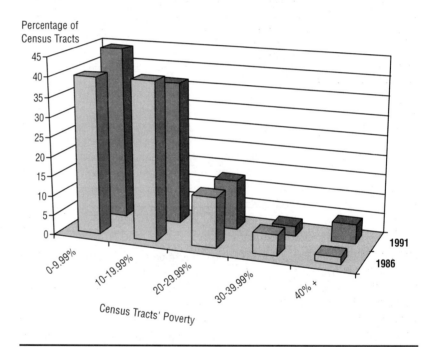

One last observation is the rising percentage of census tracts that fall into the first category, that is, those with a 0-10% poverty rate. However, it should also be noticed that this proportion varies drastically from city to city; while for some cities this percentage has been as low as 3.1 and 11.8 in 1986 and 1991, respectively, for others it has been as high as 72.7 and 69.4.

## Canadian Cities, SCOP, Population

The distribution of census tracts in different poverty areas tells us about the morphological features of a city rather than the experience of its people. Eventually, however, we are concerned with knowing how people are distributed in different neighbourhoods. Table 2-4 shows the proportional distribution of cities' populations in neighbourhoods of different poverty levels for both 1986 and 1991. The graphical representation of this data as well as additional details is contained in Appendices 1 through 4.

FIGURE 2-2
THE PROPORTION OF CENSUS TRACTS IN DIFFERENT POVERTY AREAS, 1986

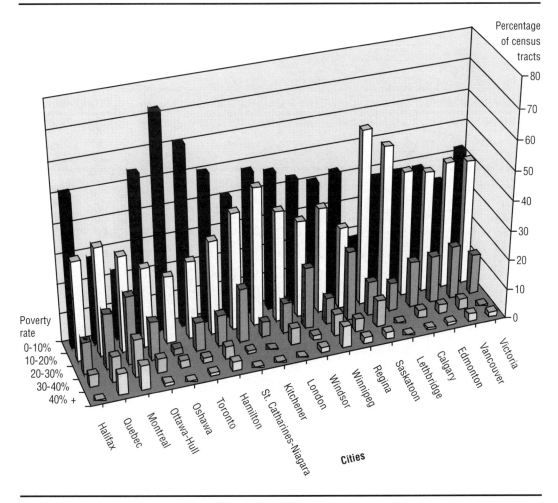

One striking fact in Table 2-4 is the situation of cities in Quebec and the Prairie provinces. Winnipeg and Montreal, for example, have the highest proportions of their population living in ghetto neighbourhoods, that is, census tracts with at least a 40% poverty rate (10.3 and 10.2, respectively). This is far higher than the national average for this category of census tracts, that is, 1.8%. In Ontario, except for Ottawa-Hull and Hamilton, the cities have either no or a low percentage of their population living in such neighbourhoods. Such a trend exists for both census years. Another interesting observation is that some cities in Ontario have a high proportion of their population living in very low poverty neighbourhoods, that is, those with less than a 10% poverty rate. At least 50% of the population in cities such as Ottawa-Hull, Kingston, Peterborough, Oshawa, and Toronto live in such neighbourhoods.

FIGURE 2-3

THE PROPORTION OF CENSUS TRACTS IN DIFFERENT POVERTY AREAS, 1991

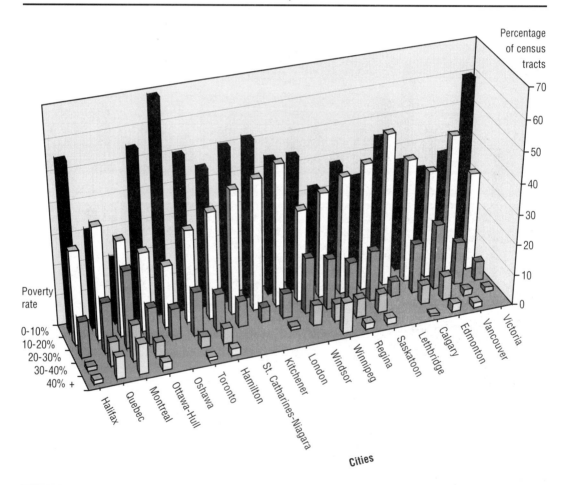

TABLE 2-4

THE PROPORTION OF CITY POPULATION LIVING IN CENSUS TRACTS (CTS) WITH DIFFERENT POVERTY LEVELS, 1986-1991

| | Poverty Rate of Census Tracts (%) | | | | | | | | | | Changes 1986-1991 (%) | | | | |
| | 0-9.99 | | 10-19.99 | | 20-29.99 | | 30-39.99 | | 40+ | | | | | | |
| Cities | 1986 | 1991 | 1986 | 1991 | 1986 | 1991 | 1986 | 1991 | 1986 | 1991 | 0-9.99 | 10-19.99 | 20-29.99 | 30-39.99 | 40+ |
|---|---|---|---|---|---|---|---|---|---|---|---|---|---|---|---|
| St. John's | 20.0 | 37.5 | 51.4 | 40.0 | 15.6 | 10.0 | 11.5 | 12.5 | 1.5 | 0.0 | 17.5 | -11.4 | -5.6 | 1.0 | -1.5 |
| Halifax | 47.8 | 54.7 | 36.1 | 30.7 | 12.0 | 12.0 | 4.1 | 1.3 | 0.0 | 1.3 | 6.9 | -5.4 | 0.0 | -2.8 | 1.3 |
| Moncton | 42.1 | 43.5 | 30.4 | 30.4 | 22.2 | 26.1 | 5.3 | 0.0 | 0.0 | 0.0 | 1.4 | 0.0 | 3.9 | -5.3 | 0.0 |
| Saint John | 25.7 | 27.9 | 38.8 | 34.9 | 20.0 | 23.3 | 11.4 | 7.0 | 4.0 | 7.0 | 2.2 | -3.9 | 3.3 | -4.4 | 3.0 |
| Chicoutimi-Jonquière | 2.9 | 28.6 | 65.3 | 45.7 | 21.6 | 17.1 | 10.1 | 8.6 | 0.0 | 0.0 | 25.7 | -19.6 | -4.5 | -1.5 | 0.0 |
| Quebec | 27.5 | 31.1 | 44.3 | 37.1 | 18.7 | 16.6 | 6.1 | 7.9 | 3.4 | 7.3 | 3.6 | -7.2 | -2.1 | 1.8 | 3.9 |
| Sherbrooke | 8.6 | 25.8 | 61.7 | 32.3 | 12.0 | 19.4 | 10.6 | 12.9 | 7.1 | 9.7 | 17.2 | -29.4 | 7.4 | 2.3 | 2.6 |
| Trois-Rivières | | 11.8 | | 55.9 | | 14.7 | | 8.8 | | 8.8 | . | . | . | . | . |
| Montreal | 23.5 | 20.9 | 39.0 | 31.3 | 22.1 | 25.5 | 9.5 | 12.1 | 5.8 | 10.2 | -2.6 | -7.7 | 3.4 | 2.6 | 4.4 |
| Ottawa-Hull | 55.2 | 54.8 | 27.2 | 26.0 | 12.6 | 12.0 | 4.1 | 4.8 | 0.8 | 2.4 | -0.4 | -1.2 | -0.6 | 0.7 | 1.6 |
| Kingston | 54.5 | 64.7 | 32.7 | 23.5 | 8.1 | 8.8 | 4.7 | 2.9 | 0.0 | 0.0 | 10.2 | -9.2 | 0.7 | -1.8 | 0.0 |
| Peterborough | 65.2 | 56.5 | 23.8 | 34.8 | 6.0 | 4.3 | 5.0 | 4.3 | 0.0 | 0.0 | -8.7 | 11 | -1.7 | -0.7 | 0.0 |
| Oshawa | 75.1 | 69.4 | 20.4 | 20.4 | 2.0 | 10.2 | 2.6 | 0.0 | 0.0 | 0.0 | -5.7 | 0 | 8.2 | -2.6 | 0.0 |
| Toronto | 59.8 | 50.5 | 26.8 | 30.5 | 10.0 | 14.3 | 2.3 | 3.6 | 1.1 | 1.1 | -9.3 | 3.7 | 4.3 | 1.3 | 0.0 |
| Hamilton | 51.4 | 45.1 | 30.8 | 35.2 | 10.7 | 12.3 | 4.5 | 4.9 | 2.6 | 2.5 | -6.3 | 4.4 | 1.6 | 0.4 | -0.1 |
| St. Catharines-Niagara | 39.3 | 50.6 | 40.2 | 41.0 | 19.9 | 8.4 | 0.6 | 0.0 | 0.0 | 0.0 | 11.3 | 0.8 | -11.5 | -0.6 | 0.0 |
| Kitchener | 49.2 | 51.9 | 46.3 | 43.2 | 4.4 | 4.9 | 0.0 | 0.0 | 0.0 | 0.0 | 2.7 | -3.1 | 0.5 | 0.0 | 0.0 |
| Brantford | 42.0 | 52.4 | 43.0 | 38.1 | 13.7 | 9.5 | 1.3 | 0.0 | 0.0 | 0.0 | 10.4 | -4.9 | -4.2 | -1.3 | 0.0 |
| Guelph | 68.4 | 71.4 | 26.9 | 19.0 | 4.7 | 9.5 | 0.0 | 0.0 | 0.0 | 0.0 | 3.0 | -7.9 | 4.8 | 0.0 | 0.0 |
| London | 47.3 | 44.3 | 38.8 | 46.6 | 9.4 | 8.0 | 4.6 | 1.1 | 0.0 | 0.0 | -3.0 | 7.8 | -1.4 | -3.5 | 0.0 |
| Windsor | 48.1 | 44.1 | 29.3 | 30.5 | 20.2 | 18.6 | 0.7 | 6.8 | 1.7 | 0.0 | -4.0 | 1.2 | -1.6 | 6.1 | -1.7 |
| Sarnia -Clearwater | 52.0 | 62.5 | 44.0 | 29.2 | 4.0 | 4.2 | 0.0 | 4.2 | 0.0 | 0.0 | 10.5 | -14.8 | 0.2 | 4.2 | 0.0 |
| North Bay | 49.4 | 45.0 | 28.0 | 30.0 | 15.3 | 15.0 | 4.9 | 10.0 | 2.3 | 0.0 | -4.4 | 2.0 | -0.3 | 5.1 | -2.3 |
| Sudbury | 22.5 | 43.2 | 65.8 | 45.9 | 7.1 | 5.4 | 4.5 | 5.4 | 0.0 | 0.0 | 20.7 | -19.9 | -1.7 | 0.9 | 0.0 |
| Sault Ste. Marie | 32.0 | 40.9 | 57.2 | 40.9 | 4.0 | 13.6 | 6.8 | 4.5 | 0.0 | 0.0 | 8.9 | -16.3 | 9.6 | -2.3 | 0.0 |
| Thunder Bay | 53.6 | 53.3 | 40.5 | 40.0 | 5.9 | 3.3 | 0.0 | 3.3 | 0.0 | 0.0 | -0.3 | -0.5 | -2.6 | 3.3 | 0.0 |
| Winnipeg | 41.7 | 32.3 | 37.3 | 34.8 | 7.8 | 16.8 | 7.4 | 5.8 | 5.8 | 10.3 | -9.4 | -2.5 | 9.0 | -1.6 | 4.5 |
| Regina | 45.6 | 38.8 | 29.2 | 38.8 | 19.9 | 14.3 | 4.5 | 6.1 | 0.9 | 2.0 | -6.8 | 9.6 | -5.6 | 1.6 | 1.1 |
| Saskatoon | 21.4 | 33.3 | 58.1 | 41.7 | 11.8 | 16.7 | 7.8 | 6.3 | 0.9 | 2.1 | 11.9 | -16.4 | 4.9 | -1.5 | 1.2 |
| Lethbridge | 23.5 | 45.0 | 62.3 | 50.0 | 14.3 | 5.0 | 0.0 | 0.0 | 0.0 | 0.0 | 21.5 | -12.3 | -9.3 | 0.0 | 0.0 |
| Calgary | 39.0 | 35.9 | 43.7 | 40.5 | 14.6 | 16.3 | 2.3 | 6.5 | 0.5 | 0.7 | -3.1 | -3.2 | 1.7 | 4.2 | 0.2 |
| Red Deer | | 37.5 | | 37.5 | | 12.5 | | 12.5 | | 0.0 | . | . | . | . | . |
| Edmonton | 37.3 | 32.3 | 41.5 | 35.5 | 16.2 | 21.5 | 3.7 | 8.1 | 1.4 | 2.7 | -5.0 | -6.0 | 5.3 | 4.4 | 1.3 |
| Kelowna | 19.6 | 53.8 | 75.6 | 34.6 | 0.0 | 11.5 | 4.8 | 0.0 | 0.0 | 0.0 | 34.2 | -41 | 11.5 | -4.8 | 0.0 |
| Kamloops | 19.0 | 40.9 | 64.3 | 40.9 | 5.8 | 18.2 | 10.9 | 0.0 | 0.0 | 0.0 | 21.9 | -23.4 | 12.4 | -10.9 | 0.0 |
| Matsqui | | 55.2 | | 34.5 | | 10.3 | | 0.0 | | 0.0 | . | . | . | . | . |
| Vancouver | 30.3 | 36.2 | 44.6 | 46.0 | 19.2 | 14.1 | 3.0 | 2.0 | 2.9 | 1.7 | 5.9 | 1.4 | -5.1 | -1.0 | -1.2 |
| Victoria | 37.9 | 60.0 | 47.5 | 32.3 | 13.4 | 6.2 | 0.0 | 1.5 | 1.3 | 0.0 | 22.1 | -15.2 | -7.2 | 1.5 | -1.3 |
| Prince George | 29.8 | 43.5 | 56.1 | 47.8 | 6.8 | 4.3 | 7.3 | 4.3 | 0.0 | 0.0 | 13.7 | -8.3 | -2.5 | -3.0 | 0.0 |
| Average | 39.12 | 44.28 | 43.03 | 36.62 | 12.00 | 12.68 | 4.64 | 4.62 | 1.22 | 1.79 | 5.20 | -6.40 | 0.70 | 0.00 | 0.60 |

Not only do the cities differ in terms of these proportions, but they also vary in terms of the pattern of change experienced between 1986 and 1991. Figure 2-4 is a graphical representation of these changes for the major Canadian cities. A careful examination of the magnitude of changes in the proportional population of neighbourhoods with different levels of poverty shows at least four distinct patterns among Canadian cities, which, in the absence of better words, we call *betterment, worsening, polarization*, and *homogenization*.

First, those cities that have experienced *betterment* in terms of their spatial concentration of poverty include Kingston, St. Catharines-Niagara, Kitchener, Vancouver, and Victoria. In almost all of these cities, the proportions of city population living in high poverty neighbourhoods have declined and those of richer neighbourhoods have increased. This development may have to do with the declining poverty in the city, as well as the possible building up of new neighbourhoods, which may facilitate a more even redistribution of the population.

A second pattern, that of a *worsening* situation, is noticeable for cities such as Montreal, Winnipeg., Edmonton, Regina, Calgary, and Toronto. In these cities the proportions of city population living in low poverty areas have declined and those of high poverty neighbourhoods have risen. Montreal and Winnipeg are the two worst cases in this category. This is not surprising at all, given the fact that these two cities have consistently been in the lower ranks of poverty measures. Another observation in this regard is the presence of almost all Prairie CMAs in this category. They vary, however, with regard to the severity of the problem.

A third pattern, which may be called a *polarization* situation, can be seen in cities such as Quebec, Halifax, Guelph, and Saskatoon. Cities in this category, for which Halifax provides a perfect example, have experienced a decline in the proportions of population in the middle categories and an increase in the two extreme ones. This means that if the 1986 to 1991 trend continues, these cities will have more and more of their population living in two types of neighbourhoods that differ drastically from each other.

The fourth pattern, *homogenization*, applies to cities such as London, Hamilton, and, to a lesser extent, Windsor. These cities have experienced rising proportions of population in neighbourhoods in the middle categories of poverty, at the expense of those in the extreme categories. This indicates that, if the trend continues, more and more people will be living in more or less similar types of neighbourhoods as far as neighbourhood poverty is concerned.

There are some cities, such as Oshawa, and smaller cities that are not included in the graphs, which do not comply with any of the mentioned patterns. They do not reveal any specific trend, at least in the period under examination.

FIGURE 2-4

CHANGES IN THE PROPORTIONAL DISTRIBUTION OF CITY POPULATION IN CTS WITH DIFFERENT
POVERTY LEVELS, 1986-91

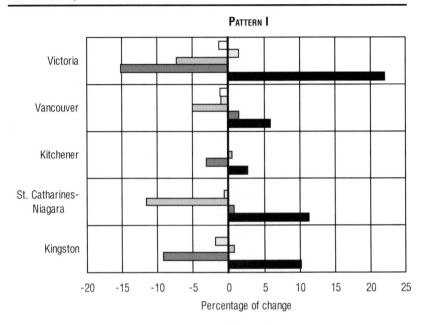

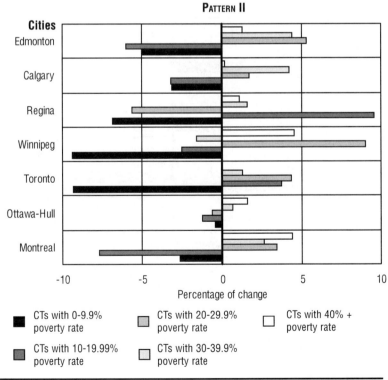

FIGURE 2-4  (continued)

CHANGES IN THE PROPORTIONAL DISTRIBUTION OF CITY POPULATION IN CTs WITH DIFFERENT POVERTY LEVELS, **1986-91**

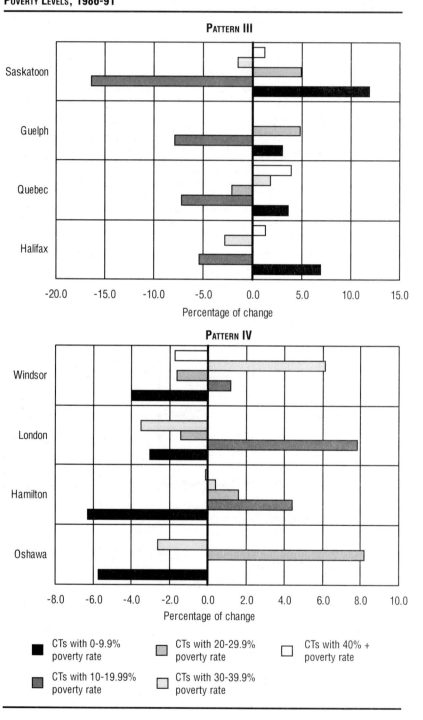

# CHAPTER THREE

# Neighbourhood: The Ethnic Dimension

T he discussion presented in Chapter Two revealed that the magnitude of neighbourhood poverty in certain Canadian cities, though not as high as those in some American cities, was noticeably high. It did not, however, provide any insight into the type of people who are most likely to live in extremely poor neighbourhoods. The American as well as European studies had already shown that racial or ethnic colour was associated with this phenomenon. This was partly due to a simultaneous awakening of racial and ethnic alignments all across the world; an unexpected phenomenon that has provoked many new studies of ethnicity internationally. This provides enough justification to study the new rise of ethnic sentiments as a whole before exploring the ethnic dimension of neighbourhood poverty in Canada. The present chapter examines this global phenomenon and, in particular, the way it is reflected in Canadian urban space.

To many social scientists, the rise of ethnic conflicts in different parts of the world during the 1980s and 1990s came as a surprise. The severe ethnic clashes in Eastern Europe were considered to be primarily domestic problems, limited in scope, and closely tied to the collapse of the Soviet bloc. The eruption of ethnic clashes in many parts of Africa and Asia, however, revealed that the rise of ethnic sentiments was not confined to Eastern Europe. Later developments, such as the alignment of public opinion along ethnic lines during the Quebec referendum in Canada and along racial lines during the O.J. Simpson trial and One-Million-Men-March in the Unites States, revealed that the ethnic and racial sentiments are quite alive also in North America. They appear to be as much alive in the First World as they were in the Second and the Third.

The rise of ethnic problems came at a time when the social sciences, and in particular, sociology, were ill prepared for it. It was both theoretically unexpected and socio-politically unprecedented. On a theoretical level, the inadequate attention paid to race and ethnicity was visible in both modern and classic sociology, but more pronounced in the latter. Mainly concerned with the transition from a traditional-agricultural-feudal society to a modern-industrial-capitalist one in Europe, the founders of sociology seemed to share a more or less similar position on ethnicity. For them, ethnicity was an issue of the past, the demise of which was marked by the newly emerging industrial society.

This "of-the-past" stature of ethnicity for nineteenth-century sociologists found its clearest expression in the historical perspective set forward by the German sociologist Max Scheler. Like Weber, Scheler was trying to invalidate what he called the "exaggeration and erroneous generalization" of Marxism in reducing complex social dynamics into a "predominantly economic" explanation (Scheler, 1980 [1926]: 62). Towards this end, Scheler suggests that there have been three distinct historical periods in each one of which only one factor has been the main cause of events: the period of blood ties, the period of the political factor, and finally, the era of the economic factor.

> [T]here are the following phases for the course of events conditioned *only by inner* causes: 1. a phase in which blood relationships of every kind and the institutions rationally regulating *them* (rights of fathers and mothers, forms of marriage, exogamy and endogamy, clan groups, integration and segregation of races, together with the "limits" set for them by law and custom) form the *independent variables* of events and determine at least primarily the *form* of groupings, i.e. determine the *latitude* for that which *can* happen through other causes of a real sort, such as political or economic ones; 2. a phase in which this effective primacy ... passes over to the *political* power factors, primarily to the workings of the state; and 3. a phase in which *economics* holds the effective primacy and in which the "economic factors" are the first to determine the conditions for real events, openings and closing the sluices' for the history of mind. In this way the old dispute among various conceptions and explanations of history would itself become *historically relativized* (Scheler, 1980 [1962]:58).

According to this classification, racial and ethnic dynamics are most important and determining only in the first phase. If there is going to be any residue of ethnicity and/or race in the succeeding stages, Scheler argues, it will be of lesser influence and will be shaped by either political or economic factors.

A similar view of ethnicity can be found among some modern sociologists. Analyzing Canadian society, Himelfarb and Richardson (1991:384), for example, point out that "ethnicity may not any longer be a very good determinant of what will happen to most people." For them, social class explains most of the social variations found in Canadian society. Surprisingly, this statement was made at a time when an intense discussion of ethnic discrimination in the job market and the resultant Employment Equity programs were under way in Canada.

A number of developments during the period since the nineteenth century contributed to the undermining of ethnic identities and the strengthening of the ethnic-blind nature of sociology. One such development was that of nation-building projects. Nation-building—which began as early as the sixteenth century in Europe, the eighteenth and nineteenth centuries in North America, and the post-World War II period for many nations in Africa, Asia, and Latin America—was a process that transformed numerous "ethnically-homogenous/politically-dispersed" local communities into fewer "politically-unified/ethnically-heterogeneous" nations (Hettne, 1995). Through this process, ethnic identities were undermined, and sometimes suppressed, in favour of national identities. Moreover, the economic development policies that followed were designed to address these artificially and forcibly shaped nations. The suppression of ethnic identities, indeed, became a prerequisite for building *nationhood.*

The second development that caused ethnic identities to appear less significant was the conspicuous post-World War II growth in economies and the improvement in living conditions, especially in the industrial nations. The economic growth rates in this period, a record high, provided an enormous economic surplus for the industrial countries; this surplus was later redistributed among the population via the welfare system. Such a development trend pushed people to leave their ethnic links behind in favour of joining nations and enjoying the associated benefits. The economic success of the United States, in particular, set an example for other nations. Fukayama, for example, went so far as to claim the "end of history" as, according to him, the whole world was converging towards what the United States had achieved; for him, there was no other imaginable stage beyond this point (Marsh, 1996). Like any other successful experience, the American experience came as a package deal; part of this was the suppression of ethnic and/or racial identities in favour of a new national one: the shaping of a "melting pot."

Ethnic identity was suppressed, not only at the socio-economic level, but also at the cultural-epistemological level. *Universalist* rationalism, as the dominant mode of thought since the Renaissance and as the spirit of the modern age, targeted all *particular* forms of knowledge, for example, religion and ethnic culture. The post-Renaissance science-religion conflict was, indeed, a conflict between universal thinking and particularism. The significant progress of science in the nineteenth and twentieth centuries and its effective linkage with technology marked an unquestionable triumph for universalism. Ethnic identities were to be sacrificed on the altar of universal reason, and so they were.

Despite all these suppressions, ethnicity re-emerged as a powerful social and political force towards the end of the twentieth century. The different dimensions of ethnicity, such as language, religion, place of birth and so on, began to gain more importance than national symbols, such as the national flag and official language. Ethnic and cultural solidarity quickly transcended national borders. Some news-breaking events of the 1990s, such as people marching in Los Angeles under the Mexican flag and those rallying in Sarajevo while waving the Saudi Arabian and Turkish flags, the bloody clashes of different ethnic groups in the former Soviet republics, and the ethnic cleansing in former Yugoslavia and Africa, were certainly not anticipated a decade prior. All these events indicated that people in different corners of the world were, according to Huntington (1996:20), "discovering new but often old identities and marching under new but often old flags, which lead to wars with new but often old enemies." This development was, and still is, quite puzzling; why such a powerful re-emergence of ethnic assertiveness? Why an ethnic resurgence?

## Why an Ethnic Resurgence? Proposed Explanations

For many, this rising ethnic assertiveness still appears to be a problem that is directly related to domestic conditions. A lack of global vision has led many to focus on the immediate conditions that may have led to this ethnic resurgence. The problem, however, is too widespread in the world to be adequately explained in terms of domestic factors. It calls for an alternative explanation, more comprehensive and global in nature.

In the following section, we will discuss two such explanations. The first, which has its own variations, points to the erosion of the nation-state as the main cause of rising ethnic assertiveness. The second, stresses the beginning of a new era in world politics, as a result of which political, ideological, and economic distinctions have given way to cultural distinctions. At the end, an effort is made to broaden the vision by suggesting some conceptual additions.

### *The Erosion of the Nation-State: McWorld vs. Jihad*

The globalization of the world economy had serious consequences for the nation-states. The rapid expansion of transportation and communication technologies in the last two to three decades made it easier for capital and labour to move across national borders. It brought about radical changes in patterns of international migration and capital investment. Geographic distance, along with the institutions closely associated with geographical units, became trivial; the nation-state was one such institution. As a consequence, the nation-state began losing its status as a major player in the international scene.

As a result of the gradual erosion of the nation-state, two other agents of social action emerged, one above the nation-state, the other below it (Mahon, 1991): transnational corporations, international organizations, and special interest groups were among the first (Morss, 1991), local and regional units, among the second. Barber (1996 [1992]) called these two rising players *McWorld* and *Jihad* forces, with the former demanding "integration and uniformity," and the latter, "retribalization of large swaths of humankind."

The empowerment of local communities inevitably led to the emergence of a stronger ethnic element, because, in many parts of the world, the small communities still have a strong ethnic or racial character. Put differently, "the ethnic groups are most commonly locally based" (Hettne, 1995:202). This is a known fact in the developing world, but it also applies, although to a lesser degree, in the industrialized countries. The recent resurgence of ethnicity in the world, therefore, can be linked to the rising significance of small-scale communities.

## Ethno-Undevelopment

Unlike the first explanation, which relates the ethnic rise to recent developments in the world economy, Hettne (1995) links it to the way economic development policies have been designed and practised since World War II. Those aspects of development policy that may have had some bearing on ethnic life are, according to Hettne (1995:195), the struggle for scarce resources, regional imbalances, infrastructural investments, labour market conflicts, and distributional conflicts.

Hettne (1995) explains these possibilities in the following way. Scarcity of natural resources may create conflicts when resources that are shared by several groups diminish, or when these resources are claimed by an external power. Sometimes the growing competition for these resources can lead to ethnocide or the exodus of marginalized groups. Regional imbalances, on the other hand, mean that certain regions are placed in more advantageous positions than others and consequently attract more investment and skills. Those excluded become reluctant citizens and often express their protests in ethnic terms, which is typically the only mode of social organization known to them. Infrastructural and industrial projects, in many cases, adversely affect the local ecosystems. In such cases, the local inhabitants must adapt to a reduced quality of life and may even be forced to abandon their traditional habitat; ecocide, in turn, leads to ethnocide. A two-tier labour market can also lead to the concentration of certain ethnic groups in disadvantaged jobs; through this, the economic structure finds an ethnic colour. Finally, governments sometimes directly contribute to the rise of ethnic assertiveness by the way in which they distribute public jobs, education, employment, and patronage. The allocation of education and public employment opportunities by quotas, for example, makes it necessary to belong to a certain community and remain a loyal member of it (Hettne, 1995). It is in this context that Hettne suggests the notion of *ethnodevelopment*–"development within a framework of cultural pluralism"–as an alternative to "national development."

## Clash of Civilizations

The *clash of civilizations* thesis, a second explanation of the recent resurgence of ethnicity, was introduced in the early 1990s, simultaneous with the end of the Cold War (Fassihian, 1998). The main tenet of this thesis is that in the post-Cold War era, ideology, politics, and economy are no longer the sources of distinction among different people; instead, culture has become more important. Global politics, Huntington (1996:125) contends, "is being reconfigured along cultural lines." The identity crisis stemming from the demise of the Cold War is being responded to with a return to traditional cultural identities.

> Peoples and nations are attempting to answer the most basic question
> humans can face: Who are we? And they are answering that question
> in the traditional way human beings have answered it, by reference to
> the things that mean most to them. People define themselves in terms
> of ancestry, religion, language, history, values, customs, and institutions
> (Huntington, 1996:21).

The cultural line that people are increasingly clustering around, and
identify themselves with, is two-fold: "civilizations" at the international
level, and "ethnic groups" at the domestic level. Huntington (1996:43)
defines civilization by common objective elements, such as "language,
history, religion, customs, institutions," and by subjective "self-identification
of people." For him, civilization marks "the highest cultural grouping of
people and the broadest level of cultural identity." Ethnicity, on the other
hand, is the same entity, but on a local scale. According to Huntington
(1996:28), "local politics is the politics of ethnicity; global politics is the
politics of civilizations." This thesis suggests that most of today's inter- and
intra-national events can be understood as realignment efforts along these
new cultural lines.[7]

Huntington (1996) suggests that there are seven contemporary
civilizations: (1) *Sinic*, which describes the common culture of China and
Chinese communities in Southeast Asia, as well as the related cultures of
Vietnam and Korea; (2) *Japanese*, which was an offspring of the Chinese
civilization but grew into a distinct one; (3) *Hindu*, referring to the most
recent civilization that emerged in the Indian subcontinent; (4) *Islamic*,
which extends from the Middle East to North Africa and the Iberian
peninsula as well as into central Asia, the Indian subcontinent, and
Southeast Asia; (5) *Orthodox*, which is centred in Russia; (6) *Western*, which
has some major components: European, North American, Australian and/
or New Zealander, and Latin American, with the last being separable as a
distinct civilization; and (7) *African*, which is not yet a distinct civilization,
but can cohere into one, consisting mainly of sub-Saharan Africa.

The boundaries of different civilizations do not match the political
boundaries. This is to say that the dividing line between two civilizations
may sometimes cross a nation, such as the former Yugoslavia, Albania,
and many African countries. This has resulted in some internal conflicts
that, due to the civilizational affiliation of confronting parties, have easily
turned into global crises. The ethnic cleansing in former Yugoslavia and
the bloody confrontations in the former Soviet Union Republics are just
some acute examples of this.

---

7. Today, the majority of the world's scholars and intellectuals, who consciously seek to
   defuse rather than incite tensions between powerful global players, reject Huntington's
   thesis. But there are many politicians who have subscribed to Huntington's divisive
   ideas, mostly for domestic consumption by their national constituency. It is important
   to note that all of these arguments are almost always presented by governments, their
   oppositions, and leading intellectuals in major capitals around the world, and rarely
   does the opportunity exist for the ordinary citizens of these societies to express their
   views about their own culture in relation to foreign cultures (Fassihian, 1998).

Civilizational distinction, however, does not necessarily mean civilizational conflict. While the different civilizations will always have some frictions, especially in the boundary areas, the severity of such frictions varies from one civilization to another. In other words, differences exist, but it is only in certain cases that they become seriously conflictual. Huntington suggests Figure 3-1 as a representation of the emerging alignments and the severity of conflicts among them.

One obvious implication of the model above is that the relatively simple, and bipolar structure of the world in the Cold War era is giving way to a much more complex, multipolar, and multicivilizational one. It should also be noted that the inter-civilizational conflicts are not the only ones that may occur; conflicts also exist within civilizations.

## Some Missing Links

As the preceding explanations suggest, the decline and re-emergence of ethnic sentiments resulted from a perplexing set of conditions, from economic to epistemological. Each of the explanations above captures one aspect of this complex trend. There are, however, two other factors that may also have had some bearing on the recent revival of ethnicity: *the evolution of the welfare system*, and the *rise of a postmodern culture*. In the following pages, these two are briefly discussed and the potential ways they may have affected ethnicity are highlighted.

FIGURE **3-1**

THE GLOBAL POLITICS OF CIVILIZATION: EMERGING ALIGNMENTS

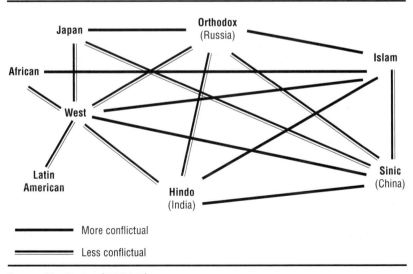

Source: Huntington (1996:245)

## Evolution of the Welfare System

Earlier, we discussed that the erasure of the welfare state had far-reaching outcomes for the social structure of some industrial nations. Rising poverty as well as escalating income inequality were two such outcomes. The withdrawal of the state from the manipulation of the market led to a situation in which certain segments of population became chronically trapped in circles of poverty and deteriorating living conditions. How can ethnicity be affected by the changes in the welfare state?

The underlying foundation of the welfare state is the notion of *decommodification* or social citizenship. *Decommodification* is defined as the degree to which the welfare states "permit people to make their living standards independent of pure market forces" (Espinding-Anderson, 1990:3). Social citizenship, on the other hand, refers to "the notion that all members of society have a right to certain social services and programs such as health care, education, old age pensions, and unemployment insurance" (Teeple, 1995:49). The application of these notions to the structure of governments led to the formation of welfare states in the industrial world during the post-World War II period.

These goals, however, were achieved through different models of the welfare state, the most important of which were liberal, social democratic, and conservative. The liberal model is perhaps the most widely known type of welfare state. In this model—the archetypical examples of which are the Unites States, Canada, and Australia—"means-tested assistance, modest universal transfers, or modest social-insurance plans predominate" (Esping-Anderson, 1990:26). Through the monitoring and support of the market, the state becomes the primary agent of the decommodification process. The social democratic model, predominant in Sweden, is different from the liberal one in that it promotes "an equality of the highest standards, not an equity of minimal needs" (Esping-Anderson, 1990:27). The conservative model, traditionally predominant in Austria, France, Germany, and Italy, is "typically shaped by Church, and hence strongly committed to the preservation of traditional family-hood." In this model, the state interferes only "when the family's capacity to service its members is exhausted" (p.27).

Out of the three types of welfare states, the last one contains a number of social elements that are strongly related to ethnicity. Religious communities as well as family and kinship ties play crucial roles in providing welfare benefits to fellow associates. This means that in societies dominated by this model of welfare state, religious and kinship networks should be strongly present; incidentally, these networks are the ones that also inspire ethnic awareness. The secondary role of the state in this model certainly makes it an attractive alternative for the liberal welfare states in an era of public sector downsizing and state expenditure cutting. Given the worldwide trend of downsizing governments and welfare systems, we are quite likely to see a gradual shift from the liberal and social democratic models to the conservative model of welfare state and, hence, more emphasis on ethnic communities.

## Postmodern Culture

Anything but a brief discussion of *postmodernism* would certainly be out of place here. At the same time, however, a brief account of postmodernism can by no means do justice to the complexity of postmodernist discourse. One source of this complexity is the fact that postmodern ideas have now penetrated a vast range of academic disciplines, from literal criticism and arts to architecture, sociology, economics, and, in some cases, even the natural sciences. In each of the disciplines listed, postmodernism has been stirred in with previous debates and has created a unique mixture. The understanding of postmodernist ideas within one discipline, therefore, does not provide much vision as to what it means in another.

Another source of complexity in postmodernist discourse is that all of the supposedly postmodern thinkers do not mean the same thing by the term *postmodernism.* This is clearly shown by the rising frequency of recent efforts to classify different types of postmodernism, i.e., deconstructive or eliminative versus constructive or revisionary (Griffin, 1988), sceptical versus affirmative (Rosenau, 1992a; 1992b), and historical, methodological, and positive (Cahoone, 1996).

But perhaps the most puzzling thing in postmodernist discourse is its core ideas and arguments, and the unconventional ways in which they are presented. All we can hope for in a brief account of postmodernism, such as this one, is to provide a bird's-eye view of postmodernist discourse with its actual and potential implications for our main issue of concern, ethnicity. To make the task easier, let us further complicate postmodernist discourse by suggesting yet another way to categorize postmodern ideas: the meanings, the levels and causes, and the implications of *postmodernism.*

### The Meanings of Postmodernism

Postmodernism is, not an extension, but a revolt against *modernity,* that is, "the new civilization developed in Europe and North America over the last several centuries and fully evident by the early twentieth century" (Cahoone, 1996:11). This is the most one can say about postmodernism without entering a grey area. Any further details are highly controversial. The source of controversy is the existence of different perceptions of what constitutes the essence of modernity and also what historical period modernity corresponds with.

Cahoone (1996) introduces four such perceptions. First, there are some who believe that the modern era began in the sixteenth century, with the Protestant Reformation. Second, there are some who consider the seventeenth-century scientific revolution of Galileo, Harvey, Hobbes, Descartes, Boyle, Leibniz, and Newton to be the prime mover of modernity. Third, there is a group who, looking at eighteenth-century developments, attach more weight to the rise of republican and democratic political ideas and the revolutions of the United States and France. Fourth, there are those who believe that modernity began in the nineteenth century, with the Industrial Revolution. Depending on which of these four one considers to be the essence of modernity, one's definition of *postmodernism* will differ.

Postmodernism is better known, however, by the challenge it has posed to the legacy of the seventeenth-century scientific revolution. The obsession the pioneers of this revolution had with the quantification of nature, the postmodern critics argue, led them to reduce the whole universe to a distorted and purely material one. In this way the world, as well as the science which dealt with it, became "disenchanted" (Griffin, 1988:2). The world was stripped of any sense of meaning, creativity, experience, feeling, and, in one word, subjectivity. In this sense, postmodern thinkers are trying to bring subjectivity back into the world. They want the world and science to be "re-enchanted."

Another group of postmodernists question the social and human, rather than the ideational and philosophical, legacy of the "modern" era: industrialization, urbanization, advanced technology, the nation state, life in the "fast lane," and so on (Rosenau, 1992a). They have also cast doubts on the legitimacy of those social systems that have led to the social disenfranchisement and marginalization of certain groups, such as sexual and racial and/or ethnic groups (Cahoone, 1996:17). It is in this sense that the emergence of postmodernism may lead to a rise of ethnic awareness and identity.

## *The Causes of Postmodernism*

The fact that postmodernism has gained more popularity among scholars in the humanities and social sciences has stimulated some controversy. In a controversial work, Gross and Levitt (1994) associated this with what they called the "new academic left," reflected in literary theory, cultural criticism, feminism, chaos theory, and postmodernism. While an inclination towards the left has always been visible among natural scientists, Gross and Levitt argued, the new academic left has targeted science itself. For them, postmodernism is a cultural manifestation of the anti-science coalition in academia.

In a similar but more moderate approach, Ward (1995) considers postmodernism as a symbolic weapon of literary fields and sub-fields in their confrontation with natural sciences as well as those social scientists who model their methodology and perspective after science. According to Ward (1995:111), what is at stake in this confrontation is not so much the grand search for determining which type of knowledge better captures the way things really are; rather, it is "the task of determining which group will be able to recruit the most allies, obtain the greatest level of funding, attract the most students, and, ultimately, gain organizational, moral, and ideological control of academia."

Finally, Rosenau (1992b:11) associates postmodernism with the changes in the position of intellectuals in the West. One example of such a change is the fact that "academicians in the 1970s and 1980s faced a very poor job market, and many were unemployed." In this sense, postmodernism is associated with the whole academic community rather than with any particular faction within it.

## Postmodernism's Implications for Ethnicity

Postmodernism seems to appeal more to those who might be perceived as desperate (Rosenau, 1992b), as it has a built-in drive to include the "marginalized" elements. This is due to a postmodernist distinction between "text" and "margin"; in the same way that "text" is understandable only in contrast to "margin," postmodernists argue, any system is perceivable only after making the margins a part of the picture. The "privileged" theme is constituted by the "excluded" margins (Cahoone, 1996:16). This logic, extended to its social imperatives, acknowledges the existence and importance of unprivileged groups and individuals.

This attention to the "marginalized" has proven to be promising for the disadvantaged. The fact that it has held more interest for graduate students and junior faculty than for those further along in their careers (Rosenau, 1992b) might be a symptom of this. For rank-and-file people, such attention may mean a wider recognition of the perception of "difference." The result of this recognition is that, as David Cheal (1998:68-69) puts it,

> it would be considered politically incorrect to suggest that one ethnocultural tradition should be given higher or lower standing than another.... Instead, every cultural tradition stands beside every other cultural tradition, on an equal footing and on the same flat plane. In a postmodern symbolic order, difference is the only justification needed for existence.

While the *postmodernist ideology* of the scholars in academia may lead to a wider study of ethnicity and particular cultures, the *postmodern culture* of ordinary people may lead them to act in a manner more closely based on their preferred cultural codes; hence, a revival of interest in ethnicity both as a subject of study and as a frame of reference for social behaviour.

The developments described above have either already strengthened ethnicity or will somehow contribute to this process. As a cultural phenomenon, the ethnic dynamic has the potential to manifest itself in a wide range of social domains, for example, inter-marriage, the job market, and political conflicts. Another domain, closely related to our discussion here, is the residential patterns in urban space. Research in Canada and the United States has established that race and ethnicity have strong bearings on the distribution of population among different neighbourhoods in North American cities.

## Ethnicity in Action: The Case of Spatial Segregation

The Chicago School researchers should be given credit for laying the ground for studying the distribution of ethnic and/or racial groups in cities. They were the first to approach and study urban space as units of analysis. The Chicago School researchers initiated this by their in-depth studies of Chicago, and by suggesting some ideas that later served as basic conceptual tools for spatial analysis. These gave birth to a rich host of studies on the spatial structure of cities. In what follows, a survey of both American and Canadian literature on spatial analysis is presented. Beside the historical similarities of the two countries, the close affinity of American and Canadian spatial analysis literature is another factor that justifies the inclusion of both countries in the section.

### *Spatial Analysis in the United States*

The research on urban space began with the study of Chicago by Park and Burgess in the early 1920s. Still under the influence of the nineteenth-century classical sociologists, Park and Burgess were trying to establish a foundation for sociology modelled after the physical sciences. This tendency is well represented in the following quotation from Robert Park:

> Reduce all social relations to relations of space and it would be possible to apply to human relations the fundamental logic of the physical sciences. Social phenomena would be reduced to the elementary movements of individuals, just as physical phenomena, chemical action, and the qualities of matter, heat, sound and electricity are reduced to the elementary movements of molecules and atoms (quoted in Peach and Smith, 1981:17).

Park believed that even cultural changes could be correlated with changes in the territorial organization of a city (Driedger, 1991). Therefore, as Thomlinson says, at the foundation of the Chicago School's studies there lies a belief in "an intimate congruity between the social order and physical space, between social and physical distance, between social equality and residential proximity" (quoted in Driedger, 1991:80).

Concerned with the spatial trends, and looking at the structure of Chicago, Burgess constructed a concentric zone model for cities and applied to this model such concepts as *segregation, competition, invasion, succession,* and *natural areas* (Gillis, 1995:13.15). *Segregation* refers to the tendency of certain activity patterns, such as commercial or residential activities or certain groups of people, different ethnic or income groups, to cluster and try to segregate themselves by excluding other activities or groups from their territory. To the extent that they are successful, they form a *natural area,* a neighbourhood that is relatively homogeneous (Gillis, 1995:13.15). *Competition* occurs when one activity or group encroaches on the territory of another. To the extent that such an invasion is successful and the incumbent activity or group is eliminated or driven out, *succession* has occurred (Gillis, 1995:13.16). The main point in the above conceptualization effort was to consider urban space as the scene for spatial trends. This was a departure from the previous studies that had traditionally focused on human entities, such as individuals, groups, and families.

The study of urban space found its definitive shape through Shevky and Williams (1949), Bell (1953), and Shevky and Bell (1955); the first two were in-depth studies of Los Angeles and San Francisco, respectively; the third, a theoretical-methodological summary of the two, with some modifications. The common aim of these studies was to provide an "ID tag" for different census tracts in terms of variables such as the extent of urbanization, social rank, family composition, racial segregation level, age structure, and so on. The major contribution they made to the research on urban space was the use of census tracts as relatively stable and comparable units, as well as the computation of composite socio-economic indices for census tracts. This initiative proved to be very helpful in future research.

One interesting finding of their analyses was that the social and residential differentiation in a city is a function of the city's level of societal develop-ment. As societies grow economically, their inhabitants become increasingly heterogeneous with respect to three fundamental dimensions: socio-economic status, family structure, and ethnic background; and these social developments are, in turn, reflected spatially (Massey, 1984:316). Shevky and Bell suggest three factors, the intersection of which defines the residential space within the urban environment (Massey, 1984): (1) social rank or socio-economic status based on occupation and education; (2) family status based on size of family, number of gainfully employed women, and type of residence; and (3) segregation of ethnic and racial groups into clusters (Driedger, 1991).

A number of subsequent studies conducted in Canada and the United States further revealed the immense impact of racial and ethnic factors on the spatial distribution of urban population. While in the United States racial groups such as whites, Blacks, Hispanics and Asians have been the focal point, in Canada there has been more attention directed towards ethnic groups such as the Jews, the Chinese, South Asians, the French, and so on. The typical research questions of these studies are similar: To what extent has common ethnic origin contributed to the concentration of people in certain neighbourhoods? Do all ethnic groups show a similar tendency to concentrate and/or segregate? How much of the spatial behaviour of a certain ethnic group is due to its ethnic characteristics as an ascriptive status, and how much is due to achieved factors such as class, education, occupation? When ethnic origin influences the spatial trends for a certain group, is it because of their genuine preference for concentration, or is the trend adopted as a defensive measure against the prejudice and discrimination they may have experienced?

The studies indicate that in the United States Blacks are the most highly segregated racial group, followed by Hispanics and Asians. It is also shown that the segregation of Blacks is, to a large extent, a result of the discrimination they face in American society, ranging from government policies and real estate agencies to neighbourhoods' inhabitants. Not only do Blacks have to concentrate in certain neighbourhoods, they must also confine themselves to the poor and deteriorated ones. The studies indicate that, although the segregation of Blacks has declined over time, it has not been in proportion to the improvements in their socio-economic status.

During the period between 1940 and 1970, the face of American cities altered drastically, due to suburbanization, that is, the loss of the growing middle and upper-middle class to the suburban zone (Choldin and Hanson, 1982:129). This development imprinted the way the urban research was conducted. While in the earlier studies the focus was traditionally on core urban areas, it was gradually acknowledged that, according to Choldin and Hanson (1982:130), "studying city areas in isolation from suburbs has been a methodological deficiency in the literature." The declining status of city areas in the period from 1940 to 1970, they argued, could be only poorly understood and explained if one did not take into consideration the enormous growth of the suburbs, "which were attracting most of the highly educated, affluent households, both newly formed ones and others" (p.134). New suburbs were indeed forming and entering the metropolitan system at the upper end of the status scale, and this affected the structure and composition of the whole scale.

The growth of suburbs sparked a new host of studies among the American spatial researchers. The main concerns in this new surge of studies have been the impact of suburbanization on the spatial distribution of ethnic and/or racial groups; whether suburbanization has occurred equally for all racial and/or ethnic groups, and when it has occurred, whether it creates a less segregated environment, or simply perpetuates the already existing patterns of ethnic concentration and segregation; and finally, whether or not there has been any noticeable differences among the different ethnic and racial groups in terms of their spatial distribution in the suburbs. The research in this area has been more concerned with Blacks, but recently the Hispanics and Asians have also received some attention.

The theoretical debates to explain the suburban spatial patterns are not qualitatively different from the ones used for the urban core. According to Logan et al. (1996:854), these theoretical debates can be organized around two broad approaches. One is the *spatial assimilation model*, which suggests that "segregation mostly reflects group differences in resources and preferences." According to this model, minorities and especially the immigrants of certain ethnic origins start from the margins of society, and, as they become more assimilated and participate more actively in the dominant culture, as well as advance in education and class status, they are expected to move out of their traditional enclaves and ghettos. The second perspective, the *place/racial stratification model*, suggests that ethnic and racial inequality is "an integral part of the social structure and is reflected in the unequal spatial distribution of groups." The unique experience of Asians in the United States, however, suggests the possibility of a third alternative, the *enclave model*; people of certain ethnic groups may remain segregated, not because of systematic discrimination against them, but because they prefer a segregated life due to its economic and cultural promises. In their segregation, as Logan et al. (1996:855) put it, "there is a high degree of voluntarism–and success–associated with the economic and residential boundaries that separate them from mainstream society."

The rise of suburbs provided a new environment to put the above perspectives to the test. While most of the previous studies had indicated that the Blacks' segregation level had remained high in cities, the question arose as to whether the process had been any different in the suburbs. The vast suburbanization of Blacks in the three decades following World War II raised the possibility that the era of Blacks' high segregation may have come to an end. Logan and Schneider (1984:875) formulated the main questions regarding the Blacks' segregation and suburbanization in the following way:

> Where it [suburbanization] has occurred, has increased black access to suburbia been accompanied by a weakening of the barriers to entry into all-white suburbs, or has black suburbanization been channeled into the familiar pattern of segregation? Has the recent renewed growth of suburban black population in several southern metropolitan regions reversed the phenomenon of displacement of blacks by whites described for the period through 1970, that is, does the South now more closely resemble the North and West in this respect? (Logan and Schneider, 1984:878).

Addressing these questions, Massey and Denton (1988a:593) found that Blacks' suburbanization does not seem to have markedly affected the extent of Black-white segregation. In 1970, they argue, racial segregation in suburbs remained quite high and could not be attributed to socio-economic factors. Other than having an initial higher proportion of Blacks, the suburbs that attract Black residents tend to be older areas, with relatively low socio-economic status, high population density, typically adjacent to or near the central city, relatively unattractive to white renters and home buyers, and, often, they are older, manufacturing suburbs characterized by weak tax bases, poor municipal services, and high degrees of debt (Massey and Denton, 1988a; Logan and Schneider, 1984). This pattern indicates that, although in a less extreme fashion, "Black suburbs replicate the conditions of inner cities" (Massey and Denton, 1988a:593-594).

The particular pattern of Blacks' segregation in suburbs is generated, or perpetuated, through a variety of individual and institutional mechanisms. Small homogeneous suburbs and ethnic blue-collar areas are more likely to resist integration through collective action, while the high-status suburbs rely on high rents or restrictive zoning to keep Blacks out (Massey and Denton, 1988a). Also, the local governments have contributed to this process through property tax regulations (Logan and Schneider, 1984).

Compared to the relatively heavy research on Blacks' segregation in the United States, there has been much less research focused on patterns of Hispanic suburbanization, and virtually no work has been done on trends in Asian suburbanization in the United States (Massey and Denton, 1988a:594). The few studies done have consistently revealed that Hispanics are significantly more suburbanized and less segregated than Blacks; also, that their segregation is "highly related to socioeconomic status" (Massey and Denton, 1988a:594). In contrast to Hispanics, Asian suburbanization has increased significantly in nearly all metropolitan areas. This combination of the high level of suburbanization and the fact that most of the Asians are relatively new immigrants to the United States, indicates that Asians, according to Massey and Denton (1988a:601), appear to deviate from the traditional American immigrant pattern by bypassing inner-city enclaves as a first step in the process of spatial assimilation. In general, they conclude, "there is little evidence of extensive Asian segregation in either cities or suburbs" (p.607).

The spatial research in the United States, however, has not evolved only conceptually; it has also improved methodologically. The availability of aggregate data on neighbourhoods was a great catalyst in this respect; it was in 1970 that the United States census made computerized data on American neighbourhoods widely available for the first time, and the continuation of this practice in 1980 corrected several weaknesses in prior research (Massey and Denton 1993:61). This ignited a whole battery of quantitative studies, with sharper policy implications.

Recently, however, the validity of the inferences based on aggregate data has been questioned. Logan et al. (1996), for example, raised the possibility of ecological fallacy, that is, "what is true of group averages may not be true for individuals." They also mentioned that "even where the theoretical question is posed at the group level, cross-regional comparisons can be misleading if they do not control for individual processes." To address this potential problem, they believe that two different types of studies need to be conducted in this area, one based on individual-level data, the other, on tract-level data (Logan et al., 1996:444). They also suggested that studies of the spatial trends need to be conducted, controlling for individual variables.

Logan et al. (1996) took the first step towards the simultaneous study of the aggregate and individual data on spatial segregation. Taking the dwelling neighbourhood as the dependent variable, they tried to see the effects and relative significance of independent variables, such as one's income, ethnic background, education, occupation, and so forth. They found that, despite some minor differences, the findings of these individual-level studies, in general, corroborated the findings of the aggregate-level studies (Logan et al., 1996; Alba et al., 1994; Alba and Logan, 1993; Logan, Alba, and Leung, 1996).

Notwithstanding their merits, these individual-tract studies are currently facing a major challenge: lack of sufficient data. Census authorities do not release such joint data due to their commitment to the confidentiality principle. Some researchers have used an unusual data set at the individual level, prepared for Douglas and Massey and Nancy Denton, which contains a 1% sample of households and individuals in the 50 largest American metropolitan areas (Alba and Logan, 1993). The problem with this data set, however, is that for the sake of anonymity, metropolitan areas are not identifiable. Also, it is not yet part of routine data generation policies, which hinders the possibility of longitudinal studies. In the case of Canada, the major limitation are that such data are not available at all.

However, this is not the only thing that differentiates the Canadian spatial research from the American research. Despite their resemblance, mostly in theoretical and methodological arenas, they vary due to differences in the population size of both their cities and ethnic groups, racial and/or ethnic composition, and historical backgrounds of ethnic groups. These differences justify a more detailed review of Canadian literature on ethnic and/or racial segregation.

## *Spatial Analysis in Canada*

Stanley Lieberson was one of the first sociologists to study residential segregation in Canadian cities (Driedger, 1991:137). In a study focused on language, and comparing 13 metropolitan centres in Canada, he found that there was a correlation between residential segregation and retention of the French language. He then concluded that French retention ratios vary inversely to the degree to which French Canadians encounter people who speak only English. While his study was the first step along this line of research, it fell short of embracing all ethnic groups.

The most extensive work on the patterns of spatial segregation of ethnic groups in Canadian cities has been done by Balakrishnan. In an initial effort to test the generalizability of Chicago School models of urban space, Balakrishnan and Jarvis (1976) tried to apply these models to the 1961 data on Canadian cities. Their study was also heavily influenced by Shevky and Bell's social area analysis. They specified three dimensions against which the patterns of spatial differentiation can be compared: socio-economic status, family size, and ethnic diversity. Balakrishnan and Jarvis (1976) found in most Canadian cities some distinct patterns with regard to the first two dimensions but none for ethnic diversity; the only weak pattern they could identify was that "in some metropolitan areas there is a tendency for ethnic diversity to decrease with distance from the centre." Balakrishnan and Jarvis (1979) repeated this study using 1971 data and found no significant change over the ten-year period.

While it was an original step towards the study of urban space along an ethnic dimension, Balakrishnan and Jarvis (1976; 1979) used only a very narrow aspect of ethnicity, that is, ethnic diversity. The Index of Ethnic

Diversity, originally proposed by Lieberson (1969), looked at the overall composition of population in census tract and city in terms of the proportion of population that belonged to the blanket category of "ethnic population" As a result, the study could not go far enough to establish the possible distinct patterns for different ethnic groups.

In a study of Montreal, Toronto, and Vancouver, Balakrishnan and Kralt (1987) found high levels of segregation for visible minority groups. They proposed two alternative explanations for this: voluntary segregation, also known as the cultural proximity model or social distance model, and involuntary segregation, known as the social class hypothesis. The ethnic segregation, according to the latter model, may be no more than one facet of social class segregation, attributable to factors such as educational background, language proficiency, and recency of immigration. It can also result from the preference of certain ethnic groups to reside in neighbourhoods populated by their compatriots.

Despite their innovative methodology and interesting findings, Balakrishnan and Kralt's (1987) study suffered from its somewhat blurred conceptual framework. As the earlier studies in the United States showed, there also exists a third potential cause for segregation, "discrimination," along with social class and cultural distance. Balakrishnan and Kralt (1987) had implicitly put discrimination under cultural distance. One can argue, however, that the existence of social distance may lead to residential segregation simply because the ethnic groups may feel more comfortable this way; it does not necessarily indicate that they suffer from discrimination. Discrimination needs to be introduced as an independent explanation. In short, the source of conceptual trouble in this study was the mismatch between a bi-dimensional theory and a tri-dimensional reality. In other words, one can consider segregation as the result of three factors: socio-economic status, cultural preference, and discrimination (see Bobo and Zubrinsky, 1996).

In a later study on the patterns of spatial distribution among immigrants in Canada's cities, Balakrishnan and Selvanathan (1990) improved the relevant conceptual framework, taking into consideration the number and size of ethnic groups. They argued that the size of a particular ethnic group may have some bearing on their segregation and concentration tendencies, because it may create a critical mass necessary for formation of ethnic neighbourhoods. Also, in this study they covered all Canadian metropolitan areas. Their findings, however, did not support the hypothesis that there might be an association between the size of ethnic population and level of segregation, indicating that the "ethnically diverse cities do not tell us much about the residential segregation prevalent in those cities" (Balakrishnan and Selvanathan, 1990:403). Among the ethnic groups, their study revealed, Natives and Italians had the highest segregation indices, and the British and Germans, the lowest. Also, the magnitude of segregation among ethnic groups appeared to be consistent with the order of social distance among them, a confirmation of the social distance hypothesis.

One of the innovative features of this study was that they developed a composite index of socio-economic status (SES) for census tracts, using income, education, and occupation. They found that, except for the Natives, who are highly segregated regardless of the level of SES, those of higher social classes are less likely to be segregated. This is to say that the segregation indices tend to decrease as the SES of census tracts increase.

Despite the inclusion of ethnic population size, however, Balakrishnan and Selvanathan (1990) did not address it adequately. The focus of their study was, indeed, on the contributions of social distance and social class in the residential behaviours of ethnic groups. Their finding that there was no significant association between the size and level of segregation may well have been affected by their choice of indices. In order to see the relationship between ethnic population size and segregation, they looked at each city's segregation index and the percentage of non-English or non-French population as a whole. This approach has an underlying deficiency: it overlooks the fact that the critical mass for one group may well be different from that of another. In other words, the particular critical mass of a group is more likely to affect the residential behaviour of that particular group and not that of the others. The hypothesis, therefore, needed to be separately formulated and tested for different groups.

Most recently, in a study of immigrants, Hou and Balakrishnan (1996) addressed the same issue with a far more transparent conceptual framework. They focused on two alternative hypotheses: "spatial concentration and segregation is the result of discrimination," or "it results from what the minorities perceive as its advantage." They also added a third hypothesis, which could be considered a variation of the second one: "new arrivals will go to ethnic enclaves first before moving to other areas as their socioeconomic conditions and ability to adjust to their new country improves." Despite the greater clarity of the new hypotheses, the study poorly addresses them. Also, despite the fact that the first two hypotheses are considered to be the main ones, it is the third corollary one that is addressed more adequately. In short, despite a more clear theoretical framework, Hou and Balakrishnan (1996) fall short in their analysis and interpretation of the findings.

Despite some inadequacies, the Hou and Balakrishnan (1996) study has some important implications for future research. First, they question the classification of ethnic groups into large blanket categories, as they contain a wide range of heterogeneous groups. Blacks, for example, contain British Caribbean, French Caribbean, and Africans, with enormous differences in terms of language, educational level, occupational skills, and cultural background. The South Asian category is another example; within this category, one can find Muslims from Pakistan and Bangladesh, as well as Hindus and Sikhs from India, and Tamils from Sri Lanka. The same is true about the West Asian category, which includes Arabic-speaking people (Muslim and Christian) from Arab countries, and Persian-speaking individuals from Iran. Further research in this area definitely needs to take this diversity into account.

Another point in the Hou and Balakrishnan (1996) study deals with suburbanization, which has received little attention in Canada. They hold that one major argument of the Chicago School researchers, that new immigrants move to the centre of the city and into poor housing, may not be applicable to the highly regulated immigrant population of Canada. This is to say that certain groups of new immigrants to Canada may bypass the inner-city neighbourhoods and settle in suburban areas. It will be interesting to see whether or not the patterns of immigrants' spatial segregation will be any different if the core-urban/sub-urban distinctions are taken into consideration. As was mentioned earlier, this has been a fast growing area of research in the United States.

The debate on the segregation or concentration trends of ethnic groups in both Canada and the United States is heavily indebted to a number of sophisticated indices developed by researchers in the field. The increasing availability of computerized data on neighbourhoods as well as more detailed ethnic categories has added to the validity of the quantitative studies of spatial trends. A review of methodological literature on this issue reveals this progressive trend. The most recently suggested indices, for example, represent more of the multidimensional nature of spatial trends. These indices will be quickly reviewed in the next section.

## How to Measure Residential Segregation: A Methodological Account

The literature on the measurement of spatial segregation, according to Blalock and Wilken (1979), contains a discussion of two questions: what is the appropriate numerical index of segregation, and what are the appropriate units or sub-units to which these measures can be applied? The settlement of these two issues will in turn determine the kind of data needed. In this chapter, we will briefly review the indices used in the segregation literature, followed by a short discussion of the units of measurement, along with a comment on the kind of data to be used. The discussion of indices of segregation in the following section is largely based on the brilliant work of Massey and Denton (1988b).

## Indices of Segregation

Since the very beginning, the spatial research was marked with an ongoing debate over the proper indices of segregation. The introduction of the Dissimilarity Index (DI) by Duncan and Duncan (1955) put an end to what Peach and Smith (1981:12) have called "the index war." For more than 20 years, the Dissimilarity Index served as the standard segregation measure, routinely employed to quantify the spatial segregation between social groups (Massey and Denton, 1988b). The DI became so popular, partly because it was simple to compute and easy to understand (Lieberson, 1981).

However, this *pax Duncana* came to an abrupt end in 1976 (Massey and Denton, 1988b:281), when a number of alternative indices began to emerge. The wide availability of computerized data on American neighbourhoods since 1970 (Massey and Denton 1993:61) allowed for more complicated indices. The application of these indices resulted in different findings, and led the field of segregation studies to, in the words of Massey and Denton (1988b:282), "a state of theoretical and methodological disarray, with different researchers advocating different definitions and measures of segregation."

The number of indices of segregation, however, is not merely due to the availability of data; it also has to do with the fact that residential segregation itself is a multidimensional phenomenon. Massey and Denton (1988b) have suggested five dimensions of ethnic segregation with which the suggested indices correspond; minority members may be distributed so that they are overrepresented in some areas and underrepresented in others (*evenness*); they may be distributed so that their exposure to the majority is limited by virtue of their rarely sharing a neighbourhood with them; they may be spatially *concentrated* within a very small area, occupying less physical space than majority members; they may be spatially *centralized*, congregating around the urban core and occupying a more central location than the majority; and finally, areas of minority settlement may be tightly clustered to form one large contiguous enclave, or be scattered widely around the urban area. What further complicates the picture is that for each one of these dimensions more than one index has been suggested. In what follows, these indices are introduced and discussed.

### Evenness

Evenness refers to the differential distribution of two social groups among areal units in a city. A minority group is segregated if it is unevenly distributed over areal units. Evenness is not measured in any absolute sense, but is scaled relative to some other group. Evenness is maximized and segregation minimized when all units have the same relative number of minority and majority members as the city as a whole (Massey and Denton, 1988b).

## Dissimilarity Index (DI):

The most widely used measure of residential evenness is the Dissimilarity Index, with the following formula:

$$DI = \frac{1}{2} \sum_{i=1}^{n} \left| \frac{N_{1i}}{N_1} - \frac{N_{2i}}{N_2} \right|$$

Where $N_{1i}$= population of group 1 in $i$th census tract, $N_{2i}$= population of groupe 2 in $i$th census tract, $N_{1}$= total population of group 1 in city, and $N_{2}$= total population of group 2 in city. The value of D is equal to the proportion of the minority (or majority) population which would have to be redistributed so that each parcel would have exactly the same composition as the city as a whole (White, 1983:1009).

FIGURE **3-2**

THE GRAPHICAL REPRESENTATION OF **DI**

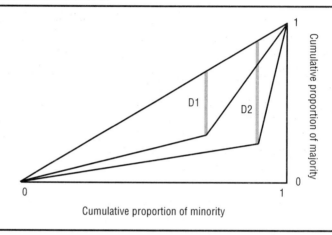

Cumulative proportion of minority

To illustrate the meaning of DI graphically, James and Taeuber (1985: 6-7) have suggested Figure 3-2, in which the cumulative proportion of minority group X is plotted against the cumulative proportion of majority group Y across areal units, ordered from smallest to largest minority proportion. The condition of zero segregation is indicated by the diagonal line. The line for a completely segregated population would lie along the x-axis from 0 to 1 and then rise along the y-axis (James and Taeuber, 1985:6). For the cases between the two extremes, "the D Index is the maximum distance between the segregation curve and the diagonal" p.6) (i.e., D1 and D2).

Using a hypothetical data set (Table 3-1), Lieberson (1981) shows a step-by-step way of calculating DI.

In Table 3-1, columns 2 and 3 express the number of Blacks and whites in each sub-area, and columns 5 and 6, the percentage of Black and white population who live in each sub-area. By converting to percentage distributions, the DI intentionally ignores the absolute numbers involved in each group, and simply compares the two percentage distributions to determine how similar they are to each other. This is done by summing differences between the Black and white percentages in each sub-area (ignoring signs). The DI is one-half the sum of these differences. In the example at hand, the index is $(|30-37| + |10-29| + |0-30| + |60-4|)/2=56$ on a scale of 0 to 100. The DI ranges from zero (in which case there is no segregation because the percentage distribution is identical for each group) to 100 (which would occur in case of maximum segregation, such that Blacks would be found only in sub-areas where whites were absent and vice versa) (Lieberson, 1981). DI has been also called the "displacement index," as it may be interpreted as the proportion of the minority population who would have to change their tract of residence to make the minority and/or majority ratio in each tract equal to the overall ratio (Duncan and Duncan, 1955:211).

**TABLE 3-1**

**A HYPOTHETICAL DATA SET FOR COMPUTATION OF SEGREGATION INDICES**

| (1)<br>Subareas | (2)<br>Number:<br>Blacks | (3)<br>Number:<br>Whites | (4)<br>Total | (5)<br>Percent:<br>Black | (6)<br>Percent:<br>White | (7)<br>Black Proportion<br>of Subarea Total |
|---|---|---|---|---|---|---|
| A | 60 | 370 | 430 | 30 | 37 | 0.140 |
| B | 20 | 290 | 310 | 10 | 29 | 0.065 |
| C | 0 | 300 | 300 | 0 | 30 | 0.000 |
| D | 120 | 40 | 160 | 60 | 4 | 0.750 |
| SUM | 200 | 1,000 | 1,200 | 100 | 100 | |

Source: Lieberson 1981: 62

DI has its shortcomings. Regarding the interpretation of DI as the proportion of the minority population that needs to be transferred in order to reach evenness, for example, Massey and Denton (1988b) point out that these transfers of minority members need to be only from areas where they are overrepresented to areas where they are underrepresented to affect DI. This means that the transfers from underrepresented areas to other underrepresented areas, or transfers from overrepresented areas to other overrepresented areas, would not make much difference.

The other weakness of DI is what was once considered to be its advantage, that is, its immunity from "compositional" influences. Referring to the preceding table, one can easily see that the Dissimilarity Index will remain intact if the white population, for example, were one-tenth of its original size, but had the same distribution; in other words, if the number of whites in each sub-area was divided by 10, that would not cause any change in DI. This feature is not always desirable, especially if one needs to measure the level of interaction between different groups (Lieberson, 1981). It follows that, when the number of minority members is small, the DI is not very reliable (Massey and Denton, 1988b). These weaknesses have led to the introduction of some other indices that account for the compositional effects, namely, the P* indices to which we will return.

## *Gini Coefficient*

Another measure of segregation, closely related to DI and lacking some of its weaknesses, is Gini Coefficient. This index is computed using the following formula:

$$G = \sum_{i=1}^{n_1} \sum_{j=1}^{n_2} \left[ t_i t_j \left| p_i - p_j \right| / 2T^2 P(1-P) \right]$$

Where $t_i$ and $t_j$ are the population of minority and majority groups in areal unit i, and n (sub$^1$) and n (sub$^2$) are the populations of city, and $P$ the population of minority in city as a proportion of total city population.

Likewise, G Index can be represented graphically in Figure 3-3; as the area between the segregation curve and the diagonal, G Index is expressed as the proportion of the total area under the diagonal (Massey and Denton, 1988b).

FIGURE 3-3

THE GRAPHICAL REPRESENTATION OF GINI INDEX

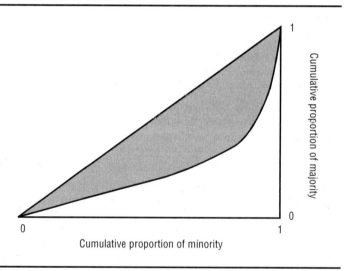

Cumulative proportion of minority

Through the comparison of the graphical illustrations of the two indices, Dissimilarity and Gini, one can see that they should be highly correlated, as the area between the curve and the diagonal is a function of the maximum distance between the curve and the diagonal.

## Entropy Index

Also known as the "Information Index," the Entropy Index measures departure from evenness by assessing each unit's departure from the racial or ethnic "entropy" of the whole city. A city's entropy is the extent of its racial or ethnic diversity, and with two groups it reaches a maximum with a 50-50 division (Massey and Denton, 1988b).

$$E = (P)\log[1/P] + (1-P)\log[1/(1-P)]$$

The above formula measures the entropy of a city. A unit's entropy is measured by the following:

$$E_i = (p_i)\log[1/p_i] + (1-p_i)\log[1/(1-p_i)]$$

The entropy index itself is the weighted average deviation of each unit's entropy from the city-wide entropy, expressed as a fraction of the city's total entropy, by the following formula:

$$H = \sum_{i=1}^{n}[t_i(E - E_i)/ET]$$

The logic of this index lies in the comparison of the information we get based on our observation of each unit and the amount of information we expect to get on the small units, based on the information we have of the overall composition of the society. Applying this index on the racial composition of schools in some American cities, James and Taeuber (1985:8) argued:

> There is little information in a statement that a student drawn at random is black if P is large because one would expect most children so selected to be black. Conversely, if P is small the message that student is black would be unexpected and the information received would be greater. The function chosen to represent the amount of information carried by such a statement, $\log_2(1/P)$, is a decreasing function of P. Thus it gives high scores to unexpected statements and low scores to those with high probabilities. The probability of receiving a message that a student is black is P, and (1-P) is the probability of receiving a message that the student is white. Hence E represents the expected information content of the message prior to its arrival and is computed by weighting the information content of each message by the probability of receiving it. In other words, E represents the expected amount of information in a message reporting the race of a student, given P.

### Atkinson Index

The Atkinson Index is similar to the Gini Index, except that it allows the researcher to decide how heavily to weight areal units at different points on the curve. In the following formula, b is a shape parameter that determines how to weight increments to segregation contributed by different portions of the curve (Massey and Denton, 1988b:286). When b=0.5, units of minority over- and underrepresentation contribute equally in computing the segregation index. For 0<b<.5, areal units where pi<P contribute more to segregation; while for 0.5<b<1.0, units where pi>P give larger increments to segregation.

$$A = 1 - \left[ P / (1 - P) \right] \left| \sum_{i=1}^{n} \left[ (1 - p_i)^{1-b} \, p_i^{b} t_i \, / \, PT \right. \right|^{1/(1-b)}$$

Despite its promises, the Atkinson Index has not been commonly used by sociologists. This may have to do with some inherent problems associated with it, one of which is that the Atkinson Index is undefined for b less than or equal to zero, that is, if there is an areal unit consisting of all-majority or all-minority members (either case produces a divide-by-zero problem) (James and Taeuber, 1985). The other problem is that the value of Atkinson Index will be different for different values of b; therefore, the comparability of research results will suffer if the different researchers select different values of the shape parameter b (Massey and Denton, 1988b:287).

### Exposure

Residential exposure refers to the degree of potential contact, or the possibility of interaction, between minority and majority group members within geographic areas of a city. Rather than measuring segregation as a departure from some abstract ideal of "evenness," exposure indices attempt to measure the experience of segregation as felt by the average minority or majority member (Massey and Denton, 1988b). It was because of on a weakness of the Dissimilarity Index that Lieberson (1981) suggested the family of P*indices as a more promising alternative. The conceptual advantage of exposure indices over the segregation indices is that the former take explicit account of the relative size of minority and majority groups, while the latter is not affected by size of minority and/or majority population ((Massey and Denton, 1988b:287). The xP*y index expresses, according to Lieberson (1981:67), "the probability that someone else [other than a randomly selected member of group X] selected from the same residential subarea will be a member of group Y." Therefore, normally the xP*y will not be equal to yP*x but in the exceptional case where the number of X and Y are identical.

## Interaction Index

There are two intertwined measures of residential exposure. The first, namely, *the Interaction Index*, measures the extent to which members of minority group *X* are exposed to members of majority group *Y*, with the following formula:

$$_xP^*_y = \sum_{i=1}^{n} \left[ x_i / X \right] \left[ y_i / t_i \right]$$

where *x*, *y*, and *t* are the numbers of *X* members, *Y* members, and the total population of unit *i*, respectively, and *X* represents the number of *X* members city-wide. *xP\*y* is interpreted as the probability that a randomly drawn *X*-member shares an area with a member of *Y* (Massey and Denton, 1988b).

## Isolation Index

The second measure, the converse of the *Interaction Index*, is the Isolation Index, which measures the extent to which minority members are exposed only to one another, rather than to majority members (Massey and Denton, 1988b:288):

$$_xP^*_x = \sum_{i=1}^{n} \left[ x_i / X \right] \left[ x_i / t_i \right]$$

In the two-group case, xP*y + xP*x =1.0; however, if more than two groups are present (X1, X2, X3 ,and a majority group Y), then only the sum of all inter-group probabilities plus the isolation index will equal 1.0, that is, x1P*x1 + x1P*x2 + x1P*x3 + x1P*y = 1.0).

To apply the *P\** indices on the hypothetical data in Table 3-1, we can compute the index in the following way:

- P*$_b$$_b$ (the Isolation Index for Blacks) = (60/200)(60/430) + (20/200)(20/310) + (0/200)(0/300) + (120/200)(120/160) =0.498

- P*$_b$$_w$ (the Interaction Index for Blacks with whites) = (60/200)(370/430)+(20/200) (290/310)+(0/200)(300/300) + (120/200)(40/160) = 0.50

- P*$_w$$_b$ (the Interaction Index for whites with Blacks) = (370/1000)(60/430) + (290/1000)(20/310) + (300/1000)(0/300)+ (40/1000)(120/160) = 0.10

## Correlation Ratio

The different values of x$P^*$y and y$P^*$x indicate that the Interaction Index is asymmetric; the values become equal only when two groups compromise the same proportion of the population. In order to remove the asymmetry, the index has been adjusted, the result of which is an equivalent to the correlation ratio, or Eta$^2$ (Massey and Denton, 1988b).

$$V = Eta^2 = \left[ \left( _xP^*_x - P \right) / \left( 1 - P \right) \right]$$

## Concentration

Concentration refers to the relative amount of physical space occupied by a minority group in the urban environment, and relatively few indices of spatial concentration have been proposed in the research literature (Massey and Denton, 1988).

## Delta Index

The only measure, which is indeed a specific application of the general Dissimilarity Index is called Delta, with the following formula:

$$DEL = (1/2)\sum_{i=1}^{n} |[x_i / X - a_i / A]$$

Delta compares the proportion of the minority group with the proportion of the overall area of the city, and is the sum of the absolute values of the differences between the two in all areal units. Like the Dissimilarity Index, it indicates the share of the minority members that would have to shift units to achieve a uniform density of minority members over all units (Massey and Denton, 19988b).

## ACO and RCO Indices

Keeping the logic of the Delta Index, Massey and Denton (1988b) have suggested two other variations of it, which take into account the minimum and maximum possible areas that could be inhabited by an ethnic group in a given city, as well as the distribution of majority group Y:

$$ACO = 1 - \left\{ \left[ \sum_{i=1}^{n}(x_i a_i / X) - \sum_{i=1}^{n1}(t_i a_i / T_1) \right] / \left[ \sum_{i=n2}^{n}(t_i a_i / T_2) - \sum_{i=1}^{n1}(t_i a_i / T_1) \right] \right\}$$

$$RCO = \left\{ \left[ \sum_{i=1}^{n}(x_i a_i / X) \right] / \left[ \sum_{i=1}^{n}(y_i a_i / Y) \right] - 1 \right\} / \left\{ \left[ \sum_{i=1}^{n1}(t_i a_i / T_1) \right] / \left[ \sum_{i=n2}^{n}(t_i a_i / T_2) \right] - 1 \right\}$$

Despite their promises, the two suggested indices may suffer from thelack of any precedence in the literature, which adversely affects the comparability of the ACO- and RCO-based studies with the ones using the more common Delta Index.

## Centralization

Centralization is the degree to which a group is spatially located near the centre of an urban area. Although in most industrialized countries, racial and ethnic minorities concentrate in centre city areas and usually tend to be spatially concentrated as well, this is not a universal pattern. A poor ethnic group may well inhabit a small share of the urban environment and yet be located in a suburban or peripheral area, as is the case in many cities of the developing world as well as in some urban areas of the southwestern United States (Massey and Denton, 1988b), and Toronto in Canada (Ley and Smith, 1997; Murdie, 1998).

## PCC Index

The simplest way to measure centralization is through the use of the following formula:

$$PCC = X_{cc} / X$$

where Xcc is the number of X members living within the boundaries of the central city. The great advantage of the PCC Index is its simplicity and the minimal data it requires; however, the other two indices suggested below make fuller use of spatial data (Massey and Denton, 19988b) and, therefore, are more informative.

## RCE Index

The Relative Centralization Index (RCE) is computed with the following formula:

$$RCE = \left( \sum_{i=1}^{n} X_{i-1} Y_i \right) - \left( \sum_{i=1}^{n} X_i Y_{i-1} \right)$$

in which X and Y are two groups in concern, and $i$ represents the areal units in the order of their distance from the central business district. This index varies between -1.0 and +1.0, with positive values indicating that X members are located closer to the city centre than are members of group Y, and negative values indicating that group X members are distributed farther from the city centre. When the index is 0, the two groups have the same spatial distribution around the central business district (Massey and Denton, 1988b).

## ACE Index

A similar index can be developed, this time measuring a group's spatial distribution against the distribution of area units around the city centre (Massey and Denton, 1988b):

$$ACE = \left( \sum_{i=1}^{n} X_{i-1} A_i \right) - \left( \sum_{i=1}^{n} X_i A_{i-1} \right)$$

## Clustering

Spatial clustering reveals whether the areal units inhabited by minority members adjoin one another, or cluster, in space. Clustering, indeed, concerns the distribution of minority areas with respect to each other, but not with other minority groups or with the majority. A high degree of clustering implies a residential structure where minority areas are contiguous and closely packed, creating a single large ethnic or racial enclave. A low level of clustering means that minority areal units are widely scattered around the urban environment, like black squares on a checkerboard (Massey and Denton, 1988b:293).

## *ACL Index*

The following formula has been used by geographers to measure the "checkerboard problem":;

$$ACL = \left\{ \left[ \sum_{i=1}^{n}(x_i/X)\sum_{j=1}^{n}(c_{ij}x_j) \right] - \left[ X/n^2 \sum_{i=1}^{n}\sum_{j=1}^{n}c_{ij} \right] \right\} / \left\{ \left[ \sum_{i=1}^{n}(x_i/X)\sum_{j=1}^{n}c_{ij}t_j \right] - \left[ X/n^2 \sum_{i=1}^{n}\sum_{j=1}^{n}c_{ij} \right] \right\}$$

However, because of the practical difficulties involved in computing cij, Massey and Denton, 1988b have suggested cij= exp(-dij), as an easier way to calculate proxy for it, where dij is the distance between areal unit centroids, and dii has been estimated as (.6ai). The index, therefore, expresses the average number of X members in nearby tracts as a proportion of the total population in nearby tracts.

## *Spatial Proximity Index*

This index, suggested by White, measures the clustering of groups in space. To calculate this measure, one begins by estimating the average proximity between members of the same group, and between members of different groups (Massey and Denton 1988b). The average proximity between group X members can be approximated by:

$$P_{XX} = \sum_{i=1}^{n}\sum_{j=1}^{n}x_i x_j c_{ij}/X^2$$

while the average proximity between members of X and Y is estimated as:

$$P_{XY} = \sum_{i=1}^{n}\sum_{j=1}^{n}x_i y_j c_{ij}/XY$$

White's Index of Spatial Proximity is simply the average of intra-group proximity, Pxx/Ptt and Pyy/Ptt, weighted by the fraction of each group in the population:

$$SP = \left( XP_{xx} + YP_{yy} \right)/TP_{tt}$$

This index equals 1.0 if there is no differential clustering between X and Y, and is greater than 1.0 when members of each group live nearer to one another than to each other. The ratio will be less than 1.0 in the unusual event that members of X and Y resided closer to each other than to members of their own group (Massey and Denton, 1988b).

## Relative Clustering Index

Based on the above indices, Massey and Denton (1988b) also suggest the Relative Clustering Index, which adopts negative values if the minority members were less clustered than the majority:

$$RCL = P_{xx} / P_{yy} - 1$$

While simple to compute and interpret, this index has the disadvantage of having no theoretical maximum or minimum.

## Distance Adjusted P* Indices

Some combined indices, called Distance-Adjusted P*, have been suggested in order to take into account the effect of clustering while measuring the evenness or exposure (Massey and Denton, 1988b). The two suggested formulas measure the probability of meeting a member of the same or another group, as a function of distance:

$$DP_{xy}^{*} = \sum_{i=1}^{n} x_i / X \sum_{j=1}^{n} K_{ij} y_j / t_j$$

where

$$K_{ij} = \exp\left(-d_{ij}\right)_j / \sum_{i=1}^{n} \exp\left(-d_{ij}\right)_j$$

and

$$DP_{XX}^{*} = \sum_{i=1}^{n} x_i / X \sum_{j=1}^{n} K_{ij} x_j / t_j$$

## The Choice of Index

The reviewing of the numerous indices of segregation leads to one inevitable question: which index to use? Indeed, as an increasing number of segregation indices began to emerge, this question became a serious concern for the scholars in the field. Duncan and Duncan (1955) made perhaps the first comprehensive comparison of the indices suggested up to their time. Although the "index war" was settled for about two decades after their contribution, it resumed in the 1970s; the wide availability of computerized census data in North America since 1970 triggered a new "rush" towards discovering more sophisticated and complicated indices. The recognition of economics in the early 1970s as a "science" and the eligibility of economists to receive the Nobel Prize reinforced the rush towards quantitative research in sociology in general, and spatial research in particular.

Among the recent evaluations of the segregation indices, that of James and Taeuber (1985) was definitely a benchmark. While the other efforts to compare the indices were limited in their scope and confined to either their theoretical logic or empirical behaviour (e.g., Allison, 1978; Winship, 1977), James and Taeuber (1985) tried to suggest some theoretical criteria to compare the different indices, and apply those in a real case, in order to observe the indices' empirical behaviours. According to James and Taeuber (1985), there are four principles that can be used to judge the different indices: organizational equivalence and size invariance, transfers, composition invariance, and the Lorenz criterion (James and Taeuber, 1985:11-15). As different indices meet these criteria differently, the resultant picture is a whole set of indices, each of which is partially reliable. Perhaps because of this complexity, and despite its creative nature, the theoretical criteria proposed by James and Taeuber (1985) were not taken very well by the researchers in the field. Besides, the theoretical part of the work, i.e., the principles suggested, left some room for subjective disagreement.

A second, and perhaps more influential, contribution in the comparison of the segregation indices was the brilliant work of Massey and Denton (1988b). While basically along the same line as James and Taeuber (1985), Massey and Denton (1988b) focused on the empirical behaviour of the segregation indices. A great advantage of the latter work was that it included most (if not all) of the indices used in the literature. The basic logic of their work was simple: to apply all the indices on all the American metropolitan areas and then compare the results using factor analysis in order to detect how different indices cluster. The final result of their study was the adoption of five indices to deal with five different dimensions of segregation: (1) Dissimilarity Index, to measure "evenness"; (2) P* Indices, to measure "exposure"; (3) RCO Index, to measure "concentration"; (4) ACE Index, to measure "centralization"; and (5) Spatial Proximity Index, to measure "clustering."

In the present study, we will use the Dissimilarity Index, due to its robustness. This also makes the current study comparable to previous works, since most if not all of them have used the same index.

## *Unit of Analysis*

The analyses of spatial segregation tend to use census tracts as their unit of analysis. Despite its popularity, the use of census tracts is not without its problems. The heart of the problems is that, according to Blalock and Wilken (1979:528), "the choice of unit boundaries will affect the magnitude of the index of dissimilarity or any other measure of segregation". This factor has led some researchers to succumb to other units of analysis, such as block, or building. The use of smaller areal units, although more accurate, violates the principle of anonymity; hence, non-availability of data. For these reasons, in this study census tracts have been used as the unit of analysis. This, however, does not undermine the fact that the findings should be approached cautiously. Conducting ethnographic and anthropological studies is also a valuable practice in order to cross-check the findings based on census data.

## Residential Segregation of Ethnic Groups in Canada

The spatial segregation research in Canada has mainly used the Dissimilarity Index to examine the extent of residential proximity of ethnic groups in urban space. In almost all of these studies, the different ethnic groups have been studied in terms of their residential patterns with regard to the majority groups, British and French (in cities with a predominantly Francophone population). In the most recent study of the segregation patterns in Canadian cities, Hou and Balakrishnan (1996:24-25) summarize their major findings as follows:

> The European groups, especially those from Western Europe who came to Canada mostly before 1961 had much lower indices of dissimilarity from the British. For instance, Germans, the earliest and the largest European group had very low indices of dissimilarity from the British, around .150 and did not show much change during the five year period. Dutch indices were only slightly higher than those for the Germans. Ukrainians, who are also early settlers, showed higher indices of dissimilarity in the Eastern cities, but had lower indices in Western cities where they were over-represented. Italians and Poles had higher indices than Western Europeans, but less than those for Black or Asian groups. Aboriginal population, though all native born, had dissimilarity indices as high as those for recent visible minority immigrants, an indication of their continued subordinate position in the Canadian social structure.

> The French-British segregation is also worth special mention. The two groups are the Charter groups in Canada. The indices are high in three CMAs, Montreal, Ottawa/Hull and Winnipeg. In Montreal, the English are concentrated in a few areas producing a high index of segregation. Hull part of Ottawa/Hull CMA is located in Quebec with a predominantly French population resulting in a segregation index as high as .6. In Winnipeg, the suburb of St. Boniface has been a French settlement for a long time. But in all the other CMAs in English Canada, the segregation index of British and French is low. Outside of Quebec province, the French seem to have been well assimilated into the Anglo culture as is evident in their residential choices. In contrast, the Jewish population, in spite of their early settlement in Canada and high socio-economic status are not only highly segregated but also showed no sign of decline in the period 1986-1991.

> It is worth noting that in Montreal, the segregation indices are uniformly high for all the ethnic groups. French language is a powerful factor in Montreal. Many ethnic groups are reluctant to adopt French rather than English as their official language and this apparently affects the parts of city in which they are residing.

While comparing different groups with the British and/or French sub-populations has its own merits, it does not tell us much about ethnic dynamics as a whole in Canada, that is, the relationship and interactions of all ethnic groups with one another. It is possible that the segregation of different ethnic groups from the British and French remain the same, but the structure of relationships among these groups themselves undergoes change. To achieve this complete picture, we need to examine the segregation patterns of all ethnic groups, using each one as the basis of comparison. This way, the overall segregation index computed for each city will be based on all possible segregation indices, rather than segregation from only the British and French. The results of using this somewhat different approach are discussed below.

## Descriptive Remarks

It would be helpful to first compare the major Canadian cities in terms of their overall segregation levels. Table 3-2 contains such information, using the Dissimilarity Index. One observation about this table is that, among the major cities with a visible ethnic population, Montreal has the highest level of segregation. The other two centres of ethnic population, that is, Toronto and Vancouver, have a medium and low segregation level, respectively. A similar pattern was found in previous research, except that it involved the segregation of ethnic groups from the British and French. It is interesting to see that the same holds true with the segregation of all ethnic groups from each other.

TABLE 3-2

THE AVERAGE SEGREGATION INDEX OF MAJOR CANADIAN CMAS, 1991

|  | Average segregation index |
|---|---|
| Halifax | 0.75 |
| Montreal | 0.74 |
| St. Catharines-Niagara | 0.67 |
| Hamilton | 0.66 |
| Ottawa-Hull | 0.65 |
| Oshawa | 0.64 |
| Kitchener | 0.64 |
| Toronto | 0.64 |
| Winnipeg | 0.63 |
| Saskatoon | 0.63 |
| Regina | 0.62 |
| London | 0.61 |
| Windsor | 0.61 |
| Edmonton | 0.59 |
| Victoria | 0.59 |
| Calgary | 0.54 |
| Vancouver | 0.53 |

Another interesting pattern in Table 3-2 is that the segregation level tends to decline as we move westward, with Quebec and Ontario cities representing the topmost ranks, Prairie cities more or less in the middle, and Vancouver at the lower end of the segregation scale. This east-west distinction has been identified with regard to many other social trends and is clearly related to the different historical paths of the two regions; eastern Canada shows more resemblance to Europe and, in many respects, has been influenced by European social traditions, while western Canada has shaped a semi-independent identity for itself because of its late development.

Due to their aggregate nature, the overall city indices do not reveal anything about the possibly diverse experiences of different ethnic groups in each city. To grasp this diversity, however, we face a problem: namely, the uneven distribution of Canadian ethnic population in Canada. Many of the non-European ethnic groups have traditionally resided in the three cities of Toronto, Vancouver, and Montreal. These three have been the pre-eminent cities of attraction for the newcomers, especially those of visible minority origin. A complete comparative picture of ethnic composition, therefore, can be more clearly acquired only for these three cities.

Table 3-3 illustrates the segregation patterns for all ethnic groups in Toronto. The average index of segregation show that the Norwegian are the most highly segregated ethnic group in Toronto, followed by the Jewish. This is in contrast to the findings of Balakrishnan and others, who specified the Jewish as the most highly segregated ethnic group. One reason for this difference is that, in previous studies, including those of Balakrishnan and others, the Finnish, Danish, Swedish, and Norwegian have been collapsed into one blanket category: "Scandinavian." This practice had veiled the real segregation of each one of these groups. Another reason may be the fact that the previous studies based their findings on the segregation of each group merely from the charter groups, that is, the British and French. In the present study, the segregation index for each group is the average of its segregation from all other ethnic groups. The inclusion of all other groups in calculating the Dissimilarity Index leads to an increase of DI values for the groups who are close to Charter groups (e.g., Norwegians), and a decrease for those highly segregated from them.

The least segregated groups are the Canadian and British, followed by the British and German, and, eventually, the British and French. Those from Eastern Europe (i.e., Hungarian, Yugoslav, Ukrainian, and Polish) are relatively clustered together, coming immediately after the first cluster of British, German, French and Canadian. Another visible pattern is that of the Swedish, Danish, and Finnish; all these groups show high degrees of segregation. Instead, the visible minority groups, such as the Black, Chinese, Korean, Indian, and Filipino, as well as the Aboriginal, all are ranked moderately. The only visible minority groups with high levels of segregation are the Vietnamese and Lebanese. The peculiar status of these two groups calls for special attention in future research.

Table 3-4 provides the information on segregation trends of ethnic groups in Vancouver. Some of the trends observed in Toronto are more clearly present in Vancouver. The Lebanese and Vietnamese are the most highly segregated groups, followed immediately by the Jewish. In contrast to Toronto, the Scandinavian ethnic groups are less segregated than others in Vancouver. The visible minority groups, as well as those from Eastern and Southern Europe, are among the highly segregated ones. Also, it is noticeable that, regardless of their ranking, almost all ethnic groups in Vancouver have lower levels of segregation in comparison to Toronto. This is reflected in Vancouver's lower average Dissimilarity Index, which is 0.53 (compared to .64 for Toronto).

**TABLE 3-3**

**THE DISSIMILARITY INDICES OF ALL ETHNIC GROUPS IN TORONTO, 1991**

| | French | British | German | Canadian | Italian | Chinese | Aboriginal | Ukrainian | Dutch | Indian | Polish | Portuguese | Jewish | Black |
|---|---|---|---|---|---|---|---|---|---|---|---|---|---|---|
| French | 0.00 | 0.22 | 0.27 | 0.25 | 0.56 | 0.54 | 0.53 | 0.44 | 0.39 | 0.50 | 0.47 | 0.59 | 0.78 | 0.49 |
| British | 0.22 | 0.00 | 0.18 | 0.14 | 0.56 | 0.57 | 0.56 | 0.42 | 0.31 | 0.52 | 0.48 | 0.63 | 0.78 | 0.52 |
| German | 0.27 | 0.18 | 0.00 | 0.22 | 0.55 | 0.58 | 0.59 | 0.41 | 0.34 | 0.53 | 0.48 | 0.63 | 0.77 | 0.53 |
| Canadian | 0.25 | 0.14 | 0.22 | 0.00 | 0.55 | 0.58 | 0.56 | 0.43 | 0.32 | 0.51 | 0.49 | 0.61 | 0.80 | 0.50 |
| Italian | 0.56 | 0.56 | 0.55 | 0.55 | 0.00 | 0.65 | 0.69 | 0.59 | 0.63 | 0.56 | 0.60 | 0.58 | 0.82 | 0.54 |
| Chinese | 0.54 | 0.57 | 0.58 | 0.58 | 0.65 | 0.00 | 0.70 | 0.63 | 0.66 | 0.50 | 0.66 | 0.69 | 0.75 | 0.53 |
| Aboriginal | 0.53 | 0.56 | 0.59 | 0.56 | 0.69 | 0.70 | 0.00 | 0.64 | 0.65 | 0.68 | 0.64 | 0.70 | 0.85 | 0.63 |
| Ukrainian | 0.44 | 0.42 | 0.41 | 0.43 | 0.59 | 0.63 | 0.64 | 0.00 | 0.54 | 0.61 | 0.36 | 0.61 | 0.81 | 0.63 |
| Dutch | 0.39 | 0.31 | 0.34 | 0.32 | 0.63 | 0.66 | 0.65 | 0.54 | 0.00 | 0.62 | 0.59 | 0.67 | 0.80 | 0.64 |
| Indian | 0.50 | 0.52 | 0.53 | 0.51 | 0.56 | 0.50 | 0.68 | 0.61 | 0.62 | 0.00 | 0.58 | 0.63 | 0.84 | 0.35 |
| Polish | 0.47 | 0.48 | 0.48 | 0.49 | 0.60 | 0.66 | 0.64 | 0.36 | 0.59 | 0.58 | 0.00 | 0.61 | 0.83 | 0.59 |
| Portuguese | 0.59 | 0.63 | 0.63 | 0.61 | 0.58 | 0.69 | 0.70 | 0.61 | 0.67 | 0.63 | 0.61 | 0.00 | 0.89 | 0.62 |
| Jewish | 0.78 | 0.78 | 0.77 | 0.80 | 0.82 | 0.75 | 0.85 | 0.81 | 0.80 | 0.84 | 0.83 | 0.89 | 0.00 | 0.85 |
| Black | 0.49 | 0.52 | 0.53 | 0.50 | 0.54 | 0.53 | 0.63 | 0.63 | 0.64 | 0.35 | 0.59 | 0.62 | 0.85 | 0.00 |
| Filipino | 0.47 | 0.49 | 0.51 | 0.49 | 0.62 | 0.50 | 0.64 | 0.58 | 0.62 | 0.39 | 0.55 | 0.65 | 0.77 | 0.44 |
| Greek | 0.51 | 0.51 | 0.52 | 0.51 | 0.57 | 0.50 | 0.68 | 0.60 | 0.64 | 0.52 | 0.61 | 0.67 | 0.79 | 0.53 |
| Hungarian | 0.41 | 0.40 | 0.39 | 0.43 | 0.59 | 0.58 | 0.63 | 0.49 | 0.52 | 0.56 | 0.51 | 0.67 | 0.67 | 0.57 |
| Vietnamese | 0.67 | 0.72 | 0.73 | 0.71 | 0.67 | 0.68 | 0.68 | 0.71 | 0.79 | 0.68 | 0.66 | 0.62 | 0.91 | 0.59 |
| Spanish | 0.54 | 0.58 | 0.57 | 0.56 | 0.51 | 0.64 | 0.60 | 0.60 | 0.68 | 0.54 | 0.57 | 0.57 | 0.84 | 0.44 |
| Lebanese | 0.64 | 0.66 | 0.65 | 0.67 | 0.72 | 0.67 | 0.76 | 0.71 | 0.73 | 0.64 | 0.69 | 0.79 | 0.82 | 0.66 |
| Norwegian | 0.83 | 0.84 | 0.83 | 0.85 | 0.91 | 0.89 | 0.85 | 0.85 | 0.84 | 0.89 | 0.85 | 0.93 | 0.86 | 0.89 |
| Japanese | 0.48 | 0.48 | 0.49 | 0.52 | 0.64 | 0.53 | 0.64 | 0.55 | 0.60 | 0.61 | 0.60 | 0.73 | 0.76 | 0.60 |
| Yugoslav | 0.44 | 0.44 | 0.43 | 0.44 | 0.57 | 0.60 | 0.63 | 0.47 | 0.54 | 0.55 | 0.48 | 0.62 | 0.80 | 0.56 |
| Korean | 0.55 | 0.56 | 0.56 | 0.57 | 0.66 | 0.56 | 0.68 | 0.58 | 0.65 | 0.57 | 0.59 | 0.72 | 0.74 | 0.59 |
| Swedish | 0.72 | 0.70 | 0.70 | 0.72 | 0.82 | 0.79 | 0.77 | 0.74 | 0.68 | 0.80 | 0.76 | 0.82 | 0.83 | 0.80 |
| Croatian | 0.60 | 0.61 | 0.58 | 0.60 | 0.64 | 0.75 | 0.73 | 0.55 | 0.63 | 0.64 | 0.55 | 0.65 | 0.90 | 0.69 |
| Danish | 0.61 | 0.57 | 0.57 | 0.59 | 0.77 | 0.74 | 0.72 | 0.68 | 0.58 | 0.76 | 0.71 | 0.80 | 0.81 | 0.75 |
| Finnish | 0.57 | 0.54 | 0.56 | 0.57 | 0.75 | 0.65 | 0.66 | 0.66 | 0.61 | 0.71 | 0.70 | 0.80 | 0.78 | 0.70 |
| **Average** | **0.52** | **0.52** | **0.52** | **0.53** | **0.64** | **0.63** | **0.67** | **0.59** | **0.60** | **0.60** | **0.60** | **0.69** | **0.81** | **0.60** |

TABLE **3-3** (concluded)

THE DISSIMILARITY INDICES OF ALL ETHNIC GROUPS IN TORONTO, 1991

| | Filipino | Greek | Hungarian | Vietnamese | Spanish | Lebanese | Norwegian | Japanese | Yugoslav | Korean | Swedish | Croatian | Danish | Finnish |
|---|---|---|---|---|---|---|---|---|---|---|---|---|---|---|
| French | 0.47 | 0.51 | 0.41 | 0.67 | 0.54 | 0.64 | 0.83 | 0.48 | 0.44 | 0.55 | 0.72 | 0.60 | 0.61 | 0.57 |
| British | 0.49 | 0.51 | 0.40 | 0.72 | 0.58 | 0.66 | 0.84 | 0.48 | 0.44 | 0.56 | 0.70 | 0.61 | 0.57 | 0.54 |
| German | 0.51 | 0.52 | 0.39 | 0.73 | 0.57 | 0.65 | 0.83 | 0.49 | 0.43 | 0.56 | 0.70 | 0.58 | 0.57 | 0.56 |
| Canadian | 0.49 | 0.51 | 0.43 | 0.71 | 0.56 | 0.67 | 0.85 | 0.52 | 0.44 | 0.57 | 0.72 | 0.60 | 0.59 | 0.57 |
| Italian | 0.62 | 0.57 | 0.59 | 0.67 | 0.51 | 0.72 | 0.91 | 0.64 | 0.57 | 0.66 | 0.82 | 0.64 | 0.77 | 0.75 |
| Chinese | 0.50 | 0.50 | 0.58 | 0.68 | 0.64 | 0.67 | 0.89 | 0.53 | 0.60 | 0.56 | 0.79 | 0.75 | 0.74 | 0.67 |
| Aboriginal | 0.64 | 0.68 | 0.63 | 0.68 | 0.60 | 0.76 | 0.85 | 0.64 | 0.63 | 0.68 | 0.77 | 0.73 | 0.72 | 0.66 |
| Ukrainian | 0.58 | 0.60 | 0.49 | 0.71 | 0.60 | 0.71 | 0.85 | 0.55 | 0.47 | 0.58 | 0.74 | 0.55 | 0.68 | 0.66 |
| Dutch | 0.62 | 0.64 | 0.52 | 0.79 | 0.68 | 0.73 | 0.84 | 0.60 | 0.54 | 0.65 | 0.68 | 0.63 | 0.58 | 0.61 |
| Indian | 0.39 | 0.52 | 0.56 | 0.68 | 0.54 | 0.64 | 0.89 | 0.61 | 0.55 | 0.57 | 0.80 | 0.64 | 0.76 | 0.71 |
| Polish | 0.55 | 0.61 | 0.51 | 0.66 | 0.57 | 0.69 | 0.85 | 0.60 | 0.48 | 0.59 | 0.76 | 0.55 | 0.71 | 0.70 |
| Portuguese | 0.65 | 0.67 | 0.67 | 0.62 | 0.57 | 0.79 | 0.93 | 0.73 | 0.62 | 0.72 | 0.82 | 0.65 | 0.80 | 0.80 |
| Jewish | 0.77 | 0.79 | 0.67 | 0.91 | 0.84 | 0.82 | 0.86 | 0.76 | 0.80 | 0.74 | 0.83 | 0.90 | 0.81 | 0.78 |
| Black | 0.44 | 0.53 | 0.57 | 0.59 | 0.44 | 0.66 | 0.89 | 0.60 | 0.56 | 0.59 | 0.80 | 0.69 | 0.75 | 0.70 |
| Filipino | 0.00 | 0.51 | 0.53 | 0.69 | 0.60 | 0.64 | 0.87 | 0.58 | 0.52 | 0.54 | 0.78 | 0.64 | 0.74 | 0.67 |
| Greek | 0.51 | 0.00 | 0.54 | 0.70 | 0.59 | 0.68 | 0.88 | 0.51 | 0.54 | 0.57 | 0.79 | 0.72 | 0.75 | 0.65 |
| Hungarian | 0.53 | 0.54 | 0.00 | 0.72 | 0.58 | 0.63 | 0.83 | 0.53 | 0.49 | 0.54 | 0.72 | 0.64 | 0.63 | 0.58 |
| Vietnamese | 0.69 | 0.70 | 0.72 | 0.00 | 0.53 | 0.80 | 0.91 | 0.73 | 0.70 | 0.74 | 0.82 | 0.74 | 0.84 | 0.80 |
| Spanish | 0.60 | 0.59 | 0.58 | 0.53 | 0.00 | 0.70 | 0.89 | 0.64 | 0.58 | 0.61 | 0.81 | 0.69 | 0.77 | 0.72 |
| Lebanese | 0.64 | 0.68 | 0.63 | 0.80 | 0.70 | 0.00 | 0.89 | 0.67 | 0.68 | 0.65 | 0.77 | 0.71 | 0.74 | 0.71 |
| Norwegian | 0.87 | 0.88 | 0.83 | 0.91 | 0.89 | 0.89 | 0.00 | 0.82 | 0.84 | 0.87 | 0.77 | 0.87 | 0.79 | 0.82 |
| Japanese | 0.58 | 0.51 | 0.53 | 0.73 | 0.64 | 0.67 | 0.82 | 0.00 | 0.56 | 0.58 | 0.73 | 0.69 | 0.66 | 0.59 |
| Yugoslav | 0.52 | 0.54 | 0.49 | 0.70 | 0.58 | 0.68 | 0.84 | 0.56 | 0.00 | 0.56 | 0.74 | 0.55 | 0.66 | 0.66 |
| Korean | 0.54 | 0.57 | 0.54 | 0.74 | 0.61 | 0.65 | 0.87 | 0.58 | 0.56 | 0.00 | 0.76 | 0.65 | 0.71 | 0.63 |
| Swedish | 0.78 | 0.79 | 0.72 | 0.82 | 0.81 | 0.77 | 0.77 | 0.73 | 0.74 | 0.76 | 0.00 | 0.76 | 0.68 | 0.73 |
| Croatian | 0.64 | 0.72 | 0.64 | 0.74 | 0.69 | 0.71 | 0.87 | 0.69 | 0.55 | 0.65 | 0.76 | 0.00 | 0.73 | 0.77 |
| Danish | 0.74 | 0.75 | 0.63 | 0.84 | 0.77 | 0.74 | 0.79 | 0.66 | 0.66 | 0.71 | 0.68 | 0.73 | 0.00 | 0.66 |
| Finnish | 0.67 | 0.65 | 0.58 | 0.80 | 0.72 | 0.71 | 0.82 | 0.59 | 0.66 | 0.63 | 0.73 | 0.77 | 0.66 | 0.00 |
| **Average** | **0.59** | **0.61** | **0.57** | **0.72** | **0.63** | **0.71** | **0.86** | **0.61** | **0.58** | **0.63** | **0.76** | **0.68** | **0.70** | **0.68** |

The indices of segregation in Montreal, Table 3-5, shows the similarly high levels of segregation among those of Scandinavian origin. The visible minority groups, intermingled with South Europeans, are located in the medium ranks. The East European groups, along with the British, German, and Polish, have a relatively low segregation. The French are ranked medium in terms of their segregation in Montreal.

One striking feature of segregation in Montreal is the high level of segregation among the French and almost all other ethnic groups. Another is the fact that the group with the lowest level of segregation from the French majority is Aboriginal; this is in contrast to the high level of segregation between the Aboriginal and the Charter groups in almost all other Canadian cities. One may speculate that one possible reason for this is a common feeling of being marginalized: both groups feel suppressed and excluded by British Canada and, therefore, feel more sympathetic towards each other.

TABLE 3-4

THE DISSIMILARITY INDICES OF ALL ETHNIC GROUPS IN VANCOUVER, 1991

| | French | British | German | Canadian | Italian | Chinese | Aboriginal | Ukrainian | Dutch | Indian | Polish | Portuguese | Jewish | Black |
|---|---|---|---|---|---|---|---|---|---|---|---|---|---|---|
| French | 0.00 | 0.21 | 0.23 | 0.29 | 0.49 | 0.57 | 0.50 | 0.21 | 0.30 | 0.54 | 0.32 | 0.52 | 0.61 | 0.44 |
| British | 0.21 | 0.00 | 0.15 | 0.23 | 0.47 | 0.56 | 0.54 | 0.19 | 0.24 | 0.52 | 0.32 | 0.53 | 0.58 | 0.48 |
| German | 0.23 | 0.15 | 0.00 | 0.23 | 0.48 | 0.55 | 0.53 | 0.20 | 0.22 | 0.46 | 0.32 | 0.51 | 0.61 | 0.47 |
| Canadian | 0.29 | 0.23 | 0.23 | 0.00 | 0.49 | 0.58 | 0.56 | 0.27 | 0.25 | 0.50 | 0.36 | 0.52 | 0.64 | 0.48 |
| Italian | 0.49 | 0.47 | 0.48 | 0.49 | 0.00 | 0.43 | 0.60 | 0.45 | 0.53 | 0.57 | 0.48 | 0.43 | 0.71 | 0.54 |
| Chinese | 0.57 | 0.56 | 0.55 | 0.58 | 0.43 | 0.00 | 0.61 | 0.54 | 0.61 | 0.53 | 0.50 | 0.42 | 0.60 | 0.55 |
| Aboriginal | 0.50 | 0.54 | 0.53 | 0.56 | 0.60 | 0.61 | 0.00 | 0.52 | 0.57 | 0.64 | 0.50 | 0.60 | 0.72 | 0.59 |
| Ukrainian | 0.21 | 0.19 | 0.20 | 0.27 | 0.45 | 0.54 | 0.52 | 0.00 | 0.27 | 0.48 | 0.30 | 0.47 | 0.63 | 0.47 |
| Dutch | 0.30 | 0.24 | 0.22 | 0.25 | 0.53 | 0.61 | 0.57 | 0.27 | 0.00 | 0.52 | 0.40 | 0.55 | 0.66 | 0.52 |
| Indian | 0.54 | 0.52 | 0.46 | 0.50 | 0.57 | 0.53 | 0.64 | 0.48 | 0.52 | 0.00 | 0.51 | 0.47 | 0.73 | 0.58 |
| Polish | 0.32 | 0.32 | 0.32 | 0.36 | 0.48 | 0.50 | 0.50 | 0.30 | 0.40 | 0.51 | 0.00 | 0.48 | 0.62 | 0.43 |
| Portuguese | 0.52 | 0.53 | 0.51 | 0.52 | 0.43 | 0.42 | 0.60 | 0.47 | 0.55 | 0.47 | 0.48 | 0.00 | 0.75 | 0.53 |
| Jewish | 0.61 | 0.58 | 0.61 | 0.64 | 0.71 | 0.60 | 0.72 | 0.63 | 0.66 | 0.73 | 0.62 | 0.75 | 0.00 | 0.69 |
| Black | 0.44 | 0.48 | 0.47 | 0.48 | 0.54 | 0.55 | 0.59 | 0.47 | 0.52 | 0.58 | 0.43 | 0.53 | 0.69 | 0.00 |
| Filipino | 0.45 | 0.45 | 0.44 | 0.49 | 0.49 | 0.37 | 0.54 | 0.43 | 0.50 | 0.43 | 0.39 | 0.42 | 0.61 | 0.46 |
| Greek | 0.55 | 0.53 | 0.54 | 0.59 | 0.61 | 0.56 | 0.66 | 0.54 | 0.61 | 0.67 | 0.55 | 0.61 | 0.55 | 0.58 |
| Hungarian | 0.31 | 0.31 | 0.30 | 0.37 | 0.50 | 0.55 | 0.52 | 0.32 | 0.38 | 0.54 | 0.36 | 0.53 | 0.62 | 0.46 |
| Vietnamese | 0.72 | 0.75 | 0.72 | 0.74 | 0.64 | 0.53 | 0.59 | 0.70 | 0.76 | 0.65 | 0.65 | 0.59 | 0.84 | 0.64 |
| Spanish | 0.51 | 0.52 | 0.51 | 0.55 | 0.56 | 0.53 | 0.57 | 0.51 | 0.58 | 0.58 | 0.46 | 0.52 | 0.70 | 0.54 |
| Lebanese | 0.72 | 0.72 | 0.76 | 0.74 | 0.72 | 0.78 | 0.78 | 0.73 | 0.75 | 0.82 | 0.73 | 0.75 | 0.79 | 0.71 |
| Norwegian | 0.31 | 0.25 | 0.27 | 0.30 | 0.51 | 0.63 | 0.57 | 0.29 | 0.31 | 0.55 | 0.37 | 0.56 | 0.66 | 0.50 |
| Japanese | 0.44 | 0.42 | 0.45 | 0.49 | 0.46 | 0.39 | 0.58 | 0.41 | 0.52 | 0.55 | 0.42 | 0.50 | 0.54 | 0.50 |
| Yugoslav | 0.42 | 0.43 | 0.42 | 0.46 | 0.47 | 0.51 | 0.58 | 0.40 | 0.46 | 0.53 | 0.45 | 0.50 | 0.69 | 0.53 |
| Korean | 0.55 | 0.52 | 0.53 | 0.53 | 0.59 | 0.59 | 0.69 | 0.52 | 0.57 | 0.63 | 0.51 | 0.58 | 0.72 | 0.56 |
| Swedish | 0.31 | 0.27 | 0.29 | 0.33 | 0.49 | 0.58 | 0.56 | 0.30 | 0.35 | 0.54 | 0.38 | 0.53 | 0.64 | 0.52 |
| Croatian | 0.59 | 0.59 | 0.58 | 0.62 | 0.44 | 0.54 | 0.67 | 0.56 | 0.62 | 0.67 | 0.59 | 0.57 | 0.75 | 0.58 |
| Danish | 0.36 | 0.28 | 0.30 | 0.35 | 0.55 | 0.63 | 0.59 | 0.34 | 0.33 | 0.56 | 0.43 | 0.58 | 0.65 | 0.54 |
| Finnish | 0.42 | 0.41 | 0.43 | 0.44 | 0.57 | 0.65 | 0.62 | 0.42 | 0.46 | 0.63 | 0.48 | 0.61 | 0.73 | 0.54 |
| **Average** | **0.44** | **0.42** | **0.43** | **0.46** | **0.53** | **0.55** | **0.59** | **0.42** | **0.48** | **0.57** | **0.46** | **0.54** | **0.67** | **0.53** |

TABLE 3-4 (concluded)

THE DISSIMILARITY INDICES OF ALL ETHNIC GROUPS IN VANCOUVER, 1991

| | Filipino | Greek | Hungarian | Vietnamese | Spanish | Lebanese | Norwegian | Japanese | Yugoslav | Korean | Swedish | Croatian | Danish | Finnish |
|---|---|---|---|---|---|---|---|---|---|---|---|---|---|---|
| French | 0.45 | 0.55 | 0.31 | 0.72 | 0.51 | 0.72 | 0.31 | 0.44 | 0.42 | 0.55 | 0.31 | 0.59 | 0.36 | 0.42 |
| British | 0.45 | 0.53 | 0.31 | 0.75 | 0.52 | 0.72 | 0.25 | 0.42 | 0.43 | 0.52 | 0.27 | 0.59 | 0.28 | 0.41 |
| German | 0.44 | 0.54 | 0.30 | 0.72 | 0.51 | 0.76 | 0.27 | 0.45 | 0.42 | 0.53 | 0.29 | 0.58 | 0.30 | 0.43 |
| Canadian | 0.49 | 0.59 | 0.37 | 0.74 | 0.55 | 0.74 | 0.30 | 0.49 | 0.46 | 0.53 | 0.33 | 0.62 | 0.35 | 0.44 |
| Italian | 0.49 | 0.61 | 0.50 | 0.64 | 0.56 | 0.72 | 0.51 | 0.46 | 0.47 | 0.59 | 0.49 | 0.44 | 0.55 | 0.57 |
| Chinese | 0.37 | 0.56 | 0.55 | 0.53 | 0.53 | 0.78 | 0.63 | 0.39 | 0.51 | 0.59 | 0.58 | 0.54 | 0.63 | 0.65 |
| Aboriginal | 0.54 | 0.66 | 0.52 | 0.59 | 0.57 | 0.78 | 0.57 | 0.58 | 0.58 | 0.69 | 0.56 | 0.67 | 0.59 | 0.62 |
| Ukrainian | 0.43 | 0.54 | 0.32 | 0.70 | 0.51 | 0.73 | 0.29 | 0.41 | 0.40 | 0.52 | 0.30 | 0.56 | 0.34 | 0.42 |
| Dutch | 0.50 | 0.61 | 0.38 | 0.76 | 0.58 | 0.75 | 0.31 | 0.52 | 0.46 | 0.57 | 0.35 | 0.62 | 0.33 | 0.46 |
| Indian | 0.43 | 0.67 | 0.54 | 0.65 | 0.58 | 0.82 | 0.55 | 0.55 | 0.53 | 0.63 | 0.54 | 0.67 | 0.56 | 0.63 |
| Polish | 0.39 | 0.55 | 0.36 | 0.65 | 0.46 | 0.73 | 0.37 | 0.42 | 0.45 | 0.51 | 0.38 | 0.59 | 0.43 | 0.48 |
| Portuguese | 0.42 | 0.61 | 0.53 | 0.59 | 0.52 | 0.75 | 0.56 | 0.50 | 0.50 | 0.58 | 0.53 | 0.57 | 0.58 | 0.61 |
| Jewish | 0.61 | 0.55 | 0.62 | 0.84 | 0.70 | 0.79 | 0.66 | 0.54 | 0.69 | 0.72 | 0.64 | 0.75 | 0.65 | 0.73 |
| Black | 0.46 | 0.58 | 0.46 | 0.64 | 0.54 | 0.71 | 0.50 | 0.50 | 0.53 | 0.56 | 0.52 | 0.58 | 0.54 | 0.54 |
| Filipino | 0.00 | 0.56 | 0.46 | 0.56 | 0.47 | 0.77 | 0.52 | 0.43 | 0.47 | 0.57 | 0.50 | 0.59 | 0.54 | 0.59 |
| Greek | 0.56 | 0.00 | 0.53 | 0.73 | 0.61 | 0.72 | 0.59 | 0.55 | 0.59 | 0.67 | 0.60 | 0.69 | 0.61 | 0.67 |
| Hungarian | 0.46 | 0.53 | 0.00 | 0.67 | 0.52 | 0.72 | 0.35 | 0.46 | 0.42 | 0.56 | 0.39 | 0.57 | 0.41 | 0.49 |
| Vietnamese | 0.56 | 0.73 | 0.67 | 0.00 | 0.60 | 0.87 | 0.75 | 0.70 | 0.69 | 0.78 | 0.75 | 0.68 | 0.76 | 0.79 |
| Spanish | 0.47 | 0.61 | 0.52 | 0.60 | 0.00 | 0.76 | 0.55 | 0.55 | 0.54 | 0.64 | 0.55 | 0.64 | 0.57 | 0.61 |
| Lebanese | 0.77 | 0.72 | 0.72 | 0.87 | 0.76 | 0.00 | 0.72 | 0.73 | 0.73 | 0.75 | 0.73 | 0.79 | 0.73 | 0.75 |
| Norwegian | 0.52 | 0.59 | 0.35 | 0.75 | 0.55 | 0.72 | 0.00 | 0.50 | 0.48 | 0.56 | 0.32 | 0.61 | 0.36 | 0.46 |
| Japanese | 0.43 | 0.55 | 0.46 | 0.70 | 0.55 | 0.73 | 0.50 | 0.00 | 0.48 | 0.55 | 0.47 | 0.56 | 0.52 | 0.58 |
| Yugoslav | 0.47 | 0.59 | 0.42 | 0.69 | 0.54 | 0.73 | 0.48 | 0.48 | 0.00 | 0.56 | 0.43 | 0.55 | 0.46 | 0.56 |
| Korean | 0.57 | 0.67 | 0.56 | 0.78 | 0.64 | 0.75 | 0.56 | 0.55 | 0.56 | 0.00 | 0.53 | 0.60 | 0.59 | 0.61 |
| Swedish | 0.50 | 0.60 | 0.39 | 0.75 | 0.55 | 0.73 | 0.32 | 0.47 | 0.43 | 0.53 | 0.00 | 0.60 | 0.38 | 0.44 |
| Croatian | 0.59 | 0.69 | 0.57 | 0.68 | 0.64 | 0.79 | 0.61 | 0.56 | 0.55 | 0.60 | 0.60 | 0.00 | 0.62 | 0.64 |
| Danish | 0.54 | 0.61 | 0.41 | 0.76 | 0.57 | 0.73 | 0.36 | 0.52 | 0.46 | 0.59 | 0.38 | 0.62 | 0.00 | 0.49 |
| Finnish | 0.59 | 0.67 | 0.49 | 0.79 | 0.61 | 0.75 | 0.46 | 0.58 | 0.56 | 0.61 | 0.44 | 0.64 | 0.49 | 0.00 |
| **Average** | **0.50** | **0.60** | **0.47** | **0.70** | **0.56** | **0.75** | **0.48** | **0.51** | **0.51** | **0.59** | **0.47** | **0.61** | **0.50** | **0.56** |

As the examination of the above tables shows, it would be difficult to capture the complete picture of ethnic relations in a city through an examination of all segregation indices. A procedure is needed to combine all this information and to illustrate it in a summarized format. In order to achieve such a picture, two statistical procedures have been used: "factor analysis" and "cluster analysis." To use factor analysis for this purpose, the different ethnic groups have been treated as different variables with their dissimilarity indices being their correlation coefficients. However, since the lower values of DI indicate more proximity (unlike what a low correlation coefficient means), all the DI values are transformed, using the formula, Corr.Coeff = 1- DI. The variables (here, ethnic groups) are then plotted in a hypothetical two-factor scenario. The output is a graph, which shows the cluster of ethnic groups in a given city. This procedure has been applied to the cities of Toronto, Vancouver, and Montreal.

Figure 3-4 illustrates the distribution of ethnic groups in the Toronto urban space. One observation about the illustrated patterns is the strikingly high level of segregation among Scandinavian groups both with the other groups and among themselves. The Norwegian, Swedish, Danish, and Finnish are all located far from the other groups. Their segregation levels are close to the Jewish, traditionally the most segregated group in Canada. This clearly indicates the need to question a common practice in census procedure as well as in previous research, that is, placing all these groups under the blanket category of "Scandinavian."

**TABLE 3-5**

**THE DISSIMILARITY INDEX OF ALL ETHNIC GROUPS IN MONTREAL, 1991**

| | French | British | German | Canadian | Italian | Chinese | Aboriginal | Ukrainian | Dutch | Indian | Polish | Portuguese | Jewish | Black |
|---|---|---|---|---|---|---|---|---|---|---|---|---|---|---|
| French | 0.00 | 0.47 | 0.47 | 0.52 | 0.59 | 0.67 | 0.34 | 0.62 | 0.65 | 0.77 | 0.59 | 0.57 | 0.90 | 0.61 |
| British | 0.47 | 0.00 | 0.30 | 0.51 | 0.62 | 0.58 | 0.54 | 0.48 | 0.49 | 0.59 | 0.44 | 0.67 | 0.79 | 0.54 |
| German | 0.47 | 0.30 | 0.00 | 0.53 | 0.63 | 0.58 | 0.55 | 0.53 | 0.48 | 0.59 | 0.48 | 0.66 | 0.77 | 0.57 |
| Canadian | 0.52 | 0.51 | 0.53 | 0.00 | 0.69 | 0.67 | 0.57 | 0.62 | 0.61 | 0.68 | 0.60 | 0.66 | 0.83 | 0.65 |
| Italian | 0.59 | 0.62 | 0.63 | 0.69 | 0.00 | 0.67 | 0.67 | 0.61 | 0.78 | 0.76 | 0.60 | 0.60 | 0.89 | 0.53 |
| Chinese | 0.67 | 0.58 | 0.58 | 0.67 | 0.67 | 0.00 | 0.71 | 0.62 | 0.70 | 0.53 | 0.53 | 0.65 | 0.75 | 0.58 |
| Aboriginal | 0.34 | 0.54 | 0.55 | 0.57 | 0.67 | 0.71 | 0.00 | 0.67 | 0.67 | 0.79 | 0.65 | 0.65 | 0.92 | 0.66 |
| Ukrainian | 0.62 | 0.48 | 0.53 | 0.62 | 0.61 | 0.62 | 0.67 | 0.00 | 0.65 | 0.65 | 0.47 | 0.67 | 0.81 | 0.62 |
| Dutch | 0.65 | 0.49 | 0.48 | 0.61 | 0.78 | 0.70 | 0.67 | 0.65 | 0.00 | 0.66 | 0.65 | 0.77 | 0.80 | 0.70 |
| Indian | 0.77 | 0.59 | 0.59 | 0.68 | 0.76 | 0.53 | 0.79 | 0.65 | 0.66 | 0.00 | 0.57 | 0.75 | 0.75 | 0.57 |
| Polish | 0.59 | 0.44 | 0.48 | 0.60 | 0.60 | 0.53 | 0.65 | 0.47 | 0.65 | 0.57 | 0.00 | 0.65 | 0.74 | 0.47 |
| Portuguese | 0.57 | 0.67 | 0.66 | 0.66 | 0.60 | 0.65 | 0.65 | 0.67 | 0.77 | 0.75 | 0.65 | 0.00 | 0.88 | 0.63 |
| Jewish | 0.90 | 0.79 | 0.77 | 0.83 | 0.89 | 0.75 | 0.92 | 0.81 | 0.80 | 0.75 | 0.74 | 0.88 | 0.00 | 0.78 |
| Black | 0.61 | 0.54 | 0.57 | 0.65 | 0.53 | 0.58 | 0.66 | 0.62 | 0.70 | 0.57 | 0.47 | 0.63 | 0.78 | 0.00 |
| Filipino | 0.85 | 0.68 | 0.68 | 0.75 | 0.82 | 0.67 | 0.86 | 0.73 | 0.73 | 0.58 | 0.68 | 0.83 | 0.66 | 0.67 |
| Greek | 0.74 | 0.68 | 0.64 | 0.73 | 0.75 | 0.64 | 0.80 | 0.71 | 0.76 | 0.60 | 0.62 | 0.72 | 0.76 | 0.65 |
| Hungarian | 0.67 | 0.53 | 0.49 | 0.64 | 0.73 | 0.61 | 0.72 | 0.61 | 0.62 | 0.62 | 0.50 | 0.72 | 0.66 | 0.62 |
| Vietnamese | 0.69 | 0.71 | 0.70 | 0.74 | 0.72 | 0.54 | 0.75 | 0.70 | 0.78 | 0.65 | 0.62 | 0.67 | 0.76 | 0.61 |
| Spanish | 0.55 | 0.56 | 0.56 | 0.63 | 0.54 | 0.55 | 0.63 | 0.60 | 0.70 | 0.65 | 0.50 | 0.58 | 0.80 | 0.50 |
| Lebanese | 0.69 | 0.65 | 0.59 | 0.70 | 0.64 | 0.64 | 0.75 | 0.68 | 0.74 | 0.70 | 0.62 | 0.72 | 0.76 | 0.65 |
| Norwegian | 0.92 | 0.86 | 0.86 | 0.89 | 0.94 | 0.88 | 0.91 | 0.89 | 0.81 | 0.89 | 0.89 | 0.93 | 0.89 | 0.93 |
| Japanese | 0.88 | 0.76 | 0.74 | 0.82 | 0.87 | 0.68 | 0.89 | 0.78 | 0.75 | 0.72 | 0.77 | 0.86 | 0.77 | 0.83 |
| Yugoslav | 0.74 | 0.66 | 0.64 | 0.69 | 0.73 | 0.67 | 0.75 | 0.68 | 0.70 | 0.65 | 0.66 | 0.76 | 0.79 | 0.65 |
| Korean | 0.90 | 0.77 | 0.77 | 0.84 | 0.89 | 0.77 | 0.89 | 0.84 | 0.80 | 0.78 | 0.80 | 0.88 | 0.81 | 0.82 |
| Swedish | 0.93 | 0.82 | 0.81 | 0.87 | 0.95 | 0.89 | 0.93 | 0.85 | 0.76 | 0.86 | 0.88 | 0.94 | 0.89 | 0.82 |
| Croatian | 0.88 | 0.83 | 0.81 | 0.82 | 0.83 | 0.79 | 0.87 | 0.81 | 0.82 | 0.76 | 0.80 | 0.85 | 0.80 | 0.91 |
| Danish | 0.93 | 0.79 | 0.81 | 0.85 | 0.93 | 0.84 | 0.91 | 0.84 | 0.78 | 0.79 | 0.86 | 0.94 | 0.90 | 0.82 |
| Finnish | 0.95 | 0.83 | 0.84 | 0.87 | 0.93 | 0.89 | 0.93 | 0.87 | 0.81 | 0.85 | 0.86 | 0.96 | 0.88 | 0.89 |
| **Average** | **0.71** | **0.64** | **0.63** | **0.70** | **0.74** | **0.68** | **0.74** | **0.69** | **0.71** | **0.69** | **0.65** | **0.75** | **0.80** | **0.68** |

TABLE **3-5** (concluded)

THE DISSIMILARITY INDEX OF ALL ETHNIC GROUPS IN MONTREAL, 1991

| | Filipino | Greek | Hungarian | Vietnamese | Spanish | Lebanese | Norwegian | Japanese | Yugoslav | Korean | Swedish | Croatian | Danish | Finnish |
|---|---|---|---|---|---|---|---|---|---|---|---|---|---|---|
| French | 0.85 | 0.74 | 0.67 | 0.69 | 0.55 | 0.69 | 0.92 | 0.88 | 0.74 | 0.90 | 0.93 | 0.88 | 0.93 | 0.95 |
| British | 0.68 | 0.68 | 0.53 | 0.71 | 0.56 | 0.65 | 0.86 | 0.76 | 0.66 | 0.77 | 0.82 | 0.83 | 0.79 | 0.83 |
| German | 0.68 | 0.64 | 0.49 | 0.70 | 0.56 | 0.59 | 0.86 | 0.74 | 0.64 | 0.77 | 0.81 | 0.81 | 0.81 | 0.84 |
| Canadian | 0.75 | 0.73 | 0.64 | 0.74 | 0.63 | 0.70 | 0.89 | 0.82 | 0.69 | 0.84 | 0.87 | 0.82 | 0.85 | 0.87 |
| Italian | 0.82 | 0.75 | 0.73 | 0.72 | 0.54 | 0.64 | 0.94 | 0.87 | 0.73 | 0.89 | 0.95 | 0.83 | 0.93 | 0.93 |
| Chinese | 0.67 | 0.64 | 0.61 | 0.54 | 0.55 | 0.64 | 0.88 | 0.68 | 0.67 | 0.77 | 0.89 | 0.79 | 0.84 | 0.89 |
| Aboriginal | 0.86 | 0.80 | 0.72 | 0.75 | 0.63 | 0.75 | 0.91 | 0.89 | 0.75 | 0.89 | 0.93 | 0.87 | 0.91 | 0.93 |
| Ukrainian | 0.73 | 0.71 | 0.61 | 0.70 | 0.60 | 0.68 | 0.89 | 0.78 | 0.68 | 0.84 | 0.85 | 0.81 | 0.84 | 0.87 |
| Dutch | 0.73 | 0.76 | 0.62 | 0.78 | 0.70 | 0.74 | 0.81 | 0.75 | 0.70 | 0.80 | 0.76 | 0.82 | 0.78 | 0.81 |
| Indian | 0.58 | 0.60 | 0.62 | 0.65 | 0.65 | 0.70 | 0.89 | 0.72 | 0.65 | 0.78 | 0.86 | 0.76 | 0.79 | 0.85 |
| Polish | 0.68 | 0.62 | 0.50 | 0.62 | 0.50 | 0.62 | 0.89 | 0.77 | 0.66 | 0.80 | 0.88 | 0.80 | 0.86 | 0.86 |
| Portuguese | 0.83 | 0.72 | 0.72 | 0.67 | 0.58 | 0.72 | 0.93 | 0.86 | 0.76 | 0.88 | 0.94 | 0.85 | 0.94 | 0.96 |
| Jewish | 0.66 | 0.76 | 0.66 | 0.76 | 0.80 | 0.76 | 0.89 | 0.77 | 0.79 | 0.81 | 0.89 | 0.80 | 0.90 | 0.88 |
| Black | 0.67 | 0.65 | 0.62 | 0.61 | 0.50 | 0.65 | 0.93 | 0.83 | 0.65 | 0.82 | 0.82 | 0.91 | 0.82 | 0.89 |
| Filipino | 0.00 | 0.77 | 0.67 | 0.63 | 0.74 | 0.75 | 0.88 | 0.75 | 0.71 | 0.77 | 0.82 | 0.82 | 0.85 | 0.86 |
| Greek | 0.77 | 0.00 | 0.61 | 0.72 | 0.66 | 0.61 | 0.91 | 0.80 | 0.70 | 0.88 | 0.90 | 0.76 | 0.90 | 0.94 |
| Hungarian | 0.67 | 0.61 | 0.00 | 0.64 | 0.61 | 0.60 | 0.86 | 0.71 | 0.66 | 0.78 | 0.83 | 0.76 | 0.85 | 0.83 |
| Vietnamese | 0.63 | 0.72 | 0.64 | 0.00 | 0.57 | 0.71 | 0.91 | 0.77 | 0.74 | 0.81 | 0.91 | 0.87 | 0.90 | 0.93 |
| Spanish | 0.74 | 0.66 | 0.61 | 0.57 | 0.00 | 0.62 | 0.91 | 0.79 | 0.66 | 0.81 | 0.92 | 0.84 | 0.93 | 0.91 |
| Lebanese | 0.75 | 0.61 | 0.60 | 0.71 | 0.62 | 0.00 | 0.90 | 0.77 | 0.69 | 0.85 | 0.89 | 0.79 | 0.92 | 0.91 |
| Norwegian | 0.88 | 0.91 | 0.86 | 0.91 | 0.91 | 0.90 | 0.00 | 0.81 | 0.88 | 0.86 | 0.84 | 0.82 | 0.83 | 0.76 |
| Japanese | 0.75 | 0.80 | 0.71 | 0.77 | 0.79 | 0.77 | 0.81 | 0.00 | 0.78 | 0.78 | 0.75 | 0.79 | 0.81 | 0.84 |
| Yugoslav | 0.71 | 0.70 | 0.66 | 0.74 | 0.66 | 0.69 | 0.88 | 0.78 | 0.00 | 0.81 | 0.86 | 0.79 | 0.83 | 0.85 |
| Korean | 0.77 | 0.88 | 0.78 | 0.81 | 0.81 | 0.85 | 0.86 | 0.78 | 0.81 | 0.00 | 0.82 | 0.83 | 0.82 | 0.79 |
| Swedish | 0.82 | 0.90 | 0.83 | 0.91 | 0.92 | 0.89 | 0.84 | 0.75 | 0.86 | 0.82 | 0.00 | 0.86 | 0.71 | 0.78 |
| Croatian | 0.82 | 0.76 | 0.76 | 0.87 | 0.84 | 0.79 | 0.82 | 0.79 | 0.79 | 0.83 | 0.86 | 0.00 | 0.87 | 0.87 |
| Danish | 0.85 | 0.90 | 0.85 | 0.90 | 0.93 | 0.92 | 0.83 | 0.81 | 0.83 | 0.82 | 0.71 | 0.87 | 0.00 | 0.76 |
| Finnish | 0.86 | 0.94 | 0.83 | 0.93 | 0.91 | 0.91 | 0.76 | 0.84 | 0.85 | 0.79 | 0.78 | 0.87 | 0.76 | 0.00 |
| **Average** | **0.75** | **0.74** | **0.67** | **0.73** | **0.68** | **0.72** | **0.88** | **0.79** | **0.73** | **0.82** | **0.86** | **0.82** | **0.85** | **0.87** |

A similar situation exists for the Vietnamese. They are highly isolated not only from the European groups but also from those who have come from the same region as they have, that is, the ethnic groups from East and Southeast Asia. This is clearly seen through the high segregation of the Vietnamese, Japanese, Chinese, and Koreans. The Chinese, in turn, reside more closely to the Filipinos and Greeks, rather than the Southeast Asian groups.

As far as other groups are concerned, the Indian, Black, Spanish, Portuguese, and Italian groups make a cluster of their own. So do the British, German, Canadian, and French, immediately followed by an orbit of East European groups, the Hungarian, Ukrainian, Yugoslav, and Polish.

Figure 3-5 illustrates the distribution of ethnic groups in the Vancouver urban space. In contrast to their situation in Toronto, the Scandinavian ethnic groups reside in close proximity to each other in Vancouver; they also live very close to the British, German, Canadian, and French. As in Toronto, this cluster of groups is immediately followed by another, consisting of East European groups such as the Polish, Hungarian, and Ukrainian. The Vietnamese and the Jewish, as well as the Lebanese, are the most highly segregated groups in Vancouver. In contrast to Toronto, the Chinese in Vancouver show a higher level of segregation, which is related to their larger population that allows for an enclave ethnic economy to grow. Except for a cluster of Indian, Italian and Spanish groups, no other cluster is distinguishable in Vancouver.

FIGURE **3-4**

SMALL SPACE ANALYSIS OF ETHNIC GROUPS, TORONTO, **1991**

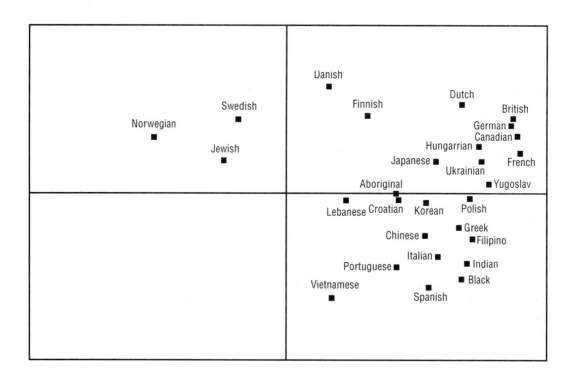

The distribution of ethnic groups in Montreal, shown in Figure 3-6, reveals some very distinct patterns. Unlike Toronto, the Scandinavian groups live very closely to one another. However, unlike Vancouver, they make their own cluster rather than residing close to the cluster of the British, German, and Canadian. Another interesting observation is that the French have distanced themselves from the other Western European groups and have become close to the Aboriginal group. This closeness may have to do with the specific political atmosphere of Quebec, causing both groups to feel unprivileged and marginalized by British Canada. It is also noticeable that, in Montreal, many groups that constituted one cluster in other cities have separated and made their own clusters; this has resulted in the formation of separate Filipino, Indian, Japanese, Yugoslav, Korean, and Black group enclaves. This situation has contributed to the comparatively significant level of segregation in Montreal, the highest among the Canadian CMAs.

**Figure 3-5**

**Small Space Analysis of Ethnic Groups, Vancouver, 1991**

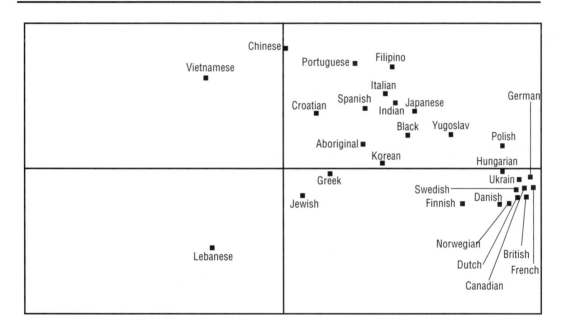

Despite the valuable information the above figures convey, they are primarily static pictures of a highly dynamic situation, as far as ethnic relations are concerned. A more dynamic picture can be achieved through the use of another statistical procedure, "cluster analysis." The underlying logic of cluster analysis is to decide which cases and/or variables can be linked together, based on a given index of distance. Such indices can be any indicator, as long as it is expressed for all cases and/or variables in a standardized way. The Dissimilarity Index used in this study is indeed a perfect example of such a standardized indicator. We therefore used the DI of all ethnic groups to capture the dynamic picture of the ethnic make-up of the three Canadian cities of Toronto, Vancouver, and Montreal.

FIGURE 3-6

SMALL SPACE ANALYSIS OF ETHNIC GROUPS, MONTREAL, **1991**

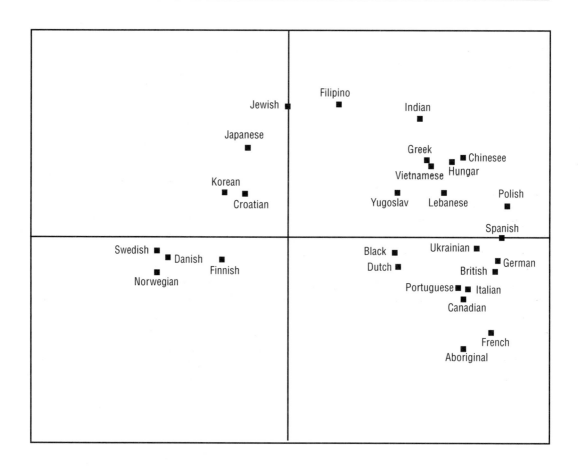

The logic of the cluster analysis is that it uses the given values as a distance indicator and tries to combine the given groups into clusters. The cluster graph needs to be read from right to left. It starts from one extreme, the situation in which each group makes its own cluster, and moves to the other extreme, when all groups join each other in one big cluster. Between the two extremes, different possible clusters are suggested, depending on the values of the distance indicator. Those groups with the lowest value of the distance indicator then collapse into clusters. At the top is indicated the number of clusters formed at each phase, and the shaded area with no empty space in between shows the groups that are part of one cluster. A sharp increase in the cluster coefficient determines the most acceptable number of clusters.

Figure 3-7 provides the clustering information of ethnic groups in Toronto. The visible increase of the cluster coefficient from the 15 to 16 cluster scenarios suggests that we should stay with 15 clusters. The first and the largest cluster is one that consists of the British, Canadian, German, French, Dutch, and Hungarian; the second, the Polish and Ukrainian; the third, the Black, East Indian and Filipino; the fourth, the Chinese, Greek, and to a lesser degree, the Japanese; the fifth, the Italian and Spanish. All the other ethnic groups are too distant from each other to share a cluster; hence, each shapes its own cluster. These groups are the Norwegian, Jewish, Portuguese, Korean, Swedish, Lebanese, Croatian, Finnish, and Aboriginal. Among all these groups, the Jewish and Norwegian are the ones that join the other clusters only in the final phase; that is, they are the most segregated groups of all.

**FIGURE 3-7**

**CLUSTER ANALYSIS OF ETHNIC GROUPS, TORONTO, 1991**

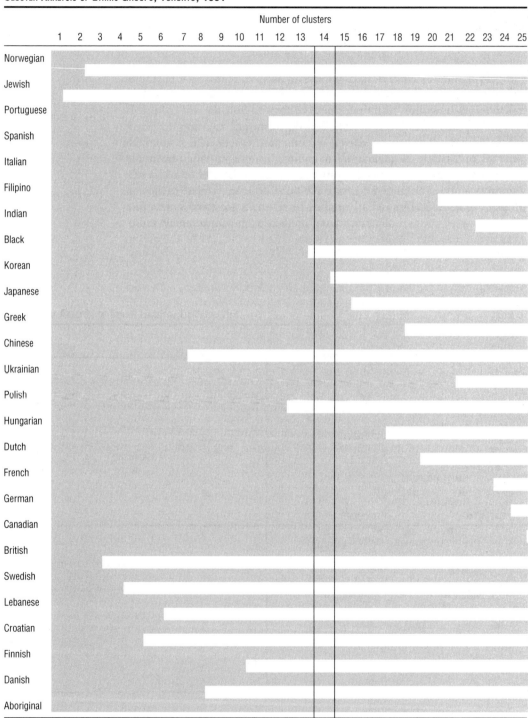

FIGURE 3-8

CLUSTER ANALYSIS OF ETHNIC GROUPS, VANCOUVER, 1991

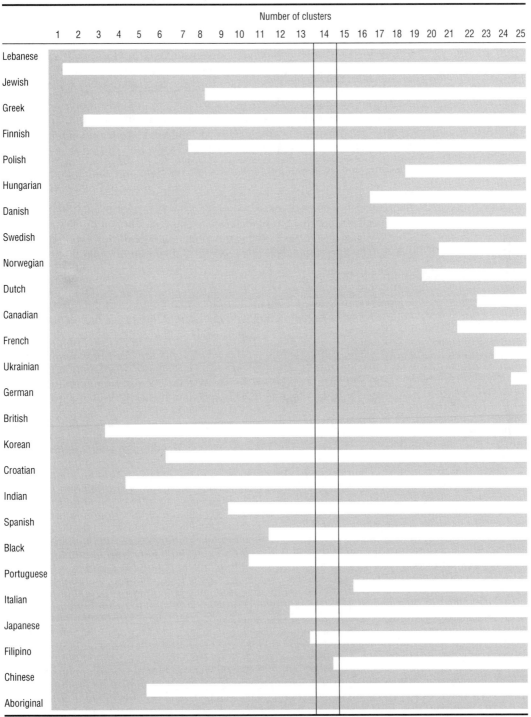

Figure 3-8 illustrates the clustering results for Vancouver. The increase of cluster coefficient after the 14th cluster suggests that it is more reasonable to consider the presence of 14 visible clusters in this city. The composition of each cluster, however, is not the same as in Toronto. The first cluster, like Toronto, includes the British, German, French, and Canadian groups, but also the Dutch, Norwegian, Swedish, Danish, Hungarian and Polish. The Portuguese and Italian make their own cluster, as do the Chinese and Filipino. These three clusters show an interesting grouping pattern, mainly centred around geographical origins, such as Europe and East Asia. The remaining ethnic groups make their own individual clusters, that is, the Aboriginal, Japanese, Black, Spanish, Indian, Croatian, Korean, Finnish, Greek, Jewish, and Lebanese. The last two groups remain the most highly segregated ones, joining in only in the last stage.

The clustering of ethnic groups for Montreal is illustrated in Figure 3-9. The changes of cluster coefficient suggest more reliability for a 12-cluster scenario. The first cluster contains a rather unusual combination of the British, German, Ukrainian, Black, Polish, Spanish, Hungarian, Chinese, and Indian. The second cluster includes the Aboriginal, French, Canadian, and, to a lesser extent, the Italian and Portuguese. These rather unusual groupings have a lot to do with the particular social and political conflicts in Quebec. Out of the three cases examined here, Montreal is the only one in which the French do not share a cluster with the British, but do so with the Aboriginal. As mentioned earlier, it may have to do with the perceived suppression that both groups experience. Out of the remaining groups, the only ones that make joint clusters are the Lebanese and Greek, and the Finnish and French do Norwegian. The rest are one-group clusters of the Japanese, Jewish, Filipino, Korean, Swedish, Danish, Croatian, and Dutch.

**FIGURE 3-9**

**CLUSTER ANALYSIS OF ETHNIC GROUPS, MONTREAL, 1991**

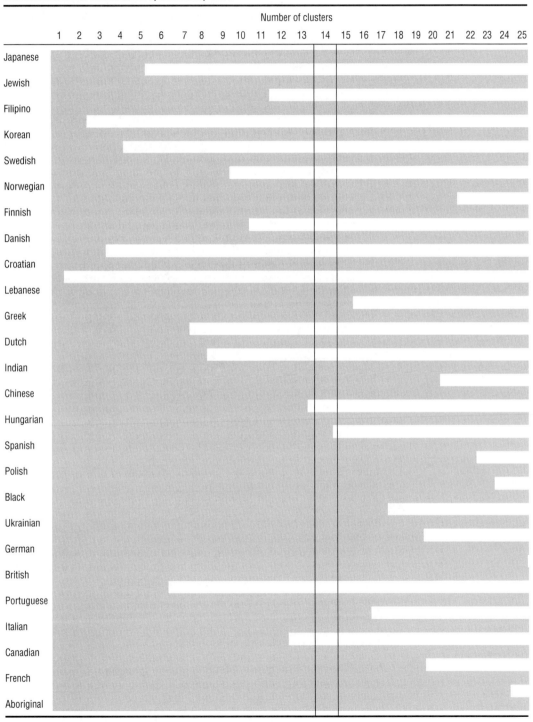

## *Explanatory Remarks*

Spatial patterns of ethnic segregation in Canada demonstrate some unique features, distinct from those observed in, say, the United States. First, the patterns do not follow racial lines. Unlike the United States, for instance, Blacks are not the most highly segregated group in Canada. This may have to do with the different history of Blacks in Canada, as there is no strong record of Black slavery in the early stages of the formation of Canada. Winks (1971:476-477) suggests that this historical feature has some origins in the way white Canadians have viewed Blacks, resulting from the way they have viewed themselves, i.e., as "transplanted Europeans."

> While the Americans had consistently asked Crevecoeur's question– "What then is the American, this new man?"–assuming that the American had become, in fact, a new man,... many Canadians continued to assert with equal vigor that they were representatives of European man and of European civilization.... To white Canadians the Negro was and is an African, even more to the degree than they are Europeans; and as such he is a sport, an exotic in a commonly shared and mutually alien environment. In short, although in the United States the Negro became an object of enslavement, discrimination, and even hatred, he came to be viewed ... as a natural part of the new American landscape; while in Canada the Negro who achieved a measure of equality nonetheless was deemed foreign to the landscape, equal but alien.

A second feature of the Canadian pattern of ethnic segregation is that the German ethnic group is one of the closest to the Charter groups and, in particular, to the British. This has led some to consider the German group as an actual member of the Charter groups (McLaughlin, 1985). This proximity resulted from two major historical developments: the role of the Germans during the formative years of Canada, and their situation in post-World War II Canada. The early Germans who came to Canada from America fought beside the British royal forces and against the revolutionaries. This gave the Germans the same historical status as the Canadian British, as they mainly comprised counter-revolutionary forces who remained loyal to the British government while fleeing America. In Post-World War II, when anti-German sentiments were at their peak, the Germans living outside of Germany had to maintain a low profile in order not to provoke any hostile reaction (McLaughlin, 1985). This resulted in the closure of German presses, clubs, and schools, as well as the geographical dispersion of Germans in an effort to reduce their visibility. The only German-origin people who maintained their original culture, continued using their language, and had a highly visible geographical concentration were groups such as the Mennonites and Hutterites, who lived mainly in small and semi-independent communities outside of the cities (Bassler, 1991).

A third unique feature of Canadian ethnic dynamics is that the Jewish are the only ethnic group with a consistently high level of segregation, regardless of the city in which they live. This tendency is partially rooted in the unique history of Jewish communities in different countries, as minorities faced with mostly hostile majorities. In order to survive in such unfavourable conditions, it was necessary to practice more caution, more discipline, and more in-group solidarity. This unique historical experience has imprinted on many of the social behaviours of Jews, evident in their high view of education, their relatively lower rates of social anomalies such as divorce and suicide (see Durkheim, 1951 [1857]) and, of course, their residential tendencies.

In the particular case of Canada, the inward orientation of the Jews is compounded by their high sense of belonging to Israel. Reporting the results of a survey, Brodbar-Nemzer and Cohen (1993), for example, point out that, compared to their American counterparts, the Canadian Jews have a more positive view of Israel, have visited there more frequently, and have a stronger desire to visit or live in Israel. These survey findings may indicate that Canadian Jews seek their preferred identity, not within the cultural boundaries of Canada, but outside of it. This may have resulted in a more conscious effort by Canadian Jews to retain their ethnic and religious identity, as well as their communal existence. Their high residential segregation strongly facilitates these tendencies.

A fourth feature of Canadian ethnic dynamics is related to the Scandinavian group. Our findings indicate that there is no adequate justification for the common research practice of treating "Scandinavian" as a homogenous group. The levels of segregation among Norwegian, Swedish, Finnish, and Danish groups in Toronto, for instance, is much higher than their segregation with other groups such as the British, French, German, and Ukrainian. Any further research on ethnic groups in Canada, therefore, needs to treat Scandinavian groups separately. The history of political conflicts among the Scandinavian nations lends support to this suggestion. Finland, for example, has been under constant pressure from two of its more powerful neighbours, namely, Russia and Sweden (Lindstrom-Best, 1985). Naturally, the flourishing of a national state in Finland was accompanied by a social movement among Finns to seek an identity distinct from the Russian and Swedish. This trend has most likely affected the way the Finns have felt about the Swedes, and it is well reflected in their high segregation index, that is, 0.73.

A fifth unique feature in Canada involves a rather complicated ethnic category: that of "Canadian." This category by no means refers to a group of people with similar ancestry, language, religion, culture, or place of birth. Viewed this way, one may argue that it could hardly be an ethnic category. However, the fact of the matter is that "Canadian" is one of the options in the census question on ethnicity, and the number of people choosing this option is soaring. While in past censuses there have been some 50,000 or 100,000 individuals who insisted on identifying themselves as Canadian, by 1996 over 5 million had identified themselves as single-origin Canadians; this is apart from the 3.5 million who selected "Canadian" as one of their multiethnicities. In terms of the distribution of "Canadians," surprisingly enough, they are highly concentrated in the east; also, the highest occurrence of "Canadians" is found in Quebec (Krotki, 1997).

The key to understanding "Canadian" as an ethnic category lies in the fact that, like other ethnic categories, it reflects subjective (or perceived), rather than objective, ethnicity. An ambiguous category such as "Canadian" provides the respondents with an opportunity to project their perceptions onto the label. There will be, therefore, little surprise, if we notice that the majority of "Canadians" are Anglophone in one city and Francophone in another; immigrants in one and non-immigrants in another; and "old" immigrants in one and "new" in another.

An interesting observation about "Canadians" is that, in Toronto and Vancouver, the overwhelming majority of them are Anglophone and have a very low level of segregation with the British. In Montreal, they are mostly Francophone, but have maintained a noticeable, physical distance between themselves and others of French origin. One possible explanation for this unique situation is that the "Canadians" in Montreal are the Francophones who do not share the separatist sentiments of the other French; hence, their spatial segregation. At the same time, this group is also distanced from the British, due to having a different mother tongue, that of French. This is reflected in the relatively identical DI of "Canadians" with both the French and British living in Montreal. The issue, however, is an interesting one and is open for further research.

# CHAPTER FOUR

# Poverty: The Ethnic Dimension

In the previous chapters, two main issues were discussed. First, it was discussed that the socio-economic developments in the industrial world since the early 1970s had led to a strong and "new" surge of poverty; the "newness" was not only in its magnitude; it was also in its facets and victims. *Neighbourhood poverty* was one such new facet, which was added to the conventional dimensions of individual, household, and family poverty. Chapter Two was, indeed, an exploration of the magnitude of this facet of new poverty in Canada. Second, it was argued that the new poverty was contemporaneous with an ethnic resurgence along sharpening racial and ethnic cleavages. This could affect the way the racial and ethnic population is distributed in urban space; it could also cause some ethnic groups to be more severely hit by poverty. The former was extensively discussed in Chapter Three. This chapter explores the latter, that is, the poverty of ethnic groups.

## The Poverty of Ethnic Groups in Canada

The pattern of poverty distribution in Canada indicates that members of different ethnic groups have considerably different poverty experiences. Table 4-1, the poverty rates of ethnic groups, shows the extent of these differences. Using as a yardstick the national poverty rate of Canada in 1991, 15.6%, the table is divided into three areas: the shaded area at the top contains the groups with poverty rates lower than the national rate, the area at the middle, those with poverty rates up to two times the national rate, and the shaded area at the bottom identifies those with poverty rates more than two times the national rate. The difference between the group with the highest poverty rate and the one with the lowest is 30.7%, about two times the national rate. This wide range corroborates that the different ethnic groups in Canada live in radically different worlds, at least as far as their poverty is concerned.

TABLE 4-1

POVERTY RATE OF ETHNIC GROUPS, **1991**

| Ethnic Group | Poverty Rate |
|---|---|
| Dutch (Netherlands) | 10.4 |
| Canadian | 11.6 |
| Italian | 11.9 |
| German | 12.5 |
| British | 13.8 |
| Jewish | 13.9 |
| Balkan origins | 14.1 |
| Portuguese | 15.1 |
| Ukrainian | 15.2 |
| French origins | 16.6 |
| South Asian | 18.6 |
| Hungarian (Magyar) | 18.7 |
| Polish | 20.5 |
| Filipino | 20.8 |
| Greek | 21.1 |
| Chinese | 23.5 |
| Black/Caribbean | 32.7 |
| Vietnamese | 35.1 |
| Spanish | 38.5 |
| Arab origins | 39.4 |
| Aboriginal | 39.1 |
| West Asian origins | 41.0 |
| Latin, Central and South American | 41.1 |

Table 4-1 reveals a few consistent patterns with regard to the poverty of ethnic groups. First, the groups located in the top area are exclusively European, except for the Jewish. Although the Jewish group cannot be specifically associated with a particular geographical location, the examination of their places of birth shows that more than 78% of them were born in Canada, the United States, and Europe. Therefore, in general, the Jews can be safely grouped with the Europeans. Second, the groups who experience the most severe type of poverty, i.e., those in the bottom area of Table 4-1, are exclusively non-European, except for the Spanish. However, the examination of place of birth for the Spanish shows that only 13.5% of them were born in Europe. About 62% of them declared a Latin American country as their place of birth. As a result, the Spanish are more closely associated with non-Europeans than Europeans. Also, except for the Aboriginal group, all the others in the bottom area of the table are visible minorities. Given that these groups consist mainly of immigrants, it is striking that some of them experience a poverty level close to the one they experienced in their home countries. Third, except for the French, which have a poverty level close to the other European groups, those in the middle area constitute a mixture of Asian and Eastern and/or Southern European, with the former being close to the bottom, and the latter, close to the top area.

**TABLE 4-2**

**Percentage of Ethnic Population Below Poverty Line, by City, 1991**

| Ethnic Group | Oshawa | Kitchener | St. Catharines-Niagara | Sudbury and Thunder Bay | Halifax | London | Victoria | Ottawa-Hull | Toronto | Hamilton | Windsor | Regina and Saskatoon | Calgary | Vancouver | Quebec | Edmonton | Winnipeg | Sherbrooke and Trois-Rivières | Montreal | Ethnic Group's Poverty Rate |
|---|---|---|---|---|---|---|---|---|---|---|---|---|---|---|---|---|---|---|---|---|
| Dutch (Netherlands) | 5.2 | 11.2 | 7.6 | 5.7 | | 7.5 | 20.6 | 11.1 | 8.3 | 10.8 | 11.4 | 8.7 | 12.9 | 13.7 | 20.0 | 11.9 | 9.8 | | 17.5 | 10.4 |
| Canadian | 7.2 | 9.2 | 12.9 | 10.0 | 14.5 | 15.6 | 14.0 | 9.8 | 8.9 | 13.3 | 20.0 | 7.9 | 15.3 | 18.9 | 38.9 | 15.2 | 11.6 | 29.0 | 27.4 | 11.6 |
| Italian | 4.2 | 9.9 | 10.7 | 7.2 | | 10.9 | 22.6 | 10.6 | 10.4 | 12.6 | 9.8 | 21.7 | 13.1 | 15.1 | 10.6 | 11.0 | 14.2 | 13.6 | 16.6 | 11.9 |
| German | 4.9 | 6.6 | 11.4 | 13.2 | 12.8 | 11.7 | 11.2 | 10.6 | 11.5 | 10.2 | 14.1 | 13.6 | 14.2 | 15.4 | 21.6 | 14.0 | 15.6 | 11.1 | 16.9 | 12.5 |
| British | 9.6 | 11.5 | 12.3 | 13.3 | 13.7 | 12.5 | 12.0 | 11.7 | 11.8 | 15.1 | 14.8 | 14.6 | 15.1 | 15.7 | 15.8 | 15.9 | 18.5 | 17.5 | 21.5 | 13.8 |
| Jewish | | | 25.0 | 30.8 | | 8.3 | 15.0 | 6.3 | 12.3 | 11.2 | 11.4 | 10.0 | 19.2 | 14.7 | | 15.7 | 12.1 | | 17.0 | 13.9 |
| Balkan origins | 2.7 | 7.4 | 15.2 | 8.6 | | 12.2 | 12.9 | 15.5 | 11.7 | 9.6 | 10.2 | 4.2 | 18.4 | 18.4 | 33.3 | 20.8 | 16.4 | | 37.7 | 14.1 |
| Portuguese | 11.9 | 14.4 | | 18.8 | | 8.6 | 9.1 | 15.2 | 13.9 | 16.2 | 19.2 | 35.3 | 11.9 | 20.8 | 27.8 | 25.2 | 14.0 | 18.2 | 23.9 | 15.1 |
| Ukrainian | 6.7 | 4.9 | 10.5 | 11.6 | | 13.9 | 14.7 | 7.6 | 12.5 | 19.4 | 9.6 | 15.1 | 16.4 | 15.3 | 25.0 | 15.0 | 19.1 | | 24.2 | 15.2 |
| French | 12.6 | 14.9 | 15.0 | 14.4 | 11.4 | 15.1 | 11.5 | 14.2 | 15.5 | 15.6 | 14.4 | 20.7 | 18.0 | 17.4 | 17.9 | 17.5 | 18.7 | 19.8 | 18.7 | 16.6 |
| South Asian | 1.2 | 11.1 | 14.8 | 4.5 | | 13.6 | 13.3 | 12.7 | 18.6 | 24.9 | 21.4 | 25.4 | 15.7 | 22.1 | 50.0 | 24.0 | 22.5 | 100.0 | 34.8 | 18.6 |
| Hungarian (Magyar) | 10.0 | 15.6 | 18.0 | 25.0 | | 19.3 | 19.4 | 14.7 | 18.5 | 20.4 | 8.1 | 14.1 | 30.0 | 18.2 | 20.0 | 16.7 | 31.7 | 40.0 | 26.0 | 18.7 |
| Polish | 16.5 | 20.9 | 12.9 | 10.9 | | 25.6 | 8.8 | 17.4 | 22.0 | 19.6 | 21.2 | 18.5 | 20.5 | 23.3 | 50.0 | 26.2 | 25.3 | 15.4 | 28.6 | 20.5 |
| Filipino | 5.9 | 9.7 | | | | 20.0 | 27.6 | 21.3 | 18.1 | 26.3 | 4.5 | 22.2 | 23.3 | 23.6 | | 22.8 | 22.8 | | 37.6 | 20.8 |
| Greek | 19.4 | 20.9 | 3.7 | 14.3 | | 8.2 | 22.7 | 15.7 | 16.3 | 23.9 | 22.6 | 7.1 | 17.5 | 25.5 | 16.7 | 17.1 | 31.8 | | 30.0 | 21.1 |
| Chinese | 20.9 | 18.4 | 28.2 | 30.0 | | 32.1 | 11.4 | 23.1 | 19.9 | 31.8 | 18.6 | 24.3 | 24.0 | 26.8 | 33.3 | 27.1 | 32.4 | 37.5 | 39.8 | 23.5 |
| Black/Caribbean | 5.2 | 24.5 | 24.2 | 27.8 | 33.8 | 30.3 | 33.3 | 37.6 | 28.4 | 25.3 | 39.5 | 20.8 | 24.7 | 44.1 | 37.5 | 39.6 | 34.9 | 43.8 | 46.9 | 32.7 |
| Vietnamese | 29.4 | 29.4 | 61.5 | 60.0 | | 30.4 | 9.1 | 20.5 | 37.8 | 42.6 | 10.7 | 20.0 | 38.8 | 29.4 | 39.3 | 42.0 | 38.0 | 36.4 | 36.1 | 35.1 |
| Spanish | 11.1 | 25.0 | | 25.0 | | 45.2 | 29.4 | 46.4 | 31.7 | 48.6 | 46.5 | 70.6 | 53.1 | 49.5 | 41.4 | 62.8 | 37.5 | 66.7 | 39.2 | 38.5 |
| Aboriginal | 33.3 | 18.5 | 11.9 | 47.2 | 44.4 | 46.7 | 39.7 | 24.0 | 25.6 | 46.8 | 69.2 | 65.0 | 45.3 | 48.3 | 32.9 | 55.3 | 60.4 | 32.5 | 31.5 | 39.1 |
| Arab | 15.8 | 37.0 | 27.8 | 50.0 | | 35.0 | 50.0 | 37.2 | 27.6 | 43.4 | 41.9 | | 32.4 | 48.6 | 69.0 | 49.5 | 4.0 | 21.1 | 47.3 | 39.4 |
| West Asian | 41.7 | 43.3 | 20.0 | 50.0 | | 34.8 | 10.0 | 38.5 | 40.0 | 37.8 | 44.8 | 20.0 | 51.0 | 44.4 | 87.5 | 54.3 | 34.4 | | 41.1 | 41.0 |
| Latin, Central and South American | 41.9 | 41.9 | | | | 34.8 | 27.3 | 41.9 | 32.4 | 42.9 | 53.8 | 34.4 | 40.6 | 30.1 | 40.0 | 42.3 | 51.4 | 42.9 | 55.0 | 41.1 |
| City's Poverty Rate | 8.7 | 11.7 | 12.6 | 12.6 | 12.9 | 13.4 | 13.5 | 13.9 | 14.4 | 14.8 | 14.9 | 17.1 | 17.1 | 17.7 | 18.3 | 18.6 | 19.5 | 20.1 | 21.7 | |

Not all members of a certain ethnic group, however, experience poverty similarly. This is because the poverty rates vary drastically from one city to another, depending on the size, economic status, and demographic composition of the city. The considerable variation in the experience of poverty by various ethnic groups in different cities, shown in Table 4-2, corroborates this argument.

Table 4-2 contains the percentage of each ethnic group in each city living below the poverty line. The last row and column signify the overall poverty rate for ethnic groups and cities, which are rank-ordered from the lowest to the highest. The national poverty rate in 1991 (15.6%) is used to distinguish the cities and ethnic groups below and above the national rate. The horizontal and vertical lines in the table divide the two sets. These lines create four distinguishable areas in Table 4-2. The areas are called 1 through 4, clockwise, starting from the shaded area in the top left. Also, the poverty rates that are higher than the city rate are highlighted. This shows the groups that are worse off than the average poverty level of the city in which they live. The rationale for this practice is that the severity of poverty is fully understood only in comparison to the immediate surrounding environment. This is to say that, for example, a group with a 40% rate, which is high compared to the national average, is considered better off if its members are living in a city with a 60% poverty rate. Given these variations, Table 4-2 reveals some interesting patterns.

First, let us have a general look at the observable trends in Table 4-2. The British living in western Canada and Quebec have poverty rates consistently higher than their countrywide poverty rate. Despite this, however, they are still better off when compared to others living in those cities, as their poverty rates are lower than the city rates (with only two exceptions). The British in Hamilton and Oshawa deviate from this trend, as their poverty rates are higher than both their nationwide and city rates. Except for these two cases, the British are better off in all other Ontario cities, such as Toronto, St. Catharine-Niagara, Kitchener, London, and Ottawa-Hull.

A similar pattern prevails for the French in Quebec and western Canada. The only exceptions are Regina, Saskatoon, and Vancouver, in which their poverty rates are higher than both their nationwide and city rates. In Ontario, the French's experience of poverty is in contrast to that of the British.

The poverty rates of the Germans show two distinct patterns. First, they have the lowest poverty rate in Ontario, that is, their poverty levels are lower than both their national rate and the city rates. Second, in almost all Quebec and western Canadian cities, they have poverty levels lower than their national average. Also, except for two cases, their poverty rates are never higher than the city rates. The same observation holds for the Dutch, too.

The poverty rates for other ethnic groups reveal a variety of patterns. The Hungarian and Polish show some similar patterns. In each case, except for three cities, their poverty rates are higher than their national rates, the city rates, or both. The Spanish constitute a unique case, as their poverty rates are either higher than the city rates or their national rate, or both. The situations of the people of Latin, Central, and South America as well as those of Black and/or Caribbean origins is the same as for the Spanish. With the exception of one city, the same holds true for those of Arab, West Asian, Chinese, and Vietnamese origins, as well as Aboriginal.

Now, let us examine the patterns in the four areas of Table 4-2. Consider the vertical line, which divides the cities with poverty rates lower than the national average from those with higher rates. Except for Vancouver, the cities on the right side of the line are located either in Quebec or the Prairies, while the other half contains cities mostly in Ontario. Using the horizontal line, we can distinguish the groups with poverty rates lower or higher than the national average. In the top half of the table are located mostly Western European groups, with the exception of those with Balkan and Ukrainian origins. The bottom half includes those of Southern and Eastern Europe, as well as the ones from developing countries, not to mention the Aboriginal. The visible minorities are mostly in this set. As can be easily noticed, the highlighted cases are more frequent at the bottom half of the table, indicating that the latter groups struggle with poverty higher than that of the city in which they live. Except for a few cases, the pattern is quite consistent.

One striking aspect of the poverty of ethnic groups in Canada, however, comes from a comparison between the two shaded areas of 1 and 3. These areas represent the poverty patterns of the Western European groups in cities with lower poverty rates, and those of developing regions in the cities with poverty rates higher than the national rate. The two areas illustrate two distinct patterns: while the highlighted cases can rarely be found in area 1, they compose the overwhelming majority of the cases in area 3. In other words, the Western European groups have poverty rates lower than the city rate, even if the city rate itself is lower than the national rate. The non-Western European groups, however, have poverty levels higher than the city rate, even if the city rate is already higher than the national rate; not only do they tend to live in the cities with high poverty rates, but they are also worse off than the average population of those cities. This indicates that the gap between the living conditions of the two groups is enormous.

Other than their higher poverty levels, and the continents they have come from, the poorer ethnic groups in Canada have at least two other things in common. First, all of these groups are recent immigrants. Table 4-3 clearly shows that the overwhelming majority of these groups have arrived in Canada since the 1970s. This is in sharp contrast to those of European origin, who settled in Canada long before the 1970s. Second, these groups are heavily concentrated in Montreal, Vancouver, and

Toronto, which have traditionally been the favourite places of residence for immigrants as well as being among the cities with high poverty rates. This raises the possibility that the poverty of these ethnic groups may be related to their status as immigrants. In other words, their poverty may result, at least partly, from the fact that they are immigrants, and that they arrived in Canada at a certain period.

**TABLE 4-3**

**IMMIGRANTS BY ETHNIC ORIGIN AND PERIOD OF IMMIGRATION (% OF ETHNIC ORIGIN), 1991**

| Ethnic Origin | Period of Immigration | | | |
|---|---|---|---|---|
| | Before 1961 | 1961-1970 | 1971-1980 | 1981-1991 |
| British | 44.8 | 24.0 | 20.5 | 10.7 |
| French | 29.8 | 25.0 | 25.6 | 19.6 |
| Dutch (Netherlands) | 74.5 | 10.8 | 8.6 | 6.1 |
| German | 65.8 | 16.6 | 9.2 | 8.3 |
| Other Western European | 57.9 | 18.9 | 13.2 | 10.0 |
| Hungarian (Magyar) | 61.6 | 15.4 | 10.1 | 12.8 |
| Polish | 33.2 | 9.7 | 7.7 | 49.4 |
| Ukrainian | 80.5 | 6.9 | 4.5 | 8.1 |
| Balkan | 29.0 | 36.7 | 23.9 | 10.4 |
| Greek | 25.4 | 44.0 | 23.2 | 7.4 |
| Italian | 51.0 | 37.3 | 9.0 | 2.7 |
| Portuguese | 8.7 | 30.3 | 40.2 | 20.7 |
| Spanish | 4.5 | 12.1 | 31.6 | 51.8 |
| Jewish | 36.4 | 16.3 | 22.6 | 24.7 |
| Other European | 52.5 | 19.0 | 11.3 | 17.1 |
| Arab | 2.8 | 12.9 | 26.0 | 58.3 |
| West Asian | 2.3 | 12.4 | 21.5 | 63.8 |
| South Asian | 0.9 | 11.3 | 43.6 | 44.2 |
| Chinese | 5.0 | 9.4 | 32.4 | 53.3 |
| Filipino | 0.3 | 8.2 | 40.0 | 51.5 |
| Vietnamese | 0.1 | 0.9 | 36.8 | 62.3 |
| Other East and South East Asian | 3.0 | 8.3 | 40.8 | 47.9 |
| Latin, Central and South America | 0.5 | 3.2 | 33.1 | 63.2 |
| Black/Caribbean | 1.5 | 16.6 | 43.2 | 38.6 |
| Canadian | 35.0 | 24.4 | 27.6 | 13.0 |

However, the relationship between immigration status and poverty is not well known. The literature on the economic performance of immigrants has produced mixed results; while some researchers have indicated a better economic performance by immigrants as compared with native Canadians (Basavarajappa and Halli, 1997), others have pointed out the diminishing economic returns for immigrants (DeVoretz, 1995). The issue, therefore, deserves closer examination.

## Poverty of Immigrants

To examine the possible contribution of immigration status to the poverty patterns in Canada, we first compare the general poverty rates of immigrants and non-immigrants (Table 4-4). In general, immigrants experience a poverty level above the national rate (19.2%), while the poverty of non-immigrants is below it (14.8%). Although somewhat revealing, this highly aggregate number conceals the fact that the immigrants' experiences in different Canadian cities are far from universal. The absolute numbers of immigrants in a city as well as the proportion of a city's population that are immigrant have considerable bearing on their poverty in a certain city.

TABLE **4-4**

POVERTY RATES, BY IMMIGRANT STATUS AND **CMA, 1991**\*

| CMA | Poverty Rate | | |
| | Immigrants | Non-Immigrants | Difference Between Immigrants and Non-Immigrants |
| --- | --- | --- | --- |
| Montreal | 31.4 | 19.1 | 12.3 |
| Quebec | 29.4 | 18.0 | 11.4 |
| Ottawa-Hull | 21.1 | 12.2 | 8.9 |
| Edmonton | 24.6 | 16.8 | 7.8 |
| Sherbrooke and Trois-Rivières | 27.4 | 19.8 | 7.6 |
| Calgary | 23.2 | 16.0 | 7.2 |
| Winnipeg | 25.2 | 18.1 | 7.1 |
| Toronto | 17.5 | 11.2 | 6.3 |
| Vancouver | 20.9 | 14.7 | 6.2 |
| London | 16.6 | 12.4 | 4.2 |
| Kitchener | 14.7 | 10.5 | 4.2 |
| Hamilton | 17.5 | 13.5 | 4.0 |
| Regina and Saskatoon | 18.9 | 16.8 | 2.1 |
| Windsor | 16.1 | 14.1 | 2.0 |
| St. Catharines-Niagara | 12.5 | 12.6 | -0.1 |
| Oshawa | 8.6 | 8.7 | -0.1 |
| Halifax | 12.6 | 12.8 | -0.2 |
| Victoria | 13.1 | 13.5 | -0.4 |
| Sudbury and Thunder Bay | 12.1 | 12.6 | -0.5 |

\*    Based on a 10% random sample of the PUMF on individuals.

Table 4-4 shows the poverty rates of immigrants, non-immigrants, and the total population in Canada's major CMAs. The cities are ranked in a descending order by the values in the last column, the difference between immigrant and non-immigrant poverty rates. There are a number of interesting observations one can make based on this table. First, except for six cities with negative values in the last column, immigrants tend to have higher poverty rates. Second, even in those six cities, the values of the last column are very small (with all values being less than half a point), indicating that immigrants have almost the same poverty level as the non-immigrants. Third, the six cities at the bottom of the table are small to mid-sized cities (with populations ranging from 120,000 to 353,000). In such cities, the immigrant population is not so high in either absolute or relative terms. The correlation between the cities' total population and their immigrant poverty rate (about 0.36) further corroborates that the poverty of immigrants is a more serious problem in the cities with a larger number of immigrants. One potential reason for this is that the range of job opportunities in small cities is not so wide as to allow for the concentration of immigrants in low-paying jobs. The pattern of internal migration of immigrants may also have a bearing. The geographically mobile immigrants tend to move from small cities to larger ones in search of better job opportunities and living conditions. As a result, the poor immigrants move to larger cities, leaving behind those who already have reasonably successful careers and living conditions.

In making sense of the trends shown in Table 4-4, region plays a key role. The top seven cities, that is, those with the highest immigrant poverty rates, are located exclusively in either Quebec or the Prairie provinces. This implies that immigrants are highly over-represented among the poor in these two regions. What makes matters worse is that the total population of these cities (that is, immigrants and non-immigrants combined) already experience a higher-than-average poverty level, compared to other CMAs. In other words, immigrant poverty levels are worse than non-immigrants, even if those non-immigrants are extremely poor themselves.

In addition to the regional aspect, there is also a strong linguistic dimension evident in Table 4-4. The three cities in which immigrants have the highest poverty rates are located either in Quebec (i.e., Montreal and Quebec City), or have a big Francophone population (Ottawa-Hull). This suggests that a language conflict may pose a serious hurdle to immigrant economic success, given that the language of choice for a large proportion of immigrants, even in French-speaking cities, is still English (e.g., about 40% in Montreal). Therefore, in such environments, immigrants are worse off not only because of their generally higher poverty levels, but also because of the further limitation posed by the mismatch between their language skills and their environments' language requirements.

The relevance of language for understanding the immigrant poverty experience points to another related, but larger, factor: ethnicity. It was earlier mentioned that, in the new surge of poverty in industrial nations, racial and ethnic factors were also part of the picture (hence, *racialization* of poverty). One potential argument here is that one should attribute the higher poverty rates, not to all immigrants universally, but only to those of certain racial and ethnic origins. In that case, it is ethnic origin that proves to be important, rather than immigration-status per se. Table 4-5, representing the poverty rates of immigrants and non-immigrants by their ethnic origin, allows us to examine the validity of such an argument.

TABLE 4-5

POVERTY RATES, BY IMMIGRANT STATUS AND ETHNICITY, 1991*

| | Poverty Rate | | |
|---|---|---|---|
| Ethnic Origin | Immigrants | Non-Immigrants | Difference Between Immigrants and Non-Immigrants |
| Other East and South East Asian | 30.8 | 14.2 | 16.6 |
| West Asian | 40.5 | 26.1 | 14.4 |
| Polish | 26.1 | 13.3 | 12.8 |
| Arab | 40.9 | 28.9 | 12.0 |
| Jewish | 20.3 | 10.1 | 10.2 |
| Chinese | 23.9 | 13.9 | 10.0 |
| Ukrainian | 20.8 | 14.4 | 6.4 |
| Hungarian (Magyar) | 21.2 | 15.0 | 6.2 |
| Other European | 17.8 | 12.2 | 5.6 |
| Balkan | 15.0 | 10.4 | 4.6 |
| South Asian | 18.0 | 14.4 | 3.6 |
| Filipino | 16.8 | 13.9 | 2.9 |
| Italian | 13.2 | 10.6 | 2.6 |
| Other Western European | 11.7 | 10.0 | 1.7 |
| Vietnamese | 35.4 | 33.9 | 1.5 |
| German | 13.6 | 12.1 | 1.5 |
| Greek | 21.6 | 20.4 | 1.2 |
| Portuguese | 15.2 | 14.2 | 1.0 |
| Canadian | 12.0 | 11.6 | 0.4 |
| French | 16.9 | 16.6 | 0.3 |
| Latin, Central and South American | 38.1 | 39.5 | -1.4 |
| Dutch (Netherlands) | 9.2 | 10.9 | -1.7 |
| Spanish | 36.8 | 38.6 | -1.8 |
| British | 11.9 | 14.0 | -2.1 |
| Black/Caribbean | 29.4 | 36.1 | -6.7 |

\* Based on a 10% random sample of the PUMF on individuals.

The last column of Table 4-5 shows the difference between the poverty rates of immigrants and non-immigrants of each ethnic origin. One striking fact in this table is that immigrants of certain ethnic origins, such as West Asian, Arab, Vietnamese, Latin/Central/South American and Spanish immigrants, have poverty rates about three times the national rate. The other groups' poverty levels, while not as high as those of the first group, are still higher than the overall poverty rate in Canada. The only exceptions to this general pattern are the five ethnic groups at the bottom of the table. But even for three out of these five groups (Latin/Central/South American, Spanish, Black and/or Caribbean), the poverty rates of non-immigrants are so unusually high (39.5%, 38.6% and 36.1%, respectively) that being an immigrant does not add too much to it.

If nothing else, the discussion made so far strongly suggests that immigration-status, ethnic origin, and city of residence have significant implications for poverty patterns in Canada. There remain, however, a number of unanswered questions. The poverty rate of immigrants in a city (i.e., Table 4-4), for example, does not say if the rate is the same or different for immigrants of different ethnic origins. Similarly, the poverty pattern of immigrants of a certain ethnic origin (i.e., Table 4-5) does not provide any insight as to whether they have similar experiences in different cities. The only way to check these possibilities is to simultaneously examine the poverty rates by immigration-status, ethnic origin, and city. Table 4-6 does that.

**TABLE 4-6**

**POVERTY RATES BY CITY, IMMIGRANT STATUS, AND ETHNICITY, 1991\***

| Ethnic Group | Halifax Non-Immigrants | Halifax Immigrants | Quebec Non-Immigrants | Quebec Immigrants | Montreal Non-Immigrants | Montreal Immigrants | Sherbrooke and Trois-Rivières Non-Immigrants | Sherbrooke and Trois-Rivières Immigrants | Ottawa-Hull Non-Immigrants | Ottawa-Hull Immigrants | Oshawa Non-Immigrants | Oshawa Immigrants |
|---|---|---|---|---|---|---|---|---|---|---|---|---|
| British | 13.9 | 9.2 | 15.5 | 26.7 | 21.6 | 19.8 | 17.3 | 16.7 | 11.8 | 11.3 | 10.1 | 6.9 |
| French | 11.5 | 10.0 | 17.9 | 18.1 | 18.7 | 19.2 | 19.7 | 25.0 | 14.3 | 10 | 12.8 | |
| Dutch (Netherlands) | | | 25.0 | | 17.0 | 13.6 | | | 9.6 | 11.9 | 6.3 | 3.7 |
| German | 14.3 | | 20.0 | 33.3 | 17.6 | 16.4 | 13.3 | | 11.4 | 9.0 | 5.6 | 4.0 |
| Other Western European | | | 11.1 | | 15.2 | 16.6 | 42.9 | | 6.7 | 11.1 | | |
| Hungarian (Magyar) | | | | 25.0 | 28.1 | 23.1 | 100.0 | | 10.7 | 17.9 | 6.3 | 12.5 |
| Polish | | | 66.7 | 47.1 | 18.1 | 32.3 | 20.0 | | 5.2 | 26.7 | 6.5 | 23.2 |
| Ukrainian | | | 25.0 | | 18.8 | 31.7 | | | 8.0 | 6.5 | 4.5 | 13.0 |
| Balkan | | | | 33.3 | 22.4 | 35 | | | 5.0 | 17.1 | 9.1 | |
| Greek | | | 12.5 | 25.0 | 28.4 | 31.2 | | | 23.3 | 10.0 | 21.1 | 16.7 |
| Italian | | | 11.4 | 8.3 | 14.0 | 19.4 | 18.8 | | 10.1 | 11.3 | 4.3 | 4.0 |
| Portuguese | | | 16.7 | 33.3 | 21.0 | 24.8 | 33.3 | 12.5 | 15.2 | 15.4 | 16.7 | 8.3 |
| Spanish | | | 20.0 | 64.3 | 40.6 | 37.6 | 33.3 | 75.0 | 50.0 | 41.9 | 33.3 | |
| Jewish | | | | | 13.2 | 22.6 | 0.0 | | 5.0 | 11.6 | | |
| Other European | | | 11.1 | 35.3 | 17.4 | 30.3 | 33.3 | 22.2 | 13.2 | 14.4 | 8.8 | 22.0 |
| Arab | | | 90.0 | 52.2 | 31.4 | 48.8 | 12.5 | 33.3 | 23.7 | 39.6 | 33.3 | 8.3 |
| West Asian | | | 50.0 | 100.0 | 24.2 | 38.9 | | | 10.0 | 39.4 | 66.7 | 28.6 |
| South Asian | | | | 75.0 | 24.5 | 32.1 | | | 13.0 | 10.5 | | 1.7 |
| Chinese | | | 50.0 | 31.3 | 26.5 | 42.1 | | 20.0 | 18.3 | 22.2 | 18.8 | 20.4 |
| Filipino | | | | | 21.2 | 32.5 | | | | 14.9 | | |
| Vietnamese | | | | 44.0 | 37.0 | 35.8 | | 44.4 | | 22.1 | | |
| Other East and South East Asian | | | 20.0 | 20.0 | 28.0 | 38.0 | | 83.3 | 27.3 | 47.8 | | |
| Latin, Central and South American | | | 60.0 | 41.9 | 52.2 | 52 | | 50.0 | 33.3 | 40.0 | | |
| Black/Caribbean | 34.6 | | 20.0 | 24.0 | 47.7 | 45.2 | | 46.7 | 38.2 | 33.9 | | 7.9 |
| Canadian | 14.6 | | 38.9 | | 27.4 | 33.3 | 29.0 | | 9.3 | 23.5 | 7.2 | 7.1 |
| Other single origins | | | 33.3 | | 36.0 | 47.5 | | | 54.2 | 68.8 | 50.0 | |

\*   Based on a 10% random sample of the PUMF on individuals.

TABLE 4-6

POVERTY RATES BY CITY, IMMIGRANT STATUS, AND ETHNICITY, 1991

| Ethnic Group | Toronto Non-Immigrants | Toronto Immigrants | Hamilton Non-Immigrants | Hamilton Immigrants | St. Catharines-Niagara Non-Immigrants | St. Catharines-Niagara Immigrants | Kitchener Non-Immigrants | Kitchener Immigrants | Windsor Non-Immigrants | Windsor Immigrants | Sudbury and Thunder Bay Non-Immigrants | Sudbury and Thunder Bay Immigrants |
|---|---|---|---|---|---|---|---|---|---|---|---|---|
| British | 11.9 | 11.0 | 15.6 | 12.8 | 12.9 | 9.2 | 11.9 | 8.5 | 15.6 | 10.0 | 13.4 | 12.0 |
| French | 15.2 | 15.0 | 15.9 | | 14.9 | 18.8 | 14.7 | 25 | 14.3 | 18.8 | 14.4 | 20.0 |
| Dutch (Netherlands) | 9.5 | 6.5 | 10.7 | 11.0 | 6.2 | 9.0 | 12.4 | 8.8 | 9.5 | 13.0 | 9.8 | |
| German | 10.0 | 12.6 | 7.0 | 12.2 | 12.9 | 9.1 | 5.4 | 10.6 | 17.6 | 9.2 | 15.8 | 8.9 |
| Other Western European | 6.9 | 10.1 | 20.0 | | 0.0 | 20.0 | 8.9 | 7.7 | 8.3 | 20.0 | 0.0 | 14.3 |
| Hungarian (Magyar) | 10.8 | 21.4 | 14.3 | 24.2 | 15.2 | 21.7 | 30.0 | 3.1 | 6.5 | 10.0 | 31.3 | 16.7 |
| Polish | 12.5 | 25.3 | 11.4 | 26.4 | 10.3 | 14.6 | 6.9 | 33.1 | 11.5 | 28.8 | 2.9 | 19.3 |
| Ukrainian | 8.5 | 18.7 | 19.2 | 20.0 | 8.6 | 17.0 | 3.8 | 11.1 | 7.1 | 16.7 | 11.5 | 12.1 |
| Balkan | 8.5 | 13.1 | 5.7 | 11.5 | 10.9 | 15.6 | 5.3 | 8.6 | 11.8 | 7.6 | 8.8 | 8.3 |
| Greek | 15.7 | 16.8 | 22.9 | 24.6 | 0.0 | 7.1 | 20.0 | 21.3 | 20.8 | 24.1 | 7.7 | 25.0 |
| Italian | 9.0 | 11.5 | 9.3 | 16.0 | 12.1 | 9.2 | 13.9 | 5.1 | 9.9 | 9.9 | 5.4 | 10.1 |
| Portuguese | 12.6 | 14.0 | 14.5 | 14.1 | | | 13.8 | 15.1 | 37.5 | 11.1 | 30.0 | 13.6 |
| Spanish | 37.6 | 27.4 | 30.8 | 43.8 | 100.0 | 77.8 | 9.1 | 25.0 | 46.7 | 42.3 | 0.0 | 28.6 |
| Jewish | 8.4 | 18.9 | 6.4 | 16.0 | 40.0 | | | | 18.8 | 7.1 | 20.0 | |
| Other European | 8.4 | 17.9 | 11.9 | 19.1 | 12.7 | 13.4 | 10.9 | 23.2 | 14.9 | 10.2 | 10.3 | 6.6 |
| Arab | 26.5 | 27.5 | 37.5 | 44.8 | 20.0 | 33.3 | 20.0 | 43.8 | 17.1 | 45.5 | 100.0 | |
| West Asian | 27.2 | 39.5 | | 40.0 | | 31.3 | 14.3 | 52.6 | 66.7 | 33.3 | | 75.0 |
| South Asian | 13.9 | 17.1 | 15.5 | 27.7 | | 15.4 | 8.0 | 11.6 | | 22.5 | | 6.3 |
| Chinese | 10.2 | 20.1 | 30.2 | 26.8 | 11.1 | 29.6 | | 15.3 | 18.5 | 14.1 | 11.1 | 40.0 |
| Filipino | 11.7 | 13.4 | 7.1 | 16.0 | | 11.1 | | | 10.0 | | | |
| Vietnamese | 44.1 | 37.4 | 33.3 | 47.2 | | | 28.6 | 30.2 | 14.3 | 10.5 | 100.0 | 71.4 |
| Other East and South East Asian | 11.9 | 25.4 | 14.6 | 50.0 | | 11.8 | 20.0 | 22.8 | 0.0 | 58.8 | 16.7 | |
| Latin, Central and South American | 37.9 | 26.5 | 100.0 | 23.1 | | | 45.5 | 39.0 | 100.0 | 50.0 | | |
| Black/Caribbean | 33.2 | 25.2 | 35.7 | 19.3 | 26.3 | 21.4 | 32.4 | 18.2 | 51.2 | 27.0 | 28.6 | 27.3 |
| Canadian | 8.8 | 10.6 | 13.2 | 14.3 | 12.8 | 20.0 | 9.4 | | 20.6 | | 8.4 | 66.7 |
| Other single origins | 26.4 | 35.6 | | 23.5 | | 26.7 | | 28.6 | 100.0 | 25.0 | | |

**TABLE 4-6**

**POVERTY RATES BY CITY, IMMIGRANT STATUS, AND ETHNICITY, 1991**

| Ethnic Group | Winnipeg Non-Immigrants | Winnipeg Immigrants | Regina and Saskatoon Non-Immigrants | Regina and Saskatoon Immigrants | Calgary Non-Immigrants | Calgary Immigrants | Edmonton Non-Immigrants | Edmonton Immigrants | Vancouver Non-Immigrants | Vancouver Immigrants | Victoria Non-Immigrants | Victoria Immigrants |
|---|---|---|---|---|---|---|---|---|---|---|---|---|
| British | 18.0 | 21.6 | 14.7 | 14.6 | 15.9 | 14.7 | 15.9 | 15.6 | 15.1 | 15.2 | 12.4 | 10.7 |
| French | 18.7 | 20.0 | 21.1 | 11.1 | 17.9 | 10.0 | 17.3 | 22.2 | 18.4 | 14.3 | 11.1 | 16.7 |
| Dutch (Netherlands) | 9.7 | 10.0 | 10.2 | 3.6 | 12.0 | 16.7 | 11.2 | 11.9 | 12.6 | 12.0 | 14.5 | 28.8 |
| German | 14.6 | 18.7 | 13.6 | 13.5 | 15.4 | 15.2 | 13.1 | 16.5 | 12.6 | 16.5 | 12.3 | 8.8 |
| Other Western European | 22.2 | 17.4 | 16.7 | 20.0 | 9.3 | 12.0 | 13.6 | 17.9 | 11.6 | 10.6 | 14.3 | |
| Hungarian (Magyar) | 27.0 | 36.4 | 10.5 | 23.1 | 16.7 | 18.5 | 9.1 | 25.0 | 28.6 | 30.4 | 30.8 | 13.0 |
| Polish | 17.2 | 36.3 | 16.9 | 22.9 | 16.3 | 26.7 | 14.9 | 36.9 | 13.9 | 25.1 | 12.1 | 4.2 |
| Ukrainian | 18.3 | 27.3 | 14.6 | 28.0 | 14.5 | 23.7 | 13.8 | 29.6 | 15.7 | 27.1 | 12.8 | 33.3 |
| Balkan | 15.0 | 17.1 | | 10.0 | 17.1 | 19.2 | 16.3 | 21.7 | 15.8 | 19.6 | 25.0 | 5.3 |
| Greek | 33.3 | 32.4 | 14.3 | | 24.1 | 26.9 | 38.5 | 4.5 | 20.2 | 15.3 | 7.1 | 50.0 |
| Italian | 12.1 | 16.2 | 26.7 | 12.5 | 13.0 | 17.2 | 8.1 | 15.1 | 13.3 | 12.4 | 24.4 | 19.0 |
| Portuguese | 11.4 | 15.5 | 14.3 | 50.0 | 20.0 | 21.2 | 31.4 | 21.1 | 10.1 | 12.9 | 16.7 | |
| Spanish | 30.0 | 39.1 | 60.0 | 75.0 | 35.7 | 50.7 | 50.0 | 66.2 | 55.0 | 52.9 | 100 | 28.6 |
| Jewish | 9.0 | 21.9 | 6.7 | 20.0 | 5.4 | 34.3 | 6.7 | 27.3 | 17.3 | 24.1 | 8.3 | 25.0 |
| Other European | 16.4 | 29.5 | 16.5 | 25.9 | 14.3 | 25.9 | 14.9 | 16.9 | 16.2 | 20.5 | 19.4 | 16.4 |
| Arab | 7.1 | | | | 49.0 | 44.9 | 42.2 | 54.2 | 40.0 | 24.7 | 100.0 | 40.0 |
| West Asian | | 34.5 | | 25.0 | 16.7 | 48.7 | 87.5 | 46.2 | 38.1 | 49.7 | | 16.7 |
| South Asian | 16.7 | 24.9 | 42.9 | 24.5 | 21.3 | 22.5 | 20.1 | 24.5 | 13.7 | 16.0 | 6.1 | 19.2 |
| Chinese | 21.4 | 29.6 | 8.3 | 21.3 | 18.5 | 28.6 | 15.8 | 26.5 | 12.7 | 25.4 | 12.3 | 9.6 |
| Filipino | 21.8 | 22.5 | 0.0 | 21.4 | 17.3 | 19.1 | 8.9 | 20.6 | 15.3 | 18.3 | 40.0 | 21.7 |
| Vietnamese | 23.1 | 38.8 | 10.0 | 23.3 | 30.0 | 29.7 | 37.1 | 42.5 | 40.4 | 38.4 | | 10.0 |
| Other East and South East Asian | 21.7 | 52.4 | 60.0 | 38.5 | 25.4 | 47.3 | 14.6 | 36.3 | 11.3 | 27.9 | 6.7 | |
| Latin, Central and South American | 22.2 | 52.5 | 20.0 | 39.1 | 25.0 | 29.0 | 62.5 | 35.7 | 21.7 | 39.3 | 50.0 | 12.5 |
| Black/Caribbean | 36.8 | 32.2 | 25.0 | 15.4 | 47.6 | 42.2 | 45.8 | 35.9 | 25.8 | 22.5 | 50.0 | 33.3 |
| Canadian | 11.0 | 40.0 | 8.0 | | 18.7 | 30.0 | 15.2 | 12.5 | 15.0 | 33.3 | 14.2 | |
| Other single origins | | 65.2 | 20.0 | 20.0 | 23.5 | 39.6 | 41.4 | 25.0 | 23.2 | 22.4 | | |

Table 4-6 reports the poverty levels of all ethnic groups by city. Also, for each ethnic group, the poverty rates of immigrant and non-immigrant members are distinguished. This allows a comparison of the poverty levels of various ethnic groups in various cities, as well as those of immigrant and non-immigrant sub-populations.

The reader needs to be reminded here about the rationale used to develop this table: the overall poverty levels of ethnic groups, immigrant and non-immigrant, could not be assumed to be equally applicable to all the members of these groups countrywide. We needed to integrate the city dimension with different groups. Using Table 4-6, we can examine the extent to which there is a consistent pattern across the cities, hence, identifying the outlier cases. Tables 4-4 and 4-5 are used as criteria to spot outliers. The outlined cells are those cases that deviate from the city's poverty pattern, as shown in Table 4-4. The shaded cells represent cases asynchronous with the ethnic group's poverty pattern, as shown in Table 4-5. The cells both outlined and shaded are those that deviated from both patterns.

As far as the poverty experiences of immigrants and non-immigrants are concerned, the trends observed for different cities are fairly consistent with the general trend described earlier. This trend is more pronounced for major centres of immigrant concentration. As mentioned earlier, Table 4-6 also reveals the deviated cases, which supplies a sound basis for further research. The examination of these cases, however, goes beyond the focus of the present study.

The poverty of immigrants also has a temporal, in addition to its spatial, dimension. The immigrants who arrived in Canada before 1961 and during 1961 to 1970, for example, have poverty rates closer to the national rate (14% and 11%, respectively). The immigrants of the 1970s and 1980s, however, were not as fortunate, with 15% and 31% poverty rates. While this may refer to different degrees of adjustment and integration into the new home country, it also has to do with the fact that many of the economic trends in Canada that had attracted immigrants began to backpedal in the early 1970s. Economic growth slowed down; recessions occurred more frequently; the welfare state began to disintegrate. Recent immigrants were, therefore, more represented among the poor, due to the timing of their arrival.

The period of immigration and the lower level of integration, however, are not the only culprits, because a more or less similar problem is faced by those immigrants who had a higher chance of integration into Canadian society by virtue of their arrival at a very early age. Table 4-7 shows the poverty levels of immigrants by their age at the time of arrival in Canada. Comparing the poverty rates for the age groups 0-4 and 5-9 years (17.2% and 18.7%, respectively) with those of the 20-24 and 25-29 years (15.6% and 16.7%, respectively) indicates that the second generation of immigrants are more likely to be poor. The higher poverty rate of the second generation of immigrants can be attributed to factors such as their lower employment rates (45% and 50%, compared to employment rates in the range of 50% and 60% for their parents), lower levels of full-time employment (40.5% and 56.9%, compared to 65.6% and 62.7%), and lower education. The reason for this lower performance, especially in education, might be that education does not produce the same output as it does for non-immigrants. According to Gordon (1995:530), "against a background of environmental disadvantages, institutional racism, and doubts about the likely rewards for qualifications, educational attainments have been uneven."

TABLE 4-7

THE POVERTY RATES OF IMMIGRANTS BY AGE AT IMMIGRATION, 1991*

| Age at Arrival | Poverty Rate |
| --- | --- |
| 0-4 years | 17.2 |
| 5-9 years | 18.7 |
| 10-14 years | 19.8 |
| 15-19 years | 18.2 |
| 20-24 years | 15.6 |
| 25-29 years | 16.7 |
| 30-34 years | 19.1 |
| 35-39 years | 22.3 |
| 40-44 years | 25.6 |
| 45-49 years | 28.6 |
| 50-54 years | 27.8 |
| 55-59 years | 29.8 |
| 60-64 years | 30.4 |
| 65 years and over | 31.4 |

\*   Based on a 10% random sample of the PUMF on individuals.

The more severe situation of younger generations of immigrants in terms of poverty runs against the expectations of those who subscribe to the assimilation and/or integration model. Based on this perspective, better proficiency in language, more compatible educational background, easily recognizable credentials, and less cultural barriers should facilitate a better performance of children of immigrants in the economic and social realms. This clear conflict calls for a more comprehensive understanding of the factors and mechanisms that have resulted in the status quo. There are other factors that may have contributed in this regard, i.e., human capital variables and labour market segmentation. Even if all of these factors prove to be relevant, the relative importance of each needs to be illustrated, as it is a crucial issue for developing anti-poverty policies.

## Causes of Poverty: The Hypotheses

Poverty is too diverse and complicated a phenomenon to be adequately explained by a uni-dimensional theory. It varies, for example, from one city to another; from one ethnic group to another; from one segment of population (e.g., immigrants) to another; and even within each segment, it varies from one generation to another. Some studies have suggested that the poor can be classified into different types: "working poor," "new poor," "disadvantaged poor," "truly needy," and so on (Jenkins and Miller, 1987). The persistent differences in variations and types of poverty indicate that the corresponding causes may also be different. The explanation of poverty, therefore, calls for a more comprehensive approach, consisting of all the major relevant factors.

The factors relevant to poverty can be associated with three approaches: assimilation and/or integration, human capital, and structural. The first approach is mainly concerned with the poverty of immigrants, as compared to non-immigrants. According to this approach, immigrants face a harsher poverty situation, due to being newcomers and the disadvantages associated with their immigration adventure, for example, language barriers, incompatibility of educational credentials, limited transferability of job skills, unfamiliarity with the market demands of new home, and lack of access to informal job-hunting networks. One logical derivation of this view is that the problem ameliorates as time passes by. The second approach tries to explain poverty based on individual qualifications, such as education. According to this approach, the occurrence of poverty is an individual event, and needs to be dealt with as such. The third approach holds the economic structure responsible: macro changes in the technological and economic make-up of society have the potential to unleash the poverty-generation forces. The problem, therefore, is social rather than individual, and so is the remedy. These three sets of factors are explained below; then, an experimental logistic regression model is developed to examine the relative importance of each.

## *Assimilation and/or Integration Factors Hypothesis*

Assimilation and integration refer to two, but not the only, scenarios when people of different cultures come into contact with each other; the former refers to the extent that an individual or a group is ready to maintain or lose cultural identity, the latter to the degree that one values relationship with members of other groups. A group of newly arrived immigrants, for example, may choose to keep themselves culturally and socially intact, or choose to expose themselves to the influence of the surrounding population. In the former scenario, the end result is separation or marginalization; in the latter, assimilation or integration (Berry, 1987).

While all the above results are possible, the latter two are more likely scenarios when it comes to immigrants. Over time, immigrants become more familiar with their new environment and the surrounding population, develop better communication skills, and become more realistic in their expectations. All these facilitate more integration or assimilation into the new society. This, of course, does not mean a full assimilation or a complete integration. The cultural orientations of the involved groups have a big influence on the extent to which assimilation and integration materialize.

Although they begin as cultural processes, assimilation and integration also have some social and economic consequences. The more assimilated and/or integrated a certain group of immigrants is, for instance, the higher its members' access to more secure and lucrative positions in the economy. Using this rationale, one can hypothesize that, in their first years of arrival, immigrants face the harshest situation; but this harshness lessens as the passage of time allows for more assimilation and integration. For the second generation of immigrants, the assimilation and/or integration process starts from childhood, and even from birth. Therefore, the degree of assimilation and/or integration of immigrants is directly related to, and can be measured by, their duration of stay, their age at migration, and their language skills. As far as poverty is concerned, the most severely hit immigrants should be found among those in their first years of arrival. Those having no knowledge of official languages as well as those who have arrived at a higher age are expected to be more vulnerable in the face of poverty.

We should note, however, that immigrants do not arrive with absolutely no commonality with the host culture. Many of them have been exposed to "modern" values by virtue of their education, for example. Through education, they may manage to secure their positions in the host society, even with a low level of assimilation and integration. This suggests that the effect of assimilation and integration can sometimes be affected by other factors, such as human capital factors.

## *Human Capital Factors Hypothesis*

Human capital refers to factors such as education, age, work experience, health, and migration, which directly affect one's status in the economic hierarchy. When it comes to improving their socio-economic status and the marketability of their skills, people consider human capital as areas of investment (Schultz, 1993). A poor socio-economic status can result from a low level of human capital, i.e., poor education, low job skills, high age, poor health, low geographical mobility. A poor education can suppress one's chance of admission into well-paying jobs that demand a highly skilled labour force. An older age can be detrimental, when the successful performance on a job requires mastery of modern technology. Migration tends to be undertaken in an effort to take advantage of job opportunities available elsewhere. This is true of both internal and international migration (Massey et al., 1994).

Those who are younger are more likely to have received a higher education, enjoy better health conditions, and experience geographical mobility. A higher age, on the other hand, is likely to produce a better work experience. Among all these, age, education, and migration provide better explanatory power. This is due to their impacts on other variables as well as the reliability of the data available for them. The model developed in the present study includes these three as the human capital factors to explain poverty status.

Immigrants' higher poverty may be attributed to their initial lower level of human capital. The fact that the immigrants who are worst off in this respect are those coming from countries already struggling to provide decent education and health services for their citizenry provides basic support for such an argument. This, however, is more valid for refugee and family class immigrants, rather than independent immigrants. The latter group is painstakingly selected through a rigorous point system, which attaches considerable weight to human capital factors such as age, education, and work experience. The selection process, as a result, has put this group of immigrants ahead of the native population, as far as human capital is concerned. These seemingly opposing trends call for a closer examination.

The issue is further complicated by some earlier findings that the human capital factors are not as rewarding for immigrants as they are for non-immigrants. This problem seems to be so established that some have even attributed the lower educational achievements of second-generation immigrants to it (Gordon, 1995:530). Big proportions of immigrants in Canada have occupations inferior, both in terms of prestige and financial gains, to those they are trained for (Basran and Li, 1998). This is far from accidental; it has partly to do with the dual structure of the labour market in industrial countries and the fact that immigrant workers are systematically directed into the segment with "unstable, poorly paid jobs and few mobility prospects" (Massey et al., 1994:716). This points to the importance of structural factors in explaining the poverty of immigrants.

## *Structural Factors Hypothesis*

In the early 1970s, Edward and associates (1973) suggested the notion of "labor market segmentation," in reference to the bifurcated structure of the American economy in the $20^{th}$ century. They described the process of bifurcation in the following way:

> Between 1890 and 1920, the American economy experienced a critical transition from a more or less open, competitive, local-market-oriented, laissez-faire, entrepreneurial capitalism dominated by giant corporate enterprise.... In this system of monopoly capitalism, the giant oligopolistic corporations that dominated the economy coexisted with a surviving peripheral competitive capitalist sector. The two sectors developed according to quite different laws of motion.... A consequence of the dualist industrial structure was a corollary dualism in labor markets ... jobs in the capitalist sector became increasingly dissimilar, and labor markets became increasingly segmented (p:xi-xii).

One key characteristic of this dualism is the superior-inferior type of relationship between the two segments, with more stable and higher-paid jobs and those with better mobility prospects tending to concentrate in the superior segment (Massey et al., 1994). Another is that it interacts with preexisting divisions by race and sex (Edwards et al., 1973).

There are at least two examples of such a segmentation process in the history of the contemporary industrial economies: "industrialization," in the early decades of this century, and "computerization," in the post-W.W.II era. In the first, the "manufacturing" sector replaced the "agriculture" sector as the engine of economy; in the second, the "service" industry grew out of "manufacturing." The first shifted a large portion of the labor force off the farms and into factories; the second moved them into offices.

Each time, it was hoped that the jobs lost in the old sector would be compensated for by those created in the new sector. This hope was even stronger with regard to the second development, as the "service" sector expanded the employment outlook extensively. Part of the reason for such an expansion was the wide application of computer technology in the "service" sector. Many new jobs were needed to make computers an integral part of office work. By the early 1980s, Alvin Toffler (1980) argued that there was only one thing to be concerned about–"computer illiteracy." The remedy–massive job re-training. The highly paid jobs in the computer industry, flexible working conditions, dispensed geographical binding to the office, and many other features all indicated that a Brave New World was about to be born.

But the optimism did not last long. A large number of the jobs that were lost in the "manufacturing" sector and that were supposed to reappear in the "service" sector, appeared, instead, in the developing countries. It was in the late 1960s that the large companies discovered the advantages of moving the labor-intensive sections of their production offshore to underdeveloped regions. According to Marchak:

> The global assembly line was selectively established in countries that had strategic geopolitical positions as well as cheap labour, mostly in former colonies where English was spoken and in regions that seemed most likely to sustain what was called "a secure atmosphere for investment" (1991:72).

The optimism that computerization would create more jobs was further shattered as computers extended their territory from "service" to "manufacturing;" an increasing number of "manufacturing" jobs were taken away from the human labor force and given to machines. What made such a transfer easier was that more than 75 percent of the manufacturing tasks were very simple and repetitive in nature; hence, they could be easily done by machines. As Rifkin (1995:5) put it, "[automated] machinery, robots, and increasingly sophisticated computers can perform many if not most of these jobs." This, indeed, happened during the 1980s and 1990s, to a large extent. Machines became, Rifkin warned, "the new proletariat" (p.7).

Instead of the high-paid, full-time, and permanent jobs vanishing from the "manufacturing" sector, many new low-paid, part-time and temporary ones emerged. Such jobs did not provide a "family wage;" that is, an income enough to support a family. Depending on whether or not they were employed, and if they were, for how many hours per week, people began falling in and out of the poverty zone. In general, however, there were more people falling into poverty than out of it.

How do such segmented labor markets affect immigrants? Some immigration researchers hold that employers in the developed societies "seek to recruit immigrants to fill secondary sector positions rejected by natives;" that is, the jobs typified by instability, low pay, limited benefits and unpleasant or hazardous working conditions (Massey et al., 1994:715). In a study of European countries' immigration policy, Gordon argues that this was a deliberate policy adopted by employers and government:

The initiation of long-distance movements of workers from cheap-labor economies was in large part the outcome of recruitment activities of major employers responding to specific labor problems and of governments acting on their behalf.... The original needs of employers related to sets of jobs that were being abandoned by an increasingly educated indigenous labor force.... The problems with these jobs might be that they were dirty, dangerous, stressful, and/ or poorly paid, but it was also crucial that employers could neither solve this labor problem at that time by transferring the activities concerned to cheap-labor area (because the goods or services were untransportable), nor by mechanization, rationalization, or paying higher wages (1995:527).

A perfect supplement to this particular labour market structure is the particular situation of immigrants. As Isajiw (1999:117) puts it, for immigrants "getting a job, any job, as soon as possible upon arrival has actually been a matter of primary importance and urgency, but the jobs that have often been most readily available to them, especially in periods of economic slumps," have been those in the secondary labour market. In a study of the position of Chinese, Blacks, and Italians in the social structure of Windsor, for instance, Helling (1965) has documented some of the mechanisms through which the wages are kept low for immigrants. The first mechanism is "the wage-split," based on the practice by which the employers pay the workers a wage lower than what they record in their books and contracts, with the implicit assurance that workers would not file complaints against them. The second mechanism, called, "sweetheart agreement," involves an agreement between the employer and a union official not to enforce the collective agreements. The third, "padrone system," is used by employers when they import their workers from abroad and manage to keep them quiet about their working conditions in return for payment of their accommodation and passage costs.

However, the research on this issue has often faced a difficulty: how to operationalize the concept "sector of economy." Lack of a consensus about the nature of jobs in each sector, as well as the inadequacy of available data, have left much room for speculation. The present study, unfortunately, is not exempt from this difficulty. In the absence of a better measure of economic sectors, we have adopted two variables to operationalize the primary/secondary sectors: the standard classification of jobs in Canadian Census, and the full-time or part-time nature of the job. If the dual labour market theory holds true, we should expect to see a clear aggravating effect of employment in the secondary sector on the poverty of individuals.

### *Summary of Hypotheses*

- The likelihood of being poor decreases with the increase of total years of schooling.

- As a human capital investment, (im)migration decreases the likelihood of being poor.

- Working part-time increases the probability of being poor.

- Having work qualifications suited to the jobs in the manufacturing sector increases the likelihood of poverty.

- For immigrants, the likelihood of being poor is correlated with their age at the time of immigration.

- The probability of poverty rises with the recency of the time (year) of immigration.

- Knowledge of one or both official languages of Canada decreases the likelihood of poverty, both for immigrants and non-immigrants.

- In terms of the type of language, the likelihood of being poor is the lowest for those who have a knowledge of both English and French, followed by those who know only English, and finally, those with knowledge of only French.

## Evaluation of Hypotheses Using Logistic Regression Models

To examine the relative significance of the three alternative explanations of poverty, we employed a logistic regression model, with the poverty status of individuals as the dependent variable. The independent variables cluster under three sets of factors: human capital, structural, and assimilation/integration. Human capital factors include age, education, immigration, and migration. Structural factors look at the impacts of full-time and/or part-time work, as well as the sector of economy in which one is employed. The assimilation and/or integration factors contain variables particularly related, but not confined, to immigrants, i.e., period of immigration, age at the time of immigration, and knowledge of official languages. Since there is a possibility that these factors affect immigrants and non-immigrants quite differently, separate models are designed for each group, in addition to one for the total population. Table 4-8 shows the results of the logistic models. The variables with values lower than 1 decrease the probability of one living in poverty; those with values higher than 1 increase it. The highlighted values in the table are the ones significant at 0.05 level. The findings are discussed in the order of the factors included.

TABLE 4-8

LOGISTIC REGRESSION MODELS OF THE PREDICTORS OF POVERTY STATUS, 1991*

| | Exp (B) | | |
|---|---|---|---|
| | Model 1: | Model 2: | Model 3: |
| Predictors | Total Population | Non-Immigrants | Immigrants |
| **Human Capital Factors** | | | |
| Age | 0.98 | 0.98 | 0.97 |
| Total Years of Schooling | 0.83 | 0.84 | 0.86 |
| Immigration Status (Being Immigrant) | 1.10 | | |
| Migration (Between 1986 and 1991) | | | |
| Within the Same Neighbourhood | 2.14 | 2.28 | 1.77 |
| Intra-propvincial (Within the Same CD) | 1.75 | 1.84 | 1.50 |
| Intra-propvincial (Between CDs) | 2.24 | 2.56 | 1.38 |
| Between Provinces | 2.88 | 2.55 | 2.26 |
| From Outside Canada | 6.80 | 3.95 | 3.98 |
| **Structural Factors** | | | |
| Part-Time Work | 1.40 | 1.59 | 1.23 |
| Economic Sector | | | |
| Other Primary Industries | 0.49 | 0.40 | 0.78 |
| Manufacturing | 0.42 | 0.36 | 0.70 |
| Construction | 0.55 | 0.52 | 0.76 |
| Transportation and Storage | 0.46 | 0.42 | 0.90 |
| Communication and Other Utilities | 0.35 | 0.28 | 0.76 |
| Wholesale Tade | 0.45 | 0.41 | 0.83 |
| Retail Trade | 0.53 | 0.52 | 0.86 |
| Finance, Insurance, and Real Estate | 0.37 | 0.34 | 0.62 |
| Business Services | 0.52 | 0.45 | 0.85 |
| Governmental Services (Federal) | 0.35 | 0.24 | 0.79 |
| Governmental Services (Other) | 0.48 | 0.39 | 0.76 |
| Educational Services | 0.51 | 0.40 | 0.84 |
| Health and Social Services | 0.55 | 0.46 | 0.84 |
| Accomodation, Food and Beverage Services | 0.89 | 0.85 | 1.26 |
| **Assimilation/Integration Factors** | | | |
| Year of Immigration | | | 1.03 |
| Age at the Time of Immigration | | | 0.99 |
| Knowledge of Official Languages | | | |
| English | 0.70 | 0.09 | 0.75 |
| French | 0.78 | 0.10 | 1.58 |
| English and French | 1.69 | 0.19 | 1.71 |

Highlighted Values Significant at .05 Level
* Based on a 10% random sample of the PUMF on individuals.

## Human Capital Factors

Except for the variable "migration," the effect of the other human capital variables, such as age, education, and immigration status, are consistent with the hypothesis outlined earlier. A higher age decreases the chance of poverty in all three models, that is, for total population, immigrants, and non-immigrants alike. This finding is consistent with the other studies on *new poverty*, which indicate that younger adults and children are more severely hit by the recent surge of poverty. However, as mentioned earlier, age matters because it provides opportunities for education, acquiring job skills, and long-term employment. This means that, if the effects of these associated variables are taken into account, age by itself should not be a very strong predictor. This justifies the fact that the values of exp(B) for age are only slightly lower than 1 (.98, .98, and .97 for the three models).

Unlike age, education has a more pronounced effect on reducing the chance of poverty, given the Exp(B) values in the range of .80s. One thing to notice here is the differential impact of education for immigrants and non-immigrants (.86 and .84, respectively). This difference indicates that, while education reduces the chance of poverty for both groups, it helps non-immigrants more than immigrants. In other words, immigrants cannot fully translate their education into income and socio-economic status. This, as previous studies have shown, has to do with the fact that immigrants tend to work in jobs for which they are overqualified.

Being an immigrant has a negative bearing on one's poverty status, as it increases the chance of being poor by .10. This inferential statistic, corroborating the earlier finding that immigrants are over-represented among the poor, indicates that, even after controlling for all the relevant variables, the aggravating impact of immigration on poverty does not disappear.

The impact of migration on poverty is puzzling. We expected migration, as a human capital investment, to lower the chance of poverty. The findings, however, indicate otherwise. While this calls for further research on migration patterns, some points can be mentioned here. First, the information provided in census data records the mobility status of respondents for the previous five years. This period may not necessarily be enough for the migrated individual or family to settle into the new environment and establish a solid socio-economic status. The search for a suitable job and adjustment to the new host of skills required may take longer than five years to produce any definite result. Second, the available data does not reveal the pre-migration poverty status of internal migrants. It is possible that most of these individuals or families had been poor before migration and that they simply carried over their poverty to their new locations. This is partly reflected in the higher poverty rates of migrant-receiving cities, such as Montreal, Vancouver, and Toronto. Third, while immigration aggravates poverty, at least in the short run, why should we expect the internal migration to operate differently? As far as the adjustment to a new environment is concerned, internal migrants face the same problems that immigrants face on a larger scale. The fact that the negative impact of migration is more pronounced for non-immigrants than immigrants could refer to this similarity; immigrants suffer less from internal migration, because they have already suffered from international migration. An additional geographic relocation at a national scale does not add much to the effects of their adventurous international migration. In light of these findings, the conceptualization of migration in the context of human capital factors seems to need major revision.

## *Structural Factors*

The variables associated with the structural make-up of society, full-time or part-time work and the economic sector one is employed in, support the hypothesized relationship, though with some modification. Along with our expectation, "part-time work" has a consistently aggravating effect on one's poverty status. In contrast to our expectation, however, all the significant values of Exp(B) for "economic sector" are less than 1, indicating that they lower the chances of poverty. This is perhaps an indication of "employment" rather than "economic sector"; all those registered for one sector or another have indeed some sort of employment, which does certainly reduce the likelihood of poverty.

The findings, however, give us some insights regarding the effect of particular economic sectors. Let us take, for example, the values of exp(B) for "manufacturing" and "communication" (0.42 and 0.35, respectively), as representatives of the traditional industrial sector and the computer-based information sector. While employment in either sector lowers the chance of poverty, such an impact is stronger for "communication" than for "manufacturing." For the former, the lowering impact on poverty is even as strong as employment in federal governmental services (0.35). This suggests that, compared to "manufacturing," the "information" sector still seems economically promising. The table shows, however, that this is not typical of all the jobs in the "service" sector, as the strength of impact is a lot lower for those in health and social, educational, and business services. In sum, the findings suggest that, while the employment in the service sector is not as promising as it is for the "manufacturing" sector, those service jobs related to "information" technology provide the strongest shield against poverty.

Interestingly enough, the structural factors are not significant in explaining the poverty of immigrants: only two out of the fifteen types of jobs, "manufacturing" and "finance, insurance, and real estate," are statistically significant. While employment in both sectors reduces the chances of poverty, such an effect is stronger for non-immigrants. In other words, even after controlling for all other variables, immigrants do not enjoy the same advantages that benefit their non-immigrant counterparts in the same economic sector. Nevertheless, the fact that the impacts of most other sectors are insignificant for immigrants implies that their poverty may be better explained by their particular immigration status. The examination of assimilation and/or integration factors will reveal this.

## *Assimilation and/or Integration Factors*

Two of the variables included under this category, "year of immigration" and "age at immigration," are exclusively related to immigrants; the third, "knowledge of official language," is relevant for non-immigrants as well. The effects of the first two variables are consistent with the hypothesis that the recent and the second generation of immigrants tend to have higher poverty rates. The magnitude of impacts (1.03 and 0.99, respectively), however, is not too high. This is because these variables act partly through education and job. Controlling for these variables minimizes the effect of recency of migration and that of generation.

The relationship between "knowledge of official languages" and poverty is a complicated one. Some previous researchers have also found the relationship between the language skills and the socio-economic status of immigrants to be puzzling. One confusing aspect of this relationship is that, while poverty is reduced as a result of knowledge of "only English," and "only French" (though to a lesser degree), knowledge of both languages raises the chance of poverty for the total population. Two things may have contributed to creating this peculiar pattern. First, the census data does specify the language an individual has more knowledge of, but not the extent of his or her knowledge. Not all of those who have considered themselves to be bilingual are proficient in both languages. Second, about 60% of those who are bilingual live in Montreal, a city with one of the highest poverty rates. Third, bilinguals tend to work in English-speaking environments, which may suppress their socio-economic status if the extent of their English knowledge is limited. In Toronto, for instance, 13.6% of bilinguals live, compared to only 0.8 percent of French speakers. For Vancouver, this proportion is 3%, ten times as large as that of French speakers.

For immigrants, only knowledge of English is helpful. Both "knowledge of only French" and "knowledge of both English and French" raise their poverty level. The hypothesis suggested in the previous paragraph may be more pertinent in the case of immigrants. Obviously, many immigrants arrive with mother tongues other than English and French. In many cases, they need to know a number of different languages and dialects in addition to the official languages of the countries they have come from. This makes English and French their third and fourth languages, at least. The number of languages they have to learn may well suppress the extent of their knowledge of, and proficiency in, English and French. This suggests that, in the case of immigrants, a "knowledge of both English and French" may simply mean a "poor knowledge of both English and French." This poses serious limits on the extent of their economic success in both French- and English-speaking environments.

## SUMMARY OF FINDINGS

Three logistic regression models are developed to unravel the mechanism of poverty generation for the whole Canadian population, in addition to immigrants and non-immigrants. The models include variables related to three modes of explanation, revolving around the human capital, structural, and assimilation and/or integration factors. The effects of human capital factors tend to be significant and compatible with what the literature on poverty suggests. The only exception was "migration." Although against the expectation derived from the literature, the effect of "migration" was in the same direction as "immigration." This suggests that our conceptual understanding of poverty may be improved by treating similarly the two variables of "migration" and "immigration."

The structural factors left mixed results. The results supported, to a certain degree, the hypothesis suggested in the literature. The aggravating impact of part-time work on poverty, for example, does invalidate some arguments that the recent increase of part-time jobs is due to the voluntary choices of workers. The findings also showed that while, in general, employment in the "service" sector raises the chance of poverty, the trend is opposite for the jobs in "information technology." Somewhat surprisingly, however, the structural factors tend to be insignificant in explaining immigrants' poverty. This is in contrast to the findings of some studies on immigrants in Europe.

The assimilation and/or integration factors revealed patterns compatible with what the literature suggested: poverty is a more serious problem for recent immigrants. This has to do with the fact that, in recent years, a large number of refugee and family-class immigrants, not qualified enough to find a decent job, have entered Canada. The present study also indicates that poverty is higher for the younger generation of immigrants. The fact that, despite their higher assimilation and integration, the younger generation of immigrants has a higher chance of living in poverty is a particularly disturbing and important phenomenon. First, the already higher poverty levels of immigrants may become a "persistent poverty," as a result of the higher poverty of the younger generation. Second, this pattern may have resulted from the social and cultural barriers the second generation of immigrants face, discouraging them from pursuing the path of education and qualification improvement. This phenomenon calls for special attention in the future research.

# CHAPTER FIVE

# Neighbourhood Poverty: The Ethnic Dimension

Ｔhe poverty surge of the 1990s in the Western Hemisphere was somewhat unique in its configurations, reflected in the wide application of the term *new poverty* in reference to it. The new poverty was unique in its high magnitude, but also in its neighbourhood dimension and visible ethnic and/or racial colour.

In the previous chapters, we examined the unique dimensions of new poverty. Chapter Two examined the magnitude of neighbourhood poverty in Canada; it also discussed some of the ways through which neighbourhood poverty might affect the life chances of individuals and families. Chapter Three addressed the relevance of the ethnic factor for the study of neighbourhood dynamics in Canadian cities. In Chapter Four, we studied the ethnic and/or racial dimension of poverty in Canada.

Our study showed that the ethnic groups with the highest poverty levels consisted mostly of Asian, African and Latin American immigrants, who had entered Canada in large numbers only recently. Aboriginal as well as French and some Southern European groups also ranked high in poverty.

The *poverty* of a certain ethnic group, however, is not the same as its *neighbourhood poverty*. While related both conceptually and experimentally, these two concepts refer to two different dimensions of poverty. Poverty, in general, looks at the income of an individual or a family: an individual or a family is considered poor if this income is not sufficient to provide the basic necessities of life, such as food, shelter, and clothing. Neighbourhood poverty, on the other hand, is decided by the proportion of a neighbourhood's population who are poor. A poor individual or family can be living in a rich or poor neighbourhood. In the former case, the individual or family experiences both poverty and neighbourhood poverty; in the latter, only poverty.

Our main concern in this study is to examine the ethnic composition of the residents of poor neighbourhoods. Here are some of the questions we are concerned with: Are there certain ethnic groups who are disproportionately over-represented in poor neighbourhoods? If yes, why?

Has there been any change in their situation over time? How much of such a disproportionate over-representation is due to the general poverty of these groups? What other factors are involved? These are the questions we address in this chapter.

The chapter begins with a discussion of the reasons behind the recent interest in neighbourhood poverty, followed by a profile of the ethnic composition of poor neighbourhoods, using 1986 and 1991 census data. It then introduces the conceptual framework for a discussion of neighbourhood poverty, along with the suggested hypotheses. A conceptual model to explain the neighbourhood poverty of ethnic groups is then developed and empirically tested.

## Why an Interest in "Neighbourhood Poverty"?

It was a new interest in the notion of the *underclass* during the 1980s that paved the way for increased attention to neighbourhood poverty. This rekindled interest in the underclass was so strong that, according to Peterson (1992), it even revived urban studies after a period of relative recession. The irony is that such a powerful concept did not have a definitive meaning upon which all the interested parties agreed.

*Underclass* meant different things to different people. In a very general way, it refers to a group of people who can hardly fit into the regular class scale of society. Such a group does not belong to the upper or middle class, but neither to the lower class. According to Jencks (1992:28-29), *underclass* has been understood "as an antonym for 'middle class,' or perhaps more broadly, for 'mainstream' (a term that has come to subsume both the middle class and working class)." But this has hardly eased the problem, as there is no agreement, neither among the scholars nor rank-and-file people, on what constitutes class. This vagueness is well reflected in the fact that, according to Clement and Myles (1994), many Canadians are not yet persuaded that classes exist and, if they do, that they really matter.

The meaning of *underclass*, therefore, has been somewhat contingent upon the meaning assigned to *class*. Based on the different criteria used to define class, Jencks (1992) identifies at least four different definitions of *underclass*: one based on income level, the other on income sources, the third on cultural skills, and the last on moral norms. Those who use income level as a yardstick have equated membership in the underclass with persistent poverty; this includes those families whose poverty is attributable to a violation of one or more widely shared social norms, such as the family head's failure to work regularly or marry before having children. For others, where people get their money is more important than how much they get; the upper class get its income from capital, the middle and working classes from regular jobs, and the underclass from irregular work, crime, public assistance, and handouts. Still others assigns people to classes on the basis of how they talk, how much they know, and how they deal with other people; the underclass, for this group, is composed of those who lack the communication skills typical of the mainstream population. Yet still others, who emphasize moral norms, refer to the middle class as a group with a concrete set of values, such as having a regular job, having no children out of wedlock, and refraining from violence; the underclass, therefore, consists of those who live their lives in violation of such norms.

Despite these different notions of the underclass, however, a consensus began to develop by the late 1980s: that the underclass was a subset of poor, that it included only those families and individuals whose poverty was somehow accompanied by anti-social behaviours, and that such behaviours are more likely to be found in certain neighbourhoods. In *When Work Disappears*, Wilson (1996), for example, argues that such behaviours are typical of certain inner-city neighbourhoods most severely affected by the loss of manufacturing jobs. In another study, Crane (1991) shows that living in certain communities would increase the chance that an adolescent will drop out or have a child out of wedlock. Examining the effect of the neighbourhood's schools, Meyer (1991) comes up with similar conclusions. Jargowsky and Bane (1991) call such neighbourhoods "ghettos" and point out that "most definitions of the underclass assume implicitly or explicitly that they live in ghetto neighbourhoods" (p.237).

How can we distinguish a "ghetto"–also called "the neighbourhoods of urban concentrated poverty," "underclass tracts," and "areas of spatial concentration of poverty"–from other neighbourhoods? A number of studies have identified ghetto neighbourhoods with their high poverty levels, decided by the proportion of their population that is living in poverty (Wilson, 1987; Jargowsky and Bane, 1991; Massey and Egger, 1990). In a study of the underclass in three cities in Canada, Ley and Smith (1997) also found a high correlation between the poverty of a neighbourhood and its social fabric, in terms of its rates of joblessness, lone parenting, welfare dependency, high school dropout, and criminal activity. The literature suggests the 40% poverty rate as the threshold in identifying a ghetto (Jargowsky and Bane, 1991; Wilson, 1987; 1996). A poverty level of 40% seems to act like a critical mass; when this critical mass is reached, "a self-sustaining chain reaction is set off that creates an explosive increase in the amount of crime, addiction and welfare-dependency" (Wilson, 1987:38). Even when holding opposing views on the dynamics of such neighbourhoods, poverty researchers of different ideological and theoretical persuasions seem to have agreed on this threshold as a yardstick.

In the present study, we use the same criterion to identify ghetto neighbourhoods in Canada. A more comprehensive view of the distribution of neighbourhoods with different poverty levels was already presented in Chapter Two. The distribution of the population of Canadian CMAs in such neighbourhoods was also discussed. What was missing from the discussion of spatial concentration of poverty in Chapter Two was its ethnic dimension. The representation of ethnic groups in ghetto neighbourhoods in Canada constitutes the heart of this chapter.

## The Ethnic Composition of Ghetto Neighbourhoods in Canada

Table 5-1 illustrates the absolute numbers as well as the proportions of ethnic groups in ghetto neighbourhoods for the census years 1986 and 1991. Since, with each new census, the categorization of ethnic groups is either expanded or changed, the data of the two census years are not perfectly comparable. The values in Table 5-1 are rank ordered by the 7th column, that is, "the percentage of each group's population in census tracts with more than 40% poverty rate" in 1991. The last column indicates the amount of change during the period from 1986 to 1991.

**TABLE 5-1**

**THE ETHNIC POPULATION IN CTs WITH 40%+ POVERTY RATE, 1991**

| Ethnic Group | 1986 | | | 1991 | | | Change 1986-91 |
| --- | --- | --- | --- | --- | --- | --- | --- |
| | Population in 40%+ CTs | Total Population | % in 40%+ CTs | Population in 40%+ CTs | Total Population | % in 40%+ CTs | |
| Vietnamese | | | | 13,275 | 80,025 | **0.170** | |
| Aboriginal | 8,715 | 91,110 | **0.096** | 16,140 | 13,7165 | **0.120** | 0.024 |
| Greek | | | | 13,050 | 144,530 | **0.090** | |
| Filipino | | | | 11,150 | 151,935 | **0.070** | |
| Spanish | | | | 5,680 | 78,475 | **0.070** | |
| Black/Caribbean | 11,065 | 166,470 | **0.066** | 14,830 | 215,125 | **0.070** | 0.004 |
| Chinese | 19,360 | 340,765 | **0.057** | 25,530 | 568,120 | **0.040** | -0.017 |
| French | 120,830 | 3,306,320 | **0.037** | 136,905 | 3,462,600 | **0.040** | 0.003 |
| Polish | 4,795 | 174,020 | **0.028** | 7,515 | 224,340 | **0.030** | 0.002 |
| Lebanese | | | | 2,100 | 68,030 | **0.030** | |
| Jewish | 2,240 | 241,320 | **0.009** | 7,150 | 241,620 | **0.030** | 0.021 |
| Portuguese | | | | 6,780 | 229,530 | **0.030** | |
| Korean | | | | 1,190 | 42,120 | **0.030** | |
| Hungarian | | | | 2,085 | 79,400 | **0.030** | |
| Ukrainian | 5,825 | 278,200 | **0.021** | 7,090 | 272,870 | **0.030** | 0.009 |
| East Indian | | | | 6,415 | 305,890 | **0.020** | |
| Yugoslav | | | | 810 | 42,360 | **0.020** | |
| Swedish | | | | 360 | 23,505 | **0.020** | |
| Italian | 11,475 | 67,1895 | **0.017** | 10,335 | 709,180 | **0.010** | -0.007 |
| Japanese | | | | 585 | 42,995 | **0.010** | |
| British | 47,105 | 3,830,010 | **0.012** | 39,915 | 3,373,800 | **0.010** | -0.002 |
| Norwegian | | | | 360 | 31,155 | **0.010** | |
| German | 4,665 | 501,145 | **0.009** | 5,925 | 522,560 | **0.010** | 0.001 |
| Croatian | | | | 410 | 39,700 | **0.010** | |
| Danish | | | | 235 | 26,850 | **0.010** | |
| Canadian | | | | 5,030 | 577,410 | **0.010** | |
| Finnish | | | | 235 | 28,375 | **0.010** | |
| Dutch (Netherland) | 1,365 | 197,000 | **0.007** | 1,370 | 20,3945 | **0.010** | 0.003 |

In 1986, the Aboriginal was the group highly over-represented in ghetto neighbourhoods, followed by the Black and/or Caribbean and Chinese (9.6, 6.6, and 5.7%, respectively). The Dutch, German, Jewish and British groups, on the other hand, were the least represented (0.7, 0.9, 1.7, and 1.2%, respectively), with values around 1%. The Italian, Ukrainian, and French were located between the two extremes (1.7, 2.1, and 3.7%, respectively).

In 1991, the status of Aboriginals deteriorated, with 12% of their population living in ghettos. The Vietnamese, however, overtook the Aboriginals (17% in ghettos). It seems that these two groups are more ore less in the same situation as the American Blacks are, as far as their spatial concentration of poverty is concerned. After these two, and except for the Greeks, the next four groups are those of visible minority origin: Filipino, Spanish, Black and/or Caribbean (each 7%), and Chinese (with 4%). In spite of their still-high rate of SCOP, the Chinese are the only group out of these four that have improved over this period. They, along with the Italians and British, constitute the only group with a declining representation in ghettos between 1986 and 1991. For the rest, the situation has worsened. The unavailability of data on other groups unfortunately hinders any further implications being drawn from Table 18. Also, the highly aggregated values in the table hinder a grasp of the situation of each group in each city.

The values in Table 5-1 are broken down by city in Table 5-2. This table shows the representation of different ethnic groups in neighbourhoods with a poverty rate higher than 40% in different cities. Comparing the numbers for each ethnic group with the averages in the second-last column indicates that the Vietnamese, Spanish, Aboriginal, Chinese, Black, Portuguese, Yugoslav, Finnish, Filipino, and Hungarian groups have higher-than-average proportions of their population living in "extremely high" SCOP areas. Four out of the five top groups are visible minorities. The fifth is the Aboriginal.

**TABLE 5-2**

**THE PROPORTION OF ETHNIC GROUP POPULATION LIVING IN CENSUS TRACTS WITH 40% AND MORE POVERTY RATE BY CITY, 1991**

| Ethnic Group | Halifax | Saint John | Que-bec | Sher-brooke | Trois-Rivières | Mon-treal | Ottawa-Hull | Toronto | Hamil-ton | Regina | Sas-katoon | Cal-gary | Winn-ipeg | Ed-monton | Van-couver | Ave-rage | Modified Ethnic Group |
|---|---|---|---|---|---|---|---|---|---|---|---|---|---|---|---|---|---|
| **Vietnamese** | 37.6 | 66.7 | 17.0 | 18.5 | 0.0 | 25.6 | 16.8 | 9.1 | 32.0 | 51.1 | 19.9 | 0.0 | 3.4 | 34.9 | 12.7 | **23.02** | **24.66** |
| **Spanish** | 0.0 | 22.2 | 5.4 | 50.6 | 23.1 | 16.8 | 0.5 | 3.5 | 11.8 | 19.0 | 5.8 | 0.0 | 1.1 | 8.1 | 5.6 | **11.57** | **11.57** |
| **Aboriginal** | 7.8 | 23.8 | 6.0 | 1.8 | 8.7 | 7.3 | 0.9 | 3.6 | 6.8 | 45.7 | 16.1 | 4.0 | 0.8 | 7.7 | 13.4 | **10.29** | **10.29** |
| **Chinese** | 2.2 | 12.2 | 8.1 | 24.1 | 0.0 | 17.3 | 3.5 | 2.4 | 8.3 | 16.4 | 2.2 | 9.5 | 1.4 | 6.7 | 4.9 | **7.95** | **8.51** |
| **Black** | 14.3 | 16.7 | 14.6 | 19.4 | 0.0 | 18.7 | 4.5 | 3.9 | 3.6 | 12.6 | 0.0 | 0.0 | 0.8 | 4.1 | 4.7 | **7.86** | **8.42** |
| **Portugese** | 0.0 | 19.0 | 4.2 | 18.5 | 0.0 | 7.9 | 1.3 | 0.6 | 10.8 | 20.8 | 0.0 | 0.0 | 0.0 | 4.3 | 1.8 | **5.95** | **6.86** |
| **Yugoslav** | 0.0 | . | 0.0 | 40.0 | . | 8.7 | 0.0 | 1.1 | 0.9 | 12.9 | 5.0 | 0.0 | 1.2 | 4.1 | 1.6 | **5.81** | **6.86** |
| **Finnish** | 0.0 | 50.0 | 0.0 | . | . | 3.4 | 0.0 | 1.0 | 0.0 | 12.8 | 0.0 | 0.0 | 1.9 | 3.4 | 1.2 | **5.67** | **9.21** |
| **Filipino** | 0.0 | 0.0 | 0.0 | 0.0 | . | 24.2 | 4.1 | 3.4 | 1.5 | 24.5 | 6.3 | 3.9 | 0.4 | 3.2 | 3.0 | **5.32** | **7.45** |
| **Hungarian** | 0.0 | 0.0 | 5.6 | 35.0 | 0.0 | 9.8 | 0.7 | 1.3 | 2.4 | 11.2 | 1.9 | 2.4 | 1.7 | 3.6 | 3.5 | **5.27** | **6.59** |
| Polish | 4.3 | 0.0 | 0.0 | 21.7 | 0.0 | 11.8 | 1.8 | 1.3 | 2.4 | 11.1 | 2.3 | 1.8 | 0.9 | 5.9 | 5.4 | 4.71 | **5.89** |
| Croatian | 10.0 | . | 0.0 | 0.0 | . | 5.9 | 0.0 | 0.4 | 0.0 | 11.2 | 22.2 | 0.0 | 0.0 | 7.1 | 2.3 | 4.55 | **5.91** |
| Dutch | 0.7 | 2.6 | 0.0 | 25.0 | 14.3 | 5.1 | 0.2 | 0.5 | 0.5 | 3.6 | 1.2 | 0.6 | 0.2 | 1.3 | 0.7 | 3.77 | 4.04 |
| Lebanese | 1.8 | 0.0 | 5.7 | 0.0 | 10.0 | 5.1 | 1.6 | 1.9 | 10.0 | 10.5 | 0.0 | 0.0 | 1.2 | 1.4 | 1.7 | 3.39 | 4.63 |
| French | 1.8 | 6.2 | 3.9 | 6.4 | 4.7 | 5.1 | 0.6 | 1.7 | 2.0 | 3.9 | 2.0 | 0.2 | 0.8 | 1.9 | 2.7 | 2.93 | 2.93 |
| Korean | 0.0 | 0.0 | 0.0 | . | . | 7.4 | 1.7 | 2.7 | 3.0 | 17.6 | 0.0 | 0.0 | 0.8 | 0.5 | 2.6 | 2.79 | 4.54 |
| English | 1.4 | 4.5 | 2.4 | 2.8 | 7.7 | 6.1 | 0.7 | 1.0 | 1.1 | 5.5 | 3.0 | 0.5 | 0.5 | 1.7 | 1.0 | 2.66 | 2.66 |
| East Indian | 0.0 | 0.0 | 0.0 | 0.0 | 0.0 | 21.7 | 1.8 | 1.2 | 5.1 | 3.3 | 2.9 | 0.0 | 0.4 | 1.3 | 0.3 | 2.53 | 3.80 |
| German | 1.2 | 5.9 | 2.9 | 6.9 | 4.3 | 4.3 | 0.5 | 0.9 | 1.1 | 4.3 | 2.0 | 0.3 | 0.4 | 1.7 | 0.8 | 2.50 | 2.50 |
| Ukrainian | 0.0 | 11.1 | 0.0 | 0.0 | 0.0 | 6.7 | 0.6 | 0.8 | 1.2 | 8.5 | 1.5 | 1.3 | 0.6 | 2.7 | 1.2 | 2.41 | 3.02 |
| Greek | 0.0 | 0.0 | 0.0 | 0.0 | . | 25.8 | 0.4 | 0.5 | 1.7 | 3.1 | 0.0 | 0.0 | 0.0 | 0.7 | 1.1 | 2.38 | 2.78 |
| Italian | 0.0 | 0.0 | 0.6 | 8.0 | 0.0 | 3.2 | 2.4 | 0.8 | 1.6 | 4.6 | 3.9 | 0.0 | 0.2 | 4.3 | 1.5 | 2.07 | 2.07 |
| Danish | 3.1 | . | 0.0 | 0.0 | . | 2.2 | 0.0 | 0.5 | 1.4 | 4.2 | 6.2 | 0.0 | 0.5 | 1.6 | 1.0 | 1.73 | 1.88 |
| Norwegian | 0.0 | 7.7 | 0.0 | 0.0 | 0.0 | 2.0 | 1.9 | 0.8 | 0.0 | 4.2 | 3.5 | 0.4 | 0.8 | 1.4 | 1.4 | 1.61 | 2.19 |
| Japanese | 0.0 | . | 0.0 | . | 0.0 | 6.5 | 1.2 | 0.7 | 0.0 | 4.1 | 0.0 | 5.9 | 0.5 | 0.9 | 1.8 | 1.54 | 2.40 |
| Swedish | 0.0 | 0.0 | 0.0 | . | . | 0.0 | 0.0 | 1.1 | 0.0 | 9.6 | 2.9 | 0.0 | 0.7 | 2.4 | 1.1 | 1.37 | 2.23 |
| Jewish | 1.3 | 0.0 | 0.0 | 0.0 | 0.0 | 8.4 | 0.1 | 0.1 | 0.0 | 3.5 | 0.0 | 0.0 | 0.0 | 0.9 | 0.5 | 0.99 | 1.35 |
| | | | | | | | | | | | | | | | | **4.91** | **5.75** |

Many of the zeros in Table 5-2 may be taken literally, as indicating that no member of the corresponding ethnic groups live in the SCOP areas. However, this might simply be so because the corresponding ethnic groups do not have a significant population in those cities. Indeed, it is now an established fact that big portions of some ethnic groups, especially those who migrated from the developing societies, are concentrated in the three major cities of Toronto, Montreal, and Vancouver. These zeros, nevertheless, distort the overall average values. Comparing the zeros against the proportional population of each group in each city led to a modification of the values in Table 5-2, reflected in the "modified average" column. This modification pushed the overall average up to 5.75 from 4.90, along with changing the individual values. The changed values altered the threshold for those ethnic groups with higher-than-average SCOP rates. As a result, the Poles and Croatians fell into the category of those ethnic groups over-represented in poverty areas.

The individual values in Table 5-2 also convey important information about the SCOP experience of some ethnic groups. Let us concentrate, for example, on those groups that have neighbourhood poverty rates higher than the highest average (i.e., 23.02%). The Vietnamese in Halifax, Saint John, Montreal, Hamilton, Winnipeg., and Edmonton are distinguishable in this respect. In two of these cities, Saint John and Winnipeg, more than 50% of the Vietnamese population lives in ghetto neighbourhoods. More or less similar to the Vietnamese in these two cities are the Spanish in Sherbrooke, the Aboriginals in Winnipeg, and the Finnish in Saint John. The high proportion of Aboriginals living in ghettos in the Prairies is also alarming, given that this area contains large concentrations of Native people. All in all, the cases of the Vietnamese and the Aboriginals call for special attention in public policy making. The groups with a ghetto representation below the national average are mostly of European origin, with the only exceptions being the Korean, Japanese, Lebanese, and East Indian groups. Given the relatively high poverty rates of these groups, their low level of neighbourhood poverty may have resulted from the distribution of their poor members in urban space.

The fact that the ranking of some ethnic groups' neighbourhood poverty and their conventional poverty do not necessarily match indicates that poverty alone does not determine neighbourhood poverty; other factors are involved. The different explanations of neighbourhood poverty offered in the literature corroborate the multifaceted nature of the spatial concentration of poverty. For a better understanding of the causes as well as the effects of neighbourhood poverty, we start with an examination of the current explanations. We then try to expand them by suggesting some additional concepts to be included.

## Predictors of Ethnic Groups' Neighbourhood Poverty: The Conceptual Framework and Research Hypotheses

The conceptual framework, as well as the resultant hypotheses, used in this study is an integration and expansion of two modes of explanation already present in the literature: Wilson's *mismatch hypothesis*, and Massey and Denton's *segregation hypothesis*. In what follows, these two modes of explanation are introduced in more detail, their shortcomings are discussed, and an effort is made to improve and expand the conceptual understanding of the ethnic groups' neighbourhood poverty.

### *Mismatch Hypothesis*

Wilson (1987) traces the high level of the SCOP in certain American cities back to the structural changes in the economy. At the heart of these structural changes lies a shift from a manufacturing-based to an information-based economy. The emerging society—also referred to as "post-industrial," "cognitariate," "service-based," and so on—is more inclined to produce "information" than manufactured "goods." The manufacturing activities have shifted to overseas, where larger markets, cheaper labour forces, and inexpensive raw materials are located. While this very development boosted some economies in the developing world and made possible the emergence of NICs (Newly Industrialized Countries) in Latin America and Southeast Asia, it robbed blue-collar Americans of many jobs in the manufacturing sector. As a result, unemployment rates soared, and the blue-collar workers experienced what Wilson (1987:41) calls a "mismatch" between their skills and the market demands; the same process struck minorities harder. An inevitable result of this mismatch was the rise of poverty among urban minorities. In Wilson's own words,

> [the] vibrant information-processing sectors are more than compensating for blue-collar job losses, reversing decades of net unemployment decline. What are the implications of this transformation of urban economy for poor minorities? First of all, cities in the North that have experienced the greatest decline of jobs in the lower-education-requisite industries since 1970 have had, at the same time, significant increases in minority residents who are seldom employed in the high-growth industries.... This has created a serious mismatch between the current education distribution of minority residents in large northern cities and the changing education requirements of their rapidly transforming industries bases (Wilson, 1987:41).

But rising poverty was not the only culprit as far as neighbourhood poverty is concerned. Another factor was the increased social mobility of American racial minorities, including Blacks, during the 1950s and 1960s. This increased mobility accelerated the out-migration of middle-class families from Black neighbourhoods, leaving behind the poor Blacks

(Wilson, 1987:50). It is the combination of rising poverty and the social isolation of Blacks, according to Wilson, that has caused their high levels of SCOP in many American cities.

Although primarily concerned with American Blacks, Wilson's account is not race specific. The structural changes, the rising unemployment, the poverty rates, the social mobility of middle-class families, and the concentration of poor in certain neighbourhoods are all general developments that equally affect other groups. The race-free nature of Wilson's analysis is also reflected in the solutions that he calls for, i.e., universal social policies as opposed to race-specific ones.

## *Segregation Hypothesis*

Unlike Wilson (1987; 1996), Massey and Denton (1993) emphasize the significance of race in explaining the high rates of neighbourhood poverty among American Blacks. They argue that the recent rise of poverty in America has led to dissimilar levels of neighbourhood poverty for different racial groups. The reason for this dissimilarity, according to Massey and Denton (1993), is that these groups have different levels of *spatial segregation.* An increase in the poverty rate of a minority group that is highly concentrated results in all poor families to live in a limited number of neighbourhoods; hence, substantial increases in the neighbourhood poverty rate.

Through a simulation model of some hypothetical data, Massey and Denton (1993:120-121) show how segregation influences the neighbourhood poverty of certain racial groups. Table 5-3 contains four sets of data, each corresponding to one hypothetical city. The four cities have similar poverty rates, but different levels of segregation for the two racial groups, whites and Blacks. As the table illustrates, although the poverty rate is the same in all four cases, various groups experience different levels of neighbourhood poverty. This difference results from different levels of segregation among the two groups included.

TABLE 5-3

THE HYPOTHETICAL DATA ON THE INTERACTION OF POVERTY AND SEGREGATION

| City 1: No Ethnic Segregation | | | | City 2: Low Ethnic Segregation | | | |
|---|---|---|---|---|---|---|---|
| B=2,000 W=6,000 | B=2,000 W=6,000 | B=2,000 W=6,000 | B=2,000 W=6,000 | B=0 W=8,000 | B=0 W=8,000 | B=0 W=8,000 | B=0 W=8,000 |
| B=2,000 W=6,000 | B=2,000 W=6,000 | B=2,000 W=6,000 | B=2,000 W=6,000 | B=2,666 W=5,334 | B=2,666 W=5,334 | B=2,666 W=5,334 | B=2,666 W=5,334 |
| B=2,000 W=6,000 | B=2,000 W=6,000 | B=2,000 W=6,000 | B=2,000 W=6,000 | B=2,666 W=5,334 | B=2,666 W=5,334 | B=2,666 W=5,334 | B=2,666 W=5,334 |
| B=2,000 W=6,000 | B=2,000 W=6,000 | B=2,000 W=6,000 | B=2,000 W=6,000 | B=2,666 W=5,334 | B=2,666 W=5,334 | B=2,666 W=5,334 | B=2,666 W=5,334 |

| | | | |
|---|---|---|---|
| Poverty Rate of Blacks | 20.0% | Poverty Rate of Blacks | 20.0% |
| Poverty Rate of Whites | 10.0% | Poverty Rate of Whites | 10.0% |
| Black-White Segregation Score | 0.0% | Black-White Segregation Score | 33.3% |
| Neighbourhood Poverty Rate | | Neighbourhood Poverty Rate: | |
| Average Black Family | 12.5% | Average Black Family | 13.3% |
| Average White Family | 12.5% | Average White Family | 12.2% |

| City 3: High Ethnic Segregation | | | | City 4: Complete Ethnic Segregation | | | |
|---|---|---|---|---|---|---|---|
| B=0 W=8,000 | B=0 W=8,000 | B=0 W=8,000 | B=00 W=8,000 | B=0 W=8,000 | B=0 W=8,000 | B=0 W=8,000 | B=0 W=8,000 |
| B=0 W=8,000 | B=0 W=8,000 | B=0 W=8,000 | B=00 W=8,000 | B=0 W=8,000 | B=0 W=8,000 | B=0 W=8,000 | B=0 W=8,000 |
| B=4,000 W=4,0000 | B=4,00 W=4,000 | B=4,000 W=4,000 | B=4,000 W=4,000 | B=0 W=8,000 | B=0 W=8,000 | B=0 W=8,000 | B=0 W=8,000 |
| B=4,000 W=4,000 | B=4,000 W=4,000 | B=4,000 W=4,000 | B=4,000 W=4,000 | B=8,000 W= 0 | B=8,000 W= 0 | B=8,000 W= 0 | B=8,000 W= 0 |

| | | | |
|---|---|---|---|
| Poverty Rate of Blacks | 20.0% | Poverty Rate of Blacks | 20.0% |
| Poverty Rate of Whites | 10.0% | Poverty Rate of Whites | 10.0% |
| Black-White Segregation Score | 66.7% | Black-White Segregation Score | 100% |
| Neighbourhood Poverty Rate: | | Neighbourhood Poverty Rate: | |
| Average Black Family | 15.0% | Average Black Family | 20.0% |
| Average White Family | 11.7% | Average White Family | 10.0% |

Source: Modified from original in Massey and Denton (1993).

## *The Expansion of the Conceptual Model*

It was earlier discussed that a high level of neighbourhood poverty leads to social isolation and, consequently, to the cultural isolation of such a neighbourhood's residents. It was pointed out that, in high poverty areas, the "culture of poverty" finds a fertile ground to germinate. Both Wilson (1987) and Massey and Denton (1993) emphasize this point. In both cases, the lifestyle and subculture resulting from neighbourhood poverty is at the heart of discussion. The difference between the two arguments is that the former emphasize social isolation while the latter underscores residential segregation as the underlying factor.

The irony is that despite the centrality of the notion of the *culture of poverty* for both modes of explanation, neither Wilson nor Massey and Denton fully articulate its true meaning or include it as an integral part of their quantitative models. In this study, we make an effort to address this shortcoming, that is, to incorporate the notion of the culture of poverty into the conceptual model. We briefly discussed the culture of poverty in Chapter Two. Here, we will have a closer look at what the culture of poverty is and how we can operationalize it.

### *What Is Culture of Poverty?*

The *culture of poverty* thesis sparked wide disagreement in the past. According to Greenstone (1991), conservative social scientists welcomed it because, in their opinion, it assigned the poverty of certain individuals and groups to its "authentic" origin: a careless lifestyle, without any futuristic view, long-term planning, hard work, risk-taking, and well-calculated decision making. For them, poverty is a result of "a culture that irrationally sanctions dysfunctional conduct" (p.399). Marxists, on the other hand, strongly opposed the notion of the culture of poverty; they felt it blamed the victims, rather than the capitalist system, for their poverty. Later on, this split found a political echo: policy makers favoured the first interpretation, social critics, the second.

However, both interpretations of the culture of poverty thesis, in my opinion, have resulted from a misconception. The two sides of the debate have based their highly ideological positions on oversimplified notions of the culture of poverty, far from the way Oscar Lewis first formulated it. Let us examine the original way in which Lewis presented the idea.

Based on his observations of Latin American immigrants to the United States, Lewis (1971 [1966]) argues that a certain type of subculture–culture of poverty, in his words–has developed among them. He clearly mentioned that such a subculture is not seen among all the poor; some exceptions he listed were the white American poor and the Cuban poor. The implications of this argument are two-fold. First, the culture of poverty appears among those who are *already* poor; that is, it is a consequence rather than a cause of poverty. Second, and even so, it is not a necessary consequence for all poor; some develop the culture of poverty and some do not. This view is in clear contrast to the simplified version of the culture of poverty mentioned earlier, which assumes a solid link between the culture of poverty and poverty, and assumes that the former causes the latter.

A second source of misconception about the culture of poverty idea is the lack of adequate attention paid to the culture of poverty as a *culture*. Culture, regardless of its variations, is essentially a coping strategy, developed among a certain group of people in their interactions with their natural and social environments; it contains a pre-packaged set of instructions that help people to rationalize their lives and assign meaning to it, and to find solutions to the problems they encounter on a regular basis (Himelfarb and Richardson, 1991). In other words, culture provides people with a justifiable vision of how life should be. Another crucial feature of culture is that is transmitted from one generation to another. Without such an inter-generational dimension, culture is reduced simply to a mere individual lifestyle. It is this commonality of culture, along space and time dimensions, which makes it a social phenomenon. This distinction if of enormous importance for an authentic understanding of the notion of culture of poverty. Many misperceptions of Oscar Lewis's culture of poverty arose from mistaking it for a "lifestyle." This indicates that we cannot talk of the presence of the culture of poverty in a population unless we see some inter-generational continuity of the particular lifestyle typical of the culture of poverty.

The above argument that poverty does not necessarily bring about the culture of poverty should not, however, be taken as suggesting that there is no relationship between the two; far from it. Lewis (1966) argues that after it comes into existence within a population, the culture of poverty finds an inertia and a life of its own. From that point on, it may act against any effort to ameliorate poverty. This is to suggest that, in the presence of the culture of poverty, a mere economic effort is inadequate for ameliorating poverty; a separate cultural measure is also needed to deal with the cultural component associated with it.

The example of a newly arrived group of immigrants in a host society may help to illustrate this cultural dynamic. Before arrival, such a group is under the influence of a culture different from that of the host society; this culture has suited their living conditions at home. Their contact with the host society means an abrupt change in these living conditions, while their cultural orientation is still intact. The cultural orientation and the new living conditions come into a mismatch. In most cases, the original culture adjusts itself to the new social environment, that is, assimilation takes place. In others, culture does not give way easily; people remain loyal to their original culture and try to insulate themselves and create similar living conditions in the host society in order to avoid the mismatch. One perfect example of this scenario is the life of the Hutterites in Canada. In their case, it is culture that dictates and, indeed, perpetuates the initial living conditions it corresponds with.

How can we capture the notion of the culture of poverty in a quantitative study like the present one? What indicators can be used as proxies for the culture of poverty? How can the inter-generational dimension of the culture of poverty be captured? These are the major practical questions surrounding the inclusion of the culture of poverty as a part of the conceptual model. Few would disagree that the best way to examine the culture of poverty is through special surveys on cultural orientations. Such surveys need to be conducted longitudinally in order to capture its inter-generational dimension. To the best of our knowledge, unfortunately, such data do not exist. Perhaps the most practical and economical way to use the available data in a preliminary study of the issue, such as the present one, is to come up with some measures, however incomplete, of the culture of poverty. Before making an effort along this line, let us first examine more closely what we need to measure.

Lewis (1971 [1966]) implies that those affected by the culture of poverty do not possess a strong desire for long-term planning. Neither are they eager to utilize available opportunities to improve their lives. These are the two essential features, and indicators, of the culture of poverty. We can, therefore, conceptualize the culture of poverty as the extent to which one utilizes the resources readily available in one's surrounding environment for betterment of one's living conditions. The question then becomes, what resources? In Canada, education can be considered to be one such resource; employment, another. The former illustrates a desire for long-term planning; the latter signifies a willingness to change current living conditions. Education and employment status, therefore, can be used as the pillars of the culture of poverty.

But what about the inter-generational dimension of the culture of poverty? Education and employment attainment, all by themselves, do not necessarily indicate the existence or absence of a cultural orientation. They can simply be the results of an individual's or even a group's decision. They can, however, turn into a culture or subculture, if they persist across generations. The only way to capture this inter-generational nature is to compare two consequent generations in terms of their education and employment status. A group in which a low level of education persists for two generations is most likely under the influence of a culture that does not promote education as a valuable means. In contrast, another group for which there has been a significant improvement in terms of education and employment from one generation to another is far from having a culture of poverty of any kind.

When comparing two generations in terms of the degree of their appreciation of educational and employment opportunities, one can think of four distinct scenarios (see Table 5-4). Cell 1 illustrates a group in which a high appreciation of such opportunities has been present for two generations. An example of such a combination might be the typical American, and to a lesser extent, Canadian, middle-class family.[8] Cell 2 represents a group in which the younger generation appreciates such opportunities, while their parents' generation did not. This signifies a social mobility from one generation to the next. Perhaps such a combination could be found among the first European immigrants who came to the New World during the eighteenth and nineteenth centuries. The whole immigration adventure of these people may be summarized as an incredible effort to utilize the opportunities available even in remote areas such as the New World.[9] Cell 3 shows a group for which the desirability of education and employment has declined over a generation. Although it may appear difficult to construct any particular example for this hypothetical scenario, the findings of this study will show that, surprisingly enough, a few examples of it do exist in Canada. Cell 4 is the one in which the lack of appreciation for educational and occupational initiatives has persisted over the generations. The last two scenarios are the ones most likely associated with the culture of poverty.

TABLE 5-4

THE PRESENCE/ABSENCE OF APPRECIATION FOR EDUCATIONAL/OCCUPATIONAL OPPORTUNITIES OVER TWO GENERATIONS

|  |  | Generation of Parents | |
|  |  | Present | Absent |
| --- | --- | --- | --- |
| **Generation** | Present | (1) Dominance of the Idea of Progress | (2) Social Mobility |
| **of Children** | Absent | (3) The "Acute" Culture of Poverty | (4) The "Moderate" Culture of Poverty |

8. Tepperman (1994), for instance, discusses the cultural differences between Americans and Canadians, one of which is a stronger success-oriented view and a more serious commitment to occupational achievements among Americans, as opposed to a stronger commitment to family values among Canadians.
9. For a historiographical account of the experiences and personalities of those first immigrants, see Johnson (1997).

## *Operationalization of the Culture of Poverty*

To capture the inter-generational aspect of the culture of poverty, we have compared the educational as well as occupational achievements of two generations and then made an overall index of the degree of change. Appendix 5, a summary of which is presented in Table 5-5, contains detailed information on the average years of schooling for the members of two age groups, 1-35 and 35+ years, as representatives of two subsequent generations.[10] The ratio of the first to the second value indicates how much educational progress or regress each ethnic group has experienced over a generation.

TABLE **5-5**

THE INDEX OF INTER-GENERATIONAL EDUCATIONAL MOBILITY, ETHNIC GROUPS BY CITY, **1991**

| City | Portu-guese | Italian | Greek | Other East and South East Asian | Balkan origins | Chinese | Ukrainian | French origins | Polish |
|---|---|---|---|---|---|---|---|---|---|
| Halifax | | | | | | | | 1.203 | |
| Quebec | 1.147 | 1.253 | 1.283 | 1.388 | 1.059 | **0.963** | **0.852** | 1.204 | **0.972** |
| Montreal | 1.540 | 1.756 | 1.621 | 1.009 | 1.161 | 1.245 | 1.421 | 1.230 | 1.152 |
| Sherbrooke and Trois-Rivières | 1.853 | **0.979** | | 6.000 | | 2.000 | | 1.251 | 1.286 |
| Ottawa-Hull | 1.690 | 1.529 | 1.289 | 1.068 | 1.236 | 1.178 | 1.097 | 1.178 | 1.084 |
| Oshawa | 1.327 | 1.576 | 1.773 | **0.875** | 1.266 | 1.166 | 1.341 | 1.275 | 1.258 |
| Toronto | 1.646 | 1.694 | 1.525 | 1.030 | 1.262 | 1.177 | 1.271 | 1.165 | 1.135 |
| Hamilton | 1.789 | 1.656 | 1.561 | 1.027 | 1.426 | 1.315 | 1.340 | 1.187 | 1.243 |
| St.Catherines-Niagara | 1.000 | 1.564 | 1.590 | **0.968** | 1.352 | 1.017 | 1.316 | 1.370 | 1.258 |
| Kitchener | 1.670 | 1.550 | 1.521 | 1.512 | 1.510 | 1.074 | 1.313 | 1.326 | 1.143 |
| London | 1.694 | 1.491 | 1.585 | 1.018 | 1.389 | 1.209 | 1.293 | 1.145 | 1.126 |
| Windsor | 1.231 | 1.615 | 1.529 | 1.116 | 1.340 | 1.326 | 1.291 | 1.262 | 1.250 |
| Sudbury and Thunder Bay | 1.557 | 1.577 | 1.579 | **0.889** | 1.265 | 1.686 | 1.318 | 1.346 | 1.508 |
| Winnipeg | 1.583 | 1.556 | 1.542 | **0.960** | 1.372 | 1.447 | 1.290 | 1.213 | 1.290 |
| Regina | 1.728 | 1.082 | 1.900 | **0.941** | 1.463 | 1.282 | 1.172 | 1.232 | 1.286 |
| Calgary | 1.000 | 1.415 | 1.117 | 1.011 | 1.143 | 1.204 | 1.140 | 1.088 | 1.202 |
| Edmonton | 1.754 | 1.484 | 1.231 | 1.006 | 1.177 | 1.239 | 1.229 | 1.161 | 1.217 |
| Vancouver | 1.543 | 1.468 | 1.409 | 1.053 | 1.239 | 1.170 | 1.168 | 1.129 | 1.142 |
| Victoria | 1.367 | 1.481 | 1.190 | 1.033 | 1.161 | 1.274 | 1.105 | 1.055 | 1.200 |
| **Average** | **1.507** | **1.485** | **1.485** | **1.328** | **1.284** | **1.276** | **1.233** | **1.212** | **1.209** |

10. The word "generation" is used here rather loosely, not to be confused with the 20-25-year period which is normally referred to as one generation.

TABLE 5-5

THE INDEX OF INTER-GENERATIONAL EDUCATIONAL MOBILITY, ETHNIC GROUPS BY CITY, 1991 (continued)

| City | West Asian | German | Hungarian (Magyar) | Other Western European Origin | Arab | Spanish | Dutch (Netherlands) | Aboriginal | Other European origins |
|---|---|---|---|---|---|---|---|---|---|
| Halifax | | 1.239 | | | | | | 0.677 | |
| Quebec | 0.606 | 1.104 | 0.981 | 1.042 | 1.009 | 1.090 | 1.125 | 1.101 | 0.939 |
| Montreal | 1.172 | 1.181 | 1.113 | 1.138 | 1.094 | 1.113 | 1.093 | 1.361 | 1.150 |
| Sherbrooke and Trois-Rivières | 0.737 | 1.378 | 1.688 | 0.969 | 1.267 | 1.667 | 0.943 | 1.310 | 0.654 |
| Ottawa-Hull | 1.094 | 1.161 | 1.013 | 1.108 | 1.288 | 1.255 | 1.035 | 1.309 | 1.017 |
| Oshawa | 1.026 | 1.198 | 1.149 | 1.034 | 1.268 | 1.000 | 1.213 | 0.646 | 1.166 |
| Toronto | 1.042 | 1.132 | 1.098 | 1.075 | 1.108 | 1.089 | 1.139 | 1.114 | 1.111 |
| Hamilton | 1.137 | 1.198 | 1.288 | 1.075 | 1.162 | 1.225 | 1.169 | 1.004 | 1.159 |
| St.Catharines-Niagara | 1.410 | 1.253 | 1.169 | 1.088 | 1.134 | | 1.337 | 1.315 | 1.288 |
| Kitchener | 1.385 | 1.227 | 1.041 | 1.437 | 1.009 | 1.238 | 1.056 | 1.167 | 1.099 |
| London | 1.131 | 1.163 | 1.182 | 1.257 | 1.290 | 0.846 | 1.194 | 1.164 | 1.044 |
| Windsor | 0.947 | 1.326 | 1.215 | 1.293 | 1.185 | 1.145 | 1.166 | 1.333 | 1.233 |
| Sudbury and Thunder Bay | 3.750 | 1.134 | 1.118 | 1.363 | | 1.556 | 1.141 | 1.246 | 1.320 |
| Winnipeg | 1.023 | 1.213 | 1.204 | 1.396 | 1.179 | 0.909 | 1.181 | 1.228 | 1.162 |
| Regina | 1.323 | 1.243 | 1.239 | 1.253 | | 0.894 | 1.149 | 1.011 | 1.160 |
| Calgary | 0.874 | 1.137 | 1.124 | 1.128 | 1.015 | 1.043 | 1.067 | 0.980 | 1.129 |
| Edmonton | 0.903 | 1.183 | 1.226 | 1.313 | 1.188 | 0.918 | 1.132 | 1.083 | 1.161 |
| Vancouver | 0.995 | 1.126 | 1.139 | 1.042 | 1.136 | 0.947 | 1.080 | 1.069 | 1.132 |
| Victoria | 0.963 | 1.063 | 1.143 | 1.108 | 1.250 | 1.246 | 1.059 | 0.975 | 1.059 |
| **Average** | **1.195** | **1.193** | **1.174** | **1.173** | **1.161** | **1.128** | **1.127** | **1.110** | **1.110** |

The ratios shown in Table 5-5 reveal some interesting patterns. First, the three groups experiencing the highest degree of inter-generational mobility in terms of education are the Portuguese, Italian and Greek, all of Southern European or Iberian Peninsula origins. Except for the Italians in Sherbrooke and Trois-Rivières, none of these groups have experienced any downward mobility as far as education is concerned. Second, the two groups that have had the worst experience, that is, have regressed over a generation, are the Filipino and Latin/Central/South American, both of Third-World origin. The index values of less than 1 for these groups indicate that the average level of education for the younger generation is less than that of their parents. This shows a very unique situation, as these groups have experienced a negative growth in their educational achievements even in big cities such as Montreal, Toronto, and Vancouver, in which all the other ethnic groups have managed to progress. Third, the groups with a progressive record in all cities include the people of Portuguese, Greek, Balkan, French, German, and Arab origin. Fourth, despite their heavy emphasis on education, the Jewish group has

TABLE 5-5

THE INDEX OF INTER-GENERATIONAL EDUCATIONAL MOBILITY, ETHNIC GROUPS BY CITY, 1991 (concluded)

| City | Canadian | British | Vietnamese | Jewish | Black Caribbean | South Asian | Filipino | Latin, Central and South American Origins | Average |
|------|----------|---------|------------|--------|-----------------|-------------|----------|-------------------------------------------|---------|
| Halifax | 1.372 | 1.107 | | | 1.213 | | | | **1.135** |
| Quebec | **0.976** | 1.217 | **0.973** | | **0.990** | **0.778** | | 0.822 | **1.036** |
| Montreal | 1.312 | 1.168 | 1.023 | 1.163 | 1.050 | **0.993** | 1.033 | 1.043 | **1.205** |
| Sherbrooke and Trois-Rivières | 1.178 | 1.162 | 1.118 | 1.636 | **0.623** | 1.000 | | 0.714 | **1.428** |
| Ottawa-Hull | 1.065 | 1.050 | 1.083 | **0.948** | 1.056 | 1.045 | **0.957** | 1.015 | **1.148** |
| Oshawa | 1.054 | 1.103 | | | 1.111 | 1.114 | 1.125 | **0.779** | **1.160** |
| Toronto | 1.063 | 1.082 | 1.055 | 1.058 | 1.063 | 1.048 | **0.986** | 1.027 | **1.161** |
| Hamilton | 1.085 | 1.123 | **0.919** | 1.192 | 1.053 | 1.053 | 1.030 | **0.921** | **1.205** |
| St.Catharines-Niagara | 1.126 | 1.117 | 1.000 | 1.080 | 1.174 | 1.017 | **0.888** | **0.450** | **1.171** |
| Kitchener | 1.122 | 1.102 | 1.500 | **0.905** | **0.999** | 1.091 | 0.829 | 0.841 | **1.218** |
| London | 1.184 | 1.110 | 1.033 | 1.182 | 1.099 | 1.092 | 1.111 | 1.044 | **1.195** |
| Windsor | 1.203 | 1.141 | **0.860** | 1.002 | 1.099 | 1.207 | **0.881** | 0.855 | **1.194** |
| Sudbury and Thunder Bay | 1.073 | 1.126 | **0.684** | **0.741** | 1.524 | **0.607** | **0.750** | 1.250 | **1.324** |
| Winnipeg | 1.051 | 1.077 | **0.995** | 1.067 | **0.978** | 1.115 | 1.095 | **0.992** | **1.197** |
| Regina | 1.090 | 1.076 | 1.567 | **0.974** | **0.954** | 1.003 | **0.994** | 1.052 | **1.203** |
| Calgary | 1.013 | 1.029 | **0.910** | 1.022 | **0.947** | 1.029 | **0.975** | 0.903 | **1.063** |
| Edmonton | 1.038 | 1.035 | 1.042 | **0.923** | **0.965** | 1.109 | 1.029 | 0.850 | **1.138** |
| Vancouver | 1.030 | 1.037 | 1.078 | **0.975** | 1.042 | 1.296 | **0.976** | 0.906 | **1.128** |
| Victoria | **0.973** | **0.997** | 1.125 | 1.009 | **0.965** | 1.216 | 1.101 | **0.766** | **1.111** |
| **Average** | **1.106** | **1.098** | **1.057** | **1.055** | **1.048** | **1.045** | **0.985** | **0.902** | |

experienced a negative growth in cities such as Ottawa-Hull, Kitchener, Sudbury/Thunder Bay, Regina, Edmonton, and Vancouver. This indicates that the stereotypical image of the Jews as a group with high education and low poverty is not necessarily an accurate picture of all the Jewish communities in different Canadian cities.

Table 5-6 looks at the inter-generational mobility in terms of employment. The census questionnaire has asked respondents about their major source of income, with five options to choose from: "wages and salaries," "self-employment," "government transfers," "investment," and "no income." The first two involve some orientation or activities marked by long-term planning, appreciation of training and education, and a desire to be independent and productive economically. The latter three, however, do not seem to have any strong relationship with a certain type of personality and work ethic. We, therefore, used the extent of the presence and/or absence of the first two categories as rough indicators of the kind of personality typical of those influenced by the culture of poverty. Table

5-6 illustrates the changes, over a generation, in the proportion of each ethnic group's population whose major source of income has been "wages and salaries" and "self-employment." Likewise, this table is a partial representation of a more detailed one in Appendix 6. The values in Table 5-6 can theoretically vary from +100 to -100, indicating the whole population having or lacking wages, salaries, and/or self-employment as their major source of income.

**TABLE 5-6**

**THE INDEX OF INTER-GENERATIONAL EMPLOYMENT MOBILITY, BY ETHNICITY AND CITY, 1991**

| City | British | French | German | Black Caribbean | Aboriginal | Canadian | Dutch (Netherlands) | Other Western European | Hungarian (Magyar) |
|---|---|---|---|---|---|---|---|---|---|
| Halifax | 14.9 | 11.0 | 1.4 | -1.3 | -50.0 | 0.3 | 0.0 | 0.0 | 0.0 |
| Quebec | 17.2 | 21.1 | 35.1 | 5.5 | 2.3 | 35.7 | 100.0 | 15.0 | -50.0 |
| Montreal | 23.3 | 20.8 | 22.3 | -1.6 | 8.0 | 31.1 | 7.8 | 10.8 | 23.8 |
| Sherbrooke and Trois-Rivières | 30.2 | 21.8 | 40.2 | -37.5 | 20.0 | -14.1 | 0.0 | 41.7 | -50.0 |
| Ottawa-Hull | 17.5 | 18.7 | 9.8 | -4.1 | -10.4 | 12.1 | 11.3 | 20.1 | 12.5 |
| Oshawa | 23.5 | -0.7 | -3.2 | 4.0 | -3.8 | 10.5 | 17.9 | -7.1 | 21.6 |
| Toronto | 20.6 | -0.3 | 10.8 | -2.2 | -9.7 | 13.7 | 10.0 | 12.2 | 14.4 |
| Hamilton | 21.9 | 19.8 | 12.1 | 6.5 | 2.9 | 14.3 | 23.6 | -12.4 | 37.5 |
| St. Catharines-Niagara | 25.9 | 21.9 | 19.7 | -7.7 | 8.6 | 24.8 | 31.1 | 45.0 | 27.2 |
| Kitchener | 22.1 | 1.9 | 30.7 | -22.6 | -13.2 | 11.2 | -8.0 | 17.0 | -0.8 |
| London | 23.5 | 0.8 | 14.2 | -14.1 | 20.9 | 12.8 | 8.7 | 21.5 | 7.7 |
| Windsor | 27.6 | 21.3 | 19.6 | -2.6 | -9.1 | 4.9 | 36.7 | 23.8 | 43.1 |
| Sudbury and Thunder Bay | 22.8 | 15.6 | 13.8 | 7.5 | -6.0 | 4.0 | 18.4 | 25.0 | -16.5 |
| Winnipeg | 28.3 | 18.4 | 16.4 | -9.0 | -6.3 | 28.6 | 35.2 | 21.4 | 14.6 |
| Regina and Saskatoon | 28.1 | 23.2 | 21.6 | -20.0 | -8.8 | 17.9 | 17.6 | 42.4 | 23.9 |
| Calgary | 16.8 | -2.4 | 7.1 | -7.4 | -16.6 | 10.9 | 14.0 | 12.0 | 6.5 |
| Edmonton | 18.6 | 11.2 | 14.3 | -6.7 | -5.9 | 15.0 | 14.1 | 31.2 | 25.0 |
| Vancouver | 25.3 | 8.2 | 12.9 | -4.5 | -2.9 | 22.5 | 15.3 | 15.8 | 13.2 |
| Victoria | 31.0 | 21.0 | 13.4 | -50.0 | 9.2 | 31.3 | 14.9 | 13.8 | -3.7 |
| **Average** | **23.1** | **13.3** | **16.4** | **-8.8** | **-3.7** | **15.1** | **19.4** | **18.4** | **7.9** |

TABLE 5-6

THE INDEX OF INTER-GENERATIONAL EMPLOYMENT MOBILITY, BY ETHNICITY AND CITY, 1991 (continued)

| City | Polish | Ukrainian | Balkan origins | Greek | Italian | Portuguese | Spanish | Jewish | Other European | Arab origins |
|---|---|---|---|---|---|---|---|---|---|---|
| Halifax | 0.0 | 0.0 | 0.0 | 0.0 | 0.0 | 0.0 | 0.0 | 0.0 | 0.0 | 0.0 |
| Quebec | -8.3 | -33.3 | -100.0 | 37.1 | 11.6 | 24.7 | -3.1 | -50.0 | 7.7 | -37.4 |
| Montreal | 22.6 | 43.8 | -11.0 | 16.5 | 21.0 | 9.9 | -5.5 | 28.5 | 16.2 | -3.7 |
| Sherbrooke and Trois-Rivières | 2.8 | 0.0 | 0.0 | 0.0 | -5.9 | -21.4 | 75.0 | -50.0 | 22.2 | 24.4 |
| Ottawa-Hull | 14.6 | 19.7 | 6.0 | 4.1 | 21.1 | 3.3 | -30.5 | 18.2 | 6.5 | 3.6 |
| Oshawa | 15.8 | 42.5 | 30.7 | 27.4 | 18.9 | -2.9 | -14.3 | -100.0 | 16.2 | 0.0 |
| Toronto | 15.3 | 25.4 | 16.7 | 14.3 | 16.8 | 12.5 | -2.1 | 24.2 | 20.9 | 2.9 |
| Hamilton | 25.8 | 26.7 | 20.2 | 29.8 | 26.7 | 18.0 | 3.0 | 29.5 | 24.1 | 4.9 |
| St. Catharines-Niagara | 31.3 | 47.3 | 17.6 | 25.0 | 22.5 | -50.0 | 53.8 | -12.7 | 28.2 | 25.0 |
| Kitchener | 15.6 | 29.8 | 20.3 | 27.5 | 20.0 | 10.9 | 1.0 | -41.7 | 13.3 | -12.1 |
| London | 20.5 | 5.5 | -4.9 | 3.3 | 12.2 | 0.0 | -33.8 | 26.5 | 8.9 | -1.1 |
| Windsor | 5.9 | 50.6 | 8.5 | 22.9 | 28.3 | 10.7 | -6.9 | 11.7 | 36.0 | 1.3 |
| Sudbury and Thunder Bay | 33.1 | 31.0 | 16.7 | 15.5 | 30.8 | -0.8 | 57.1 | -25.0 | 33.9 | 0.0 |
| Winnipeg | 31.2 | 30.1 | -0.2 | 26.1 | 20.2 | 8.9 | -2.1 | 38.9 | 28.8 | 25.6 |
| Regina and Saskatoon | 16.7 | 21.6 | 40.0 | 4.2 | 1.8 | 38.9 | 65.1 | 9.6 | 26.9 | 37.5 |
| Calgary | 20.4 | 1.1 | 15.7 | 5.0 | 13.9 | -17.1 | 1.4 | 34.8 | 16.5 | -3.8 |
| Edmonton | 17.9 | 21.6 | 8.3 | -11.7 | 18.9 | -6.0 | 11.2 | 17.6 | 18.5 | 0.3 |
| Vancouver | 23.6 | 18.0 | 20.6 | 14.1 | 18.3 | 5.0 | -10.1 | 21.7 | 26.7 | -18.1 |
| Victoria | 23.5 | 34.1 | 24.5 | 25.0 | 7.3 | 3.9 | 8.6 | 23.8 | 15.7 | -40.0 |
| **Average** | **17.3** | **21.9** | **6.8** | **15.1** | **16.0** | **2.6** | **8.8** | **0.3** | **19.3** | **0.5** |

The average changes in major source of income shows that the Aboriginals, Vietnamese, and Blacks and/or Caribbeans are the groups with negative values, that is, the proportion of their population who make their living through a productive source of income has declined. On the other hand, the British, Ukrainian, Dutch, Polish, German, Italian, Greek, and French show double-digit rates of improvement. Groups such as the Spanish, Filipino, Hungarian, Chinese, and Portuguese, though in the plus side, are doing not as well as the European origin groups. The Arabs, Latin Americans, and Jews show only trivial improvement. Unlike the case of education, the Jews are not among those with the highest proportion of their population relying on productive sources of income. This may have to do with the Jews' higher reliance on investment income (with 7% of their population having "investment" as their major source of income, the highest level in Canada).

TABLE **5-6** (concluded)

THE INDEX OF INTER-GENERATIONAL EMPLOYMENT MOBILITY, BY ETHNICITY AND CITY, **1991**

| City | West Asian origins | South Asian origins | Chinese | Filipino | Viet- namese | Other East and South East Asian origins | Latin, Central and South American Origins | Other single origins | Average |
|---|---|---|---|---|---|---|---|---|---|
| Halifax | 0.0 | 0.0 | 0.0 | 0.0 | 0.0 | 0.0 | 0.0 | 0.0 | -0.9 |
| Quebec | -50.0 | 0.0 | -45.5 | 100.0 | -4.8 | 26.5 | -9.6 | 33.4 | 3.0 |
| Montreal | 5.8 | -1.6 | 7.4 | 8.1 | 9.5 | 7.7 | -3.0 | -0.3 | 11.8 |
| Sherbrooke and Trois-Rivières | 0.0 | 0.0 | 25.0 | 0.0 | 26.7 | 42.9 | -16.7 | 0.0 | 6.6 |
| Ottawa-Hull | -23.0 | -4.8 | 0.0 | -7.1 | -16.2 | -16.1 | 0.3 | -19.5 | 2.5 |
| Oshawa | 17.1 | 25.0 | 3.8 | 9.7 | 0.0 | 9.0 | 27.8 | 27.5 | 8.0 |
| Toronto | -3.8 | 4.6 | 7.6 | 1.4 | -6.3 | 8.8 | -2.1 | -12.5 | 7.9 |
| Hamilton | -6.9 | 5.7 | 3.7 | 5.3 | -8.5 | 11.4 | -13.9 | -60.0 | 10.1 |
| St. Catharines- Niagara | 13.0 | 6.6 | 0.0 | 0.9 | 0.0 | 7.1 | 50.0 | -15.7 | 16.5 |
| Kitchener | 31.8 | 3.9 | -14.1 | -1.8 | 19.9 | -4.7 | -31.9 | 46.7 | 6.4 |
| London | -24.4 | -5.4 | -14.3 | -10.0 | -32.9 | 32.8 | -9.9 | -10.0 | 2.2 |
| Windsor | -6.0 | 16.1 | -5.7 | 8.8 | -13.0 | -1.7 | 46.7 | 16.7 | 14.7 |
| Sudbury and Thunder Bay | 60.0 | 4.3 | 16.9 | 0.0 | -37.5 | 20.0 | 0.0 | 0.0 | 12.6 |
| Winnipeg | -20.3 | 11.4 | 3.0 | 5.5 | -14.2 | 21.9 | -10.3 | -1.1 | 13.0 |
| Regina and Saskatoon | 66.7 | -6.9 | 13.2 | 2.9 | 27.7 | -22.2 | -28.0 | 10.6 | 17.5 |
| Calgary | -13.0 | 5.4 | 11.8 | 6.6 | 0.0 | -5.0 | 4.7 | 9.9 | 5.5 |
| Edmonton | -21.4 | 11.4 | 8.8 | 8.7 | -5.1 | -3.0 | -12.5 | 11.2 | 7.8 |
| Vancouver | 9.0 | 14.5 | 10.4 | 0.5 | 9.8 | 2.1 | -13.8 | 7.6 | 9.8 |
| Victoria | 0.0 | 14.8 | 24.2 | 13.7 | -37.5 | -8.5 | 23.3 | -6.7 | 8.5 |
| **Average** | **1.8** | **5.5** | **3.0** | **8.1** | **-4.3** | **6.8** | **0.1** | **2.0** | |

The discussed approach to operationalize the culture of poverty enables us to use cross-sectional Census data to measure a phenomenon that is longitudinal in nature. One advantage of this approach is the high compatibility of data sets used in this study, as census data is also the data source for other parts of the study. All this, however, should not blind us to the fact that our approach is, at best, only an alternative in the absence of longitudinal survey data on cultural orientations. Unless original and adequate data is produced to explore the culture of poverty, one should approach the results cautiously.

## *The Causal Model and the Research Hypotheses*

The particular way to conceptualize and operationalize the culture of poverty offered above also contributes to our understanding of inter-generational mobility in Canada. The few studies concerned with this issue have almost exclusively concentrated on income. Corak and Heisz (1996), for instance, have studied the likelihood that children can improve the status they inherit from their parents in financial terms. Mata (1997) has explored the extent to which the members of different racial groups in Canada can equally translate their education and occupation statuses into income. Since these studies have not viewed inter-generational mobility against the background of the culture of poverty, they reveal more about current structural hurdles to utilizing available opportunities than the effect of cultural orientation. The inclusion of the culture of poverty into the conceptual framework of this study, therefore, adds a new layer to the models suggested by Wilson (1987) and Massey and Denton (1993). While their analyses focus on ethnic groups' neighbourhood poverty and its causes, our model also includes one of its possible consequences, i.e., the spread-out of the culture of poverty. These three layers are introduced in the causal model illustrated in Figure 5-1.

FIGURE **5-1**

THE CAUSAL MODEL OF CAUSES AND EFFECTS OF **SCOP**

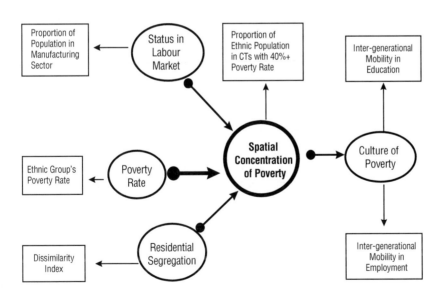

Three major predictors of neighbourhood poverty, each representing a certain mode of explanation, are included in the model: the ethnic group's poverty rate, its proportion of population working in the manufacturing sector, and its segregation level. The first predictor represents the commonsensical perception that a group's degree of neighbourhood poverty is a function of its general poverty; the second represents Wilson's thesis that neighbourhood poverty results from structural changes in the economy; the third illustrates Massey and Denton's emphasis on the group's spatial segregation. The model also explores the relationship between the SCOP and the inter-generational mobility of ethnic groups. This conceptual framework can be summarized in the form of the following specific hypotheses, later tested by a series of multiple regression models:

- The general poverty of an ethnic group has an effect on the group's neighbourhood poverty. The higher the general poverty of the group, the higher its neighbourhood poverty level.

- The level of spatial segregation of an ethnic group from the majority (represented by the value of Dissimilarity Index for the group and Charter Groups) also contributes to the group's neighbourhood poverty. The higher the extent of spatial segregation, the higher the level of neighbourhood poverty.

- Given the gradual decline of the manufacturing sector in advanced industrial societies such as Canada, the higher the proportion of a group's population in this sector, the higher its level of neighbourhood poverty.

- The ethnic groups with a higher level of neighbourhood poverty are more likely to develop a culture of poverty, represented by a lower level of educational and occupational inter-generational mobility.

## Ethnic Groups' Neighbourhood Poverty: A Multiple Regression Model

The study of spatial trends faces a serious limitation, due to the nature of publicly available data. Census data are organized in two formats: (1) data on Individuals/Families/Households, with no reference to their geographical location (e.g., only the large geographical units such as cities are mentioned); and (2) aggregate data on small geographical units such as census tracts, with no reference to individual/family/household characteristics. The reason for such a practice is the census authorities' commitment to the principle of confidentiality. This practice, however, poses a serious hurdle to the multivariate study of *neighbourhood poverty*, which is concerned with both spatial trends and individual characteristics. The study of neighbourhood poverty, therefore, needs to proceed using only the census tract aggregate data. Using such data, two regression model are developed, the results of which are discussed below.

## *Predictors of Neighbourhood Poverty*

Table 5-7 shows the results of running a multiple regression model in which the percentage of an ethnic group's population in census tracts with at least a 30% poverty rate is regressed against the ethnic group's Dissimilarity Index, proportion of their population in the manufacturing sector, and their poverty rate. The suggested model is acceptable, as it explains about 57% of total variance, and all the regression coefficients are statistically significant at a 0.05 level. The examination of Beta coefficients shows that the most important factor explaining the concentration of ethnic groups in high poverty neighbourhoods is their poverty rate, followed by their segregation from the Charter groups (.375, and .119, respectively). This finding clearly supports the *segregation hypothesis* suggested by Massey and Denton (1993). The involvement of a higher proportion of an ethnic group's population in manufacturing jobs also increases their representation in high poverty neighbourhoods, though to a limited degree (.114). This shows that the structural shift from a manufacturing-based to a service-based economy is not as influential a factor in the ethnic group's concentration in neighbourhoods with a 30% and more poverty rate.

TABLE **5-7**

THE MULTIPLE REGRESSION MODEL: PREDICTORS OF **SCOP30+**

| Variables | Beta Coefficient | Significance Level |
|---|---|---|
| Dissimilarity Index (From Charter Groups) | 0.119 | 0.02 |
| Proportion of Population in Manufacturing Sector | 0.114 | 0.02 |
| Poverty Rate | 0.375 | 0.00 |

R=0.756
R Square=0.571

The same set of predictors is used to explain an ethnic group's representation in areas with an even higher level of poverty, that is, 40% and more. Table 5-8 reveals some interesting trends. Although the overall pattern here is more or less the same, the direction of changes in some of the coefficients is different. In this model, the impacts of all variables increase. The point, however, is that the magnitude of increase is not the same for all; the change is far more pronounced for economic variables, such as poverty and structural change, than the ethnicity-related variable of segregation. This is to say that, as we move towards the extremely high poverty neighbourhoods, the effects of economic factors such as poverty and the structural shift become more pronounced than that of ethnicity-related factors such as segregation. This is a confirmation of Wilson's *mismatch hypothesis.*

TABLE 5-8

THE MULTIPLE REGRESSION MODEL: PREDICTORS OF **SCOP40+**

| Variables | Beta Coefficient | Significance Level |
|---|---|---|
| Dissimilarity Index (From Charter Groups) | 0.124 | 0 |
| Proportion of Population in Manufacturing Sector | 0.154 | 0 |
| Poverty Rate | 0.407 | 0 |

R=.689
R Square=.475

The trends observed above point to an interesting synthesis. They not only qualify both the *segregation* and the *mismatch* hypotheses, but they also imply that the two hypotheses are complementary. Rather than being two conceptual alternatives, the two seem to deal with different aspects of the same phenomenon. Unfortunately, this hypothesis cannot be readily tested now, because the number of ethnic groups as well as census tracts sharply drops as we move towards the extremely high poverty zones. However, it provides an interesting point of departure for further research. As the population of ethnic groups and the number of census tracts are constantly increasing, it may be possible to further explore this issue in the near future.[11]

A separate model was developed to examine the effects of an ethnic group's level of neighbourhood poverty on its inter-generational mobility. This model was not very revealing, as the resultant regression coefficients were mostly insignificant, and those that were significant did not reveal any identifiable pattern. One possible reason for this is the simultaneous inclusion of all ethnic groups in the model. As the direction of effects may have been different for various ethnic groups, it is possible that the simultaneous inclusion of all groups has led to a situation in which the effect of neighbourhood poverty on the *culture of poverty* for one group is cancelled out by an opposite effect for another group.

We may, therefore, need to examine such trends for each ethnic group, separately. However, this is not possible at present, due to the data limitation mentioned earlier. Since the census tract data come in aggregate form, they do not allow us to control for a variable such as ethnicity, which is included only in the census data on individuals. For this problem, a temporary, and somewhat problematic, method has been suggested: to link the two sets of data (Alba and Logan, 1992, 1993; Alba et al., 1994; Logan et al., 1996). The underlying logic of this method is that a community feature enters the model as the dependent variable. This variable, then, is regressed against a set of individual variables. Although this method relates the data on individuals and communities (ethnic groups, cities, and so on), it has two potential sources of concern. The first concern is the

---

11. Some parts of the 1996 census data that have been recently released to the public show that this census data is far richer than previous data in terms of ethnic variables. The hope, therefore, remains that it facilitates further research on this issue.

confusion and difficulty of interpretation caused by the dual units of analysis, individual and group. The second concern arises from the fact that the values of community variables are stable for all the affiliated individuals, hence, the problem of low variation and auto-correlation. Neither of these problems, as Logan et al. (1996:445) suggests, has any direct solution "because we do not possess a data set that is complete at the case level, containing both individual and locational scores."

We have used a similar approach, despite its limitations, to examine the possible relationships between neighbourhood poverty and the culture of poverty. Against the background of the inherent methodological flaw of this approach, the results of this exercise should be considered very cautiously. What the results of such an approach can give us is some possible hypotheses for further research.

## Neighbourhood Poverty and Culture of Poverty

It was hypothesized earlier that high levels of (say, 40% and more) can lead to a rise in the culture of poverty, represented by the inter-generational mobility in terms of education and employment. This relationship is illustrated in Table 5-9. For the hypothesis to hold, the coefficients in Table 5-9 need to be negative. As far as education is concerned, the hypothesis seems to be true for five groups, i.e., the Black, Vietnamese, Spanish, Portuguese, and German groups. Except for the German, all these groups are visible minorities. This is indeed a very interesting contrast, to which we will return later.

TABLE 5-9

THE REGRESSION BETA COEFFICIENTS: THE EFFECT OF NEIGHBOURHOOD POVERTY ON INTER-GENERATIONAL MOBILITY

| Ethnic Group | Employment Mobility | | Educational Mobility | |
| --- | --- | --- | --- | --- |
| | Proportion of population in neighbourhoods with 40%+ poverty rate | Proportion of population in neighbourhoods with 30-40% poverty rate | Proportion of population in neighbourhoods with 40%+ poverty rate | Proportion of population in neighbourhoods with 30-40% poverty rate |
| Black/Caribbean | -0.910 | | -0.660 | 0.577 |
| Vietnamese | | | -0.620 | -0.150 |
| Filipino | -0.240 | 0.791 | 0.657 | 0.295 |
| Chinese | -0.030 | -0.253 | 0.490 | 0.345 |
| Jewish | 0.811 | -0.286 | | -0.740 |
| Spanish | -0.188 | 0.247 | -0.454 | 0.580 |
| Portuguese | 0.128 | -0.359 | -0.081 | -0.033 |
| Italian | 0.496 | 0.201 | | |
| Greek | 0.527 | -0.437 | 0.918 | -0.367 |
| Ukrainian | 0.642 | | 0.497 | 0.122 |
| Polish | 0.852 | -0.241 | 0.385 | 0.099 |
| Hungarian | 0.249 | | 0.184 | 0.095 |
| British | 0.811 | -0.707 | 0.511 | 0.063 |
| French | 0.520 | 0.232 | 0.758 | 0.157 |
| Dutch | | | | |
| German | 0.591 | 0.283 | -0.111 | 0.987 |

\*    Beta Coefficients included are Significant at .05 level

The hypothesis is further corroborated by a comparison between the effects of ghetto neighbourhoods (those having at least a 40% poverty rate) and poor neighbourhoods (those with a 30-40% poverty rate). By moving from the former to the latter, that is, by moving to a better neighbourhood, the negative effect of neighbourhood poverty (or SCOP) on educational mobility either entirely disappears or decreases: it decreases for the Vietnamese (from -0.62 to -0.15) and Portuguese (from –0.08 to –0.03), and disappears for the Black and/or Caribbean (from –0.66 to 0.577), Spanish (from –0.454 to 0.58), and German (from –0.11 to 0.987).

The effect of the ghetto neighbourhood on occupational inter-generational mobility follows a similar pattern. Again, the negative impact of neighbourhood poverty on inter-generational mobility can be seen only for some visible minority groups, i.e., the Black, Filipino, Chinese, and Spanish groups. This contrast confirms the hypothesis that high levels of neighbourhood poverty may nurture the culture of poverty, but it also clearly shows that this is far from a universal trend. It is, perhaps, a good point to remind the reader that, in his thesis on the culture of poverty, Oscar Lewis also notes that this culture can be seen only among certain groups of poor, but not all.

The above observations support our argument that ghettos provide a fertile ground for the growth of the culture of poverty. Unlike what we expected, however, this is true only for visible minority groups. Why is there such a contrast, and how can this difference be explained? In addressing this issue, the lack of adequate data is a serious handicap. In the absence of data, all we can do is to propose a potential explanation for the observed contrast, without being able to test it empirically.

### Neighbourhood Poverty and Culture of Poverty: Why a Contrast between Ethnic Groups?

To explain the observed contrast between visible minorities and other ethnic groups, we found relevant the Multiple Discrepancies Theory (MDT) of Michalos, as well as the idea of "reference group" suggested by Merton. Addressing the source of life dissatisfaction, Michalos holds that the more our *real life* departs from the *ideal life* that we have imagined for ourselves, the more dissatisfied we will be (Tepperman, 1994). This dissatisfaction, in turn, triggers change. In other words, the lack of discrepancy between the *real* and the *ideal* life results in a lack of motivation to change the status quo. Out of these two, the *real life* and the *ideal life*, the former tends to be more stable than the latter; one's living conditions cannot change overnight, but his or her expectations can. This very quality of expectations makes them subject to external influences.

A number of factors contribute to the shaping of one's expectations: one's past life or what one has had in the past, what one thinks one deserves, and more important, what the "relevant others" have (Tepperman, 1994). The last factor indicates that life satisfaction is not merely an individual process; it is affected by what happens around us. We often adjust, that is, raise or lower, our expectations through the constant comparison of our situation with that of those whom we think are in similar situations. These "relevant others" act as a "reference group" with whom we constantly compare ourselves.[12]

In order to show the relevance of these theories for our study, we need to look at the culture of poverty in a slightly different light. It was mentioned earlier that the culture of poverty leads to a perpetuation of poverty. This means that the poor who are influenced by this culture do not make any effective attempts to free themselves from the poverty trap. We also noticed that such a trend does exist for visible minority ethnic groups, but not for those of European origin. This contrast exists, probably because the two have different "reference groups." The visible minorities may have a "reference group" (or "relevant others") who are in a situation not much different from their own, hence, no sense of discrepancy and no desire to change. The European origin groups living in ghetto neighbourhoods, on the other hand, may have a "reference group" with whom they feel a discrepancy, hence, efforts to change the situation and no subscription to the culture of poverty. The end result: presence of culture of poverty among the visible minority groups, and the lack thereof among the European origin groups.

The question that may arise here is that of how the groups that share the same ghetto neighbourhood can have different "reference groups." This may be so because the two groups, while sharing the same neighbourhood and perhaps having similar economic experiences, differ in terms of their social experiences in such neighbourhoods. While living in ghettos means the same thing for all economically, it may mean different thing, socially. For those of European ethnic origin, living in a poor neighbourhood means a higher level of interaction with other poor, mostly of non-European ethnic origin. This interaction is not necessarily a pleasant experience for those of European origin. It puts them in the same neighbourhood with immigrants whom they see as rivals in the job market. Previous studies have already shown that racist ideas are stronger among the lower class people of the mainstream population, because of their economic vulnerability (Satzewich, 1998). For the groups of European origin, such rivals can never act as a "reference group"; instead, their reference groups may well be the non-poor of European origin. In other

---

12. The dynamics of "reference group" influence is certainly more complicated than this. In his *Social Theory and Social Structure*, Merton (1968:286-287) identifies the situations in which "individuals take as a base for self-reference the situation of people with whom they are in direct social interaction.... At others, the assumed frame of reference is yielded by social categories of people ... with whom the individual is not in sustained social relations." This reveals a very complicated process that Merton calls "the dynamics of selection of reference groups."

words, the poor of European origin who live in poor neighbourhoods look beyond their immediate environments to find their ideal lives. This creates a discrepancy between their current situation and the one they would like to have; hence, their not giving in to the culture of poverty, and their efforts to improve their economic status in order to move out of ghettos.

Those of non-European ethnic origin, however, undergo an entirely different experience. For them, the "reference group" is likely to be those of European ethnic origin with whom they have interaction at the neighbourhood level, that is, the poor of European origin. While different ethnically, they are more or less the same economically. The fact that they live in the same poor neighbourhoods along with those of European origin may act as a false assurance for them; assurance that the chances of improvement are not great, and that there is nothing abnormal and undesirable about their living conditions. Such a feeling deadens any sense of discrepancy for them. Hence, they make no major effort to ameliorate their current living conditions, that is, they subscribe to the culture of poverty.

## SUMMARY OF FINDINGS

The distribution of ethnic population in high-poverty neighbourhoods in Canadian cities showed some alarmingly high levels of over-representation for certain groups, mostly of visible minority origins. As literature had suggested, the main contributors to this particular situation are the ethnic groups' poverty rate, the sector of economy in which they mostly work, and their residential segregation from the majority population, with the first factor being the most important and the other two being, alternately, second and third.

We had also hypothesized that the high concentration of ethnic groups in extremely poor neighbourhoods may lead to the development of a "culture of poverty" among them. This meant, in our view, that the neighbourhood poverty could be one, and not the only, factor that may cause the "culture of poverty." Interestingly enough, such a hypothesis turned out to be true mostly for visible minority groups. This contrast between the two sets of groups was quite noteworthy and not easily explainable.

Using Michalos' *multiple discrepancy theory of life satisfaction* and Merton's *theory of reference groups,* we attempted to explain the observed discrepancy between visible minorities and other groups by proposing a conceptual hypothesis to be examined empirically in future research. Based on both these theories, one's level of life satisfaction is determined by one's constant comparison between what one has and what the "relevant others" have.

Depending on who the "relevant others" or the "reference group" is, one may feel happy or unhappy with his or her current life. The greater the discrepancy between one's current life and the life of the "relevant others," the more dissatisfied with life one is; hence, the more effort one is willing to make to change one's living conditions. In the case of the two sets of ethnic groups, the possibility exists that the two have different "reference groups." The European origin groups may compare themselves with other wealthier groups of European origin, while visible minority groups may compare themselves with their fellow countrymen who are still back home. These different reference groups may have different results. For Europeans, it may bring a dissatisfaction with life, which may motivate them to change their current situation. For visible minorities, it may bring a satisfaction with life, which can hinder any additional effort to change their living conditions; hence, the development of a "culture of poverty."

# CHAPTER SIX

# Conclusion, Implications and Limitations of the Study

**A** few points highlighted in Chapters One through Five should be reiterated here in order to set up the discussion on the implications and limitations of the study. First and foremost is the fact that the *spatial concentration of poverty* in Canada has not followed the patterns detected in the research on American cities. Previous research had already illustrated that, in many respects, the social trends found in Canadian society stand closer to European countries than to the United States. The spatial concentration of poverty appears to be in accord with such an observation. This means that the problem of concentrated urban poverty is not deforming the morphology of Canadian cities as severely as it is doing south of the border. The sharp cleavage between inner city and suburb, with the high level of SCOP in the former and affluent dwellers in the latter, does not exist in Canada. In some Canadian cities, the high SCOP areas are even located in suburbs.

Despite its overall moderate levels, spatial concentration of poverty has been quite visibly high in two cities, Montreal and Winnipeg. Not only were the proportions of these cities' populations living in ghetto neighbourhoods quite high in 1986, they had almost doubled by 1991. The other larger cities also have alarmingly high levels of SCOP, compared to the smaller cities, but the problem was not as severe as it is for Montreal and Winnipeg. Also, a provincial dimension seems to be involved, with Quebec and the Prairie provinces facing considerably higher rates of spatial concentration of poverty.

Another departure from the American scenario is due to the influence of ethnic, rather than racial, origin. Unlike the United States, in which the spatial trends seem to have a very strong racial dimension, race does not influence social trends drastically in Canada. The examination of residential patterns in Canada, for example, showed that in many cities, Canadian Blacks share neighbourhoods with the Asian and Hispanic. Ethnicity seems to be more influential in Canada, but even that is far from creating rigid boundaries among people. An example of this is the

Scandinavian origin groups, i.e., the Swedish, Finnish, Danish, and Norwegians; in one city, they are closely clustered into a separate group, in another, they are a part of the Western European groups, and in third, each of them makes its own cluster.

The examination of spatial concentration of poverty along ethnic lines revealed that, although it is not a universal problem in all Canadian cities, it seems to be an inevitable trap for certain groups, regardless of where they live. The Vietnamese, Spanish, and Aboriginals, with the first two being the newly arrived groups of immigrants (mostly refugees) and the last one, a domestic sub-population, are the three groups most seriously suffering from high SCOP levels. In some cities, close to 50% of the population of these groups live in ghettos. The immigrant groups seem to be doubly disadvantaged; they not only suffer from the general poverty due to the economic sectors they are employed in, as well as the low-paid jobs they are qualified for, but they are also hampered by factors related to their immigration status, such as their limited knowledge of official languages and the mismatch of their skills and market demands.

In addition to limiting the social progress of the current generation, a high level of SCOP raises hurdles for the social mobility of the next generations. Based on a theoretical standpoint, we expected to see some sort of culture of poverty being nourished among those groups with a high representation in ghetto neighbourhoods. Through an empirical test, such a hypothesis turned out to be true only for certain ethnic groups: those of visible minorities. The settlement in ghetto neighbourhoods primarily hampered the inter-generational mobility of the non-European ethnic groups. While puzzling, this differential effect corroborated once more that cultural orientations are not linear functions of socio-economic conditions. Factors other than poverty and neighbourhood poverty are involved.

In an effort to make conceptual sense of the trends observed, we found merit in the theories of "life satisfaction" and "reference group." The reason why, in contrast to non-Europeans, the European ethnic groups do not lose their socio-economic ambitions to improve their living conditions through legitimate means, such as education, job training, and hard work, may be related to their different "reference group". We assumed that these groups of poor, or residents of poor neighbourhoods, would look up to the non-poor fellow Europeans as their reference group; the discrepancy between the living conditions of the two groups put the former in a state of constant dissatisfaction, hence, more motivation to fill the gap between their current life and their desired life. The non-European ethnic groups, in contrast, feel more satisfied when observing European-origin people in the same situation as theirs; hence, the loss of ambition to improve their living conditions.

## Policy Implications

The policy implications of a study of spatial concentration of poverty in Canada heavily depends on the vision such a study offers on the causes and consequences of SCOP. The consequences indicate how important the issue is, and the causes highlight the targets for potential policy-making efforts. The simple fact that an alarming level of SCOP may bear a distinct culture of poverty that has little in common with the general culture is enough for a country as culturally diverse and strongly committed to cultural pluralism as Canada is to consider the issue seriously. Multiculturalism works only when it co-exists with a common cultural ground. Otherwise, it can easily lead to cultural disintegration. The causes of spatial concentration of poverty in Canada, on the other hand, single out three major areas of concern for policy makers: poverty, residential segregation, and structural changes.

Our study showed that, notwithstanding the difference between general *poverty* and *neighbourhood poverty*, the former is a strong predictor of the latter. No matter which areas are considered to be poor neighbourhoods, the poverty of ethnic groups appeared as the single most important factor, explaining about 50% of the SCOP variation. This implies that poverty alleviation measures could be the most effective means to mitigate the problem of spatial concentration of poverty. The rising poverty level in Canada during the 1990s, however, questions the effectiveness of the measures taken thus far. The high poverty rates of certain sub-populations, such as young lone parents, women and children, as well as certain ethnic groups, sometimes up to three times the national rate, suggest that such measures need to be more specifically focused. They need to more sharply address the specific groups who are particularly vulnerable.

The residential segregation of ethnic groups has been another factor contributing to their representation in areas of high spatial concentration of poverty. Policy recommendation in this area is somewhat difficult, given the inadequacy of the available information on the factors associated with ethnic groups' residential segregation. The spatial research in the United States has shown that discriminatory real estate regulations have streamed Blacks into certain neighbourhoods. However, such a factor has not been detected or documented for Canada. The only known case for which such a practice has been spotted is the Aboriginal. Some studies have suggested that as the Aboriginal population of a neighbourhood increases, the real estates prices fall, and so does the desirability of the neighbourhood. This has resulted in some invisible practices by real estate agents, who direct Natives to certain neighbourhoods and not to others. The outcome of this practice has been the extremely high concentration of Natives in a small number of neighbourhoods in most Canadian cities. The existence of such discriminatory practices, therefore, remains an open topic for further investigation.

However, the residential segregation of certain ethnic groups has been also influenced by governments' public housing projects. Some previous research cited in this study has shown that the location of highly poor neighbourhoods closely follow the location of public housing projects. The erection of such projects in already poor neighbourhoods has further intensified the spatial poverty. Also, since many of the beneficiaries of such projects are low-income, visible minority, recent immigrants, it has changed the social fabric of poor neighbourhoods, i.e., the concentration of immigrants and visible minorities in such neighbourhoods. The location-seeking strategies for public housing projects, therefore, need to be revised in order to ameliorate the problem of spatial concentration of poverty in Canadian cities.

Equally influential in raising SCOP for certain ethnic groups has been the structural changes in the economy, i.e., a shift from a manufacturing-based to a service-oriented economy. Further, out of all the possible areas of activity in the service sector, information technology has been the most promising in terms of providing income. Given the fast computerization of life, from education to economy, the limited access and knowledge of computer technology among visible minorities is a serious handicap. Their initial poverty, which impedes any investment in acquiring such skills and knowledge, further aggravates poverty. This vicious circle needs to be broken through some sort of governmental intervention and public policy. The traditional training courses currently available for new immigrants, for example, need to be radically changed in order to meet this need.

Along with the above economic decisions, some cultural measures also need to be taken. We know that, in Canada, the different ethnic groups have been able to retain their distinct ethnic culture. Our study showed that, at least for visible minorities, concentration in ghettos also contributes to the shaping of yet another distinct subculture, the culture of poverty, among them. The big risk here is that if such a culture lacks necessary links with the general culture, it may lead to social isolation of those it influences from mainstream society. The interaction of the two, the ethnic culture and the culture of poverty, compounds such isolation. This can jeopardize the principle of ethnic diversity, as it can trigger a trend towards social disintegration. Such a trend can become particularly acute and problematic during periods of economic hardship.

The traditional commitment to ethnic diversity and multiculturalism, therefore, is not adequate in dealing with the problem we have discussed. The maintenance of ethnic identities needs to be accompanied by a commitment to promote inter-cultural contacts. Certainly, this can be partly accomplished through non-cultural measures, such as appropriate urban space planning and poverty alleviation measures. But all such measures only escalate the likelihood of inter-cultural contacts; actual contacts also need to be promoted through concrete cultural measures.

Given the complex set of social, economic, spatial, and cultural relationships involved, the feasibility of the measures suggested or the actions taken needs to be constantly examined against the research findings. The paucity of research on spatial concentration of poverty in Canada seriously limits the applicability of the findings. As one of the primary steps in this direction, the present study enables us to predicate the un- or under-investigated areas that need to be addressed in future research. Below, we discuss the implications of this study for future research.

## RESEARCH IMPLICATIONS

Each study builds upon a host of assumptions, from abstract and philosophical ones on the general nature of the subject matter to more concrete ones on the specific concepts and methods to apply. Such assumptions are often taken for granted, with no attempt to verify them. This is inevitable, as without such assumptions, no research is possible. If each research study had to start over from the first step, human knowledge would hardly progress. It is, however, essential for the researcher as well as the audience to be aware of such assumptions, to identify and introduce them painstakingly, and to suggest the possible loopholes they may contain. It is only through this practice that we can expect to further our knowledge.

The present study is not an exception to this general rule. Primarily concerned with the magnitude and seriousness of spatial concentration of poverty in Canadian cities, we had to sidestep a number of related issues, treating them as the assumptions of our study. The first and foremost is the definition of poverty. The review of poverty literature in Chapter 2 illustrated the enormous difficulty involved in this enterprise, manifested in a wide range of poverty definitions suggested and applied by poverty researchers: from relative to absolute measures, from income-based to consumption-based indicators, and from economic to social perceptions. The application of each of the suggested measures results in an image of poverty different from the others. Although we adopted the Statistics Canada Low-Income Cut-Offs as the poverty indicator, due to its better data availability and wider national coverage, the need remains to examine the spatial concentration of poverty using alternative measures.

Another issue, closely related to the one just mentioned, is the definition of poor or *ghetto* neighbourhood. Previous research, especially in the United States, had suggested the 40% poverty threshold, beyond which the neighbourhood's social organization would begin disintegrating. Although the many socio-economic similarities between Canada and the United States may encourage us to safely use the same threshold in Canada, such a practice lacks a much needed empirical foundation. Given the fact that the social breakdown of neighbourhoods tends to lead to higher crime rates, the generally lower rates of crime in Canadian, compared to American, cities may suggest that the thresholds are different in Canadian cities. As a consequence, in Canada, the ghetto behaviours may not necessarily start emerging at the 40% poverty threshold, as they do south of the border.

Even if a 40%, or any other, threshold can be securely established, there is no systematic and empirically founded evidence that they will necessarily trigger the sort of behaviours typical of American ghettos. This is an issue beyond the reach of a quantitative study like the present one; it requires comprehensive ethnographic and anthropological studies utilizing direct observatory methods. This also remains as a needed complement to the current study.

The time span this study covers, the period from 1986 to 1991, is simultaneously advantageous and problematic. It is advantageous, as it captures a period of change in recent Canadian history. It is also problematic, because the period ends in 1991, the year in which Canada experienced one of its most severe economic recessions ever. It is hard to imagine which portions of our findings are attributable to this unusual recession and which to the general trends of the 1980s and 1990s.

In the last couple of months before the completion of this book, Statistics Canada began releasing the 1996 census data. This can help the efforts to overcome the limitations of the present study in a number of ways. First, it expands the time span of study to ten years. This not only improves the longitudinal dimension of the study, but it also enables researchers to have a more stable image of spatial concentration of poverty in Canada, less affected by temporal economic fluctuations. Second, in the 1996 Census, the previously collapsed ethnic categories are decomposed into more specific ones, allowing for a more accurate evaluation of the influence of ethnicity. Third, and perhaps most important, Canadian census authorities have began reviewing and considering the possibility of forming a linked individual-census tract data set. With such data, the research on spatial concentration of poverty would make a great leap forward. We hope that the present study has managed to provide, if nothing else, a stepping stone for that leap.

# REFERENCES

Adams, Ian, William Cameron, Brian Hill, and Peter Penz. 1971. *The Real Poverty Report*. Edmonton: M.G. Hurtig Limited.

Alba, Richard D., and John R. Logan. 1992. Analyzing Locational Attainments. *Sociological Methods and Research* 20 (3): 367-397.

–––. 1993. Minority Proximity to Whites in Suburbs: An Individual-Level Analysis of Segregation. *American Journal of Sociology* 98 (6): 1388-1427.

Alba, Richard D., John R. Logan, and Paul E. Bellair. 1994. Living with Crime: The Implications of Racial/Ethnic Differences in Suburban Location. *Social Forces* 73 (2): 395-434.

Allison, Paul.1978. Measures of Inequality. *American Sociological Review* 43 (December): 865-880.

Anderson, Martin. 1978. *Welfare: The Political Economy of Welfare Reform in the United States*. USA: Stanford Hoover Institutions Press.

Aron, Raymond. 1970. *Main Currents in Sociological Thought*. Vol. 2. New York: Anchor Books Doubleday.

Balakrishnan, T.R., and K. Jarvis. 1976. Socioeconomic Differentiation in Urban Canada. *Canadian Review of Sociology and Anthropology* 13 (2): 204-216.

–––. 1979. Changing Patterns of Spatial Differentiation in Urban Canada, 1961-1971. *Canadian Review of Sociology and Anthropology* 16 (2): 218-227.

Balakrishnan, T.R., and John Kralt. 1987. Segregation of Visible Minorities in Montreal, Toronto, and Vancouver. In *Ethnic Canada: Identities and Inequalities*, edited by Leo Driedger. Toronto: Copp Clark Pitman.

Balakrishnan, T.R., and K. Selvanathan. 1990. Ethnic Residential Segregation in Metropolitan Canada. In *Ethnic Demography*, edited by S. Halli, F. Trovato, and L. Driedger. Ottawa: Carleton University Press.

Barber, Benjamin R. [1992] 1996. JIHAD vs. McWORLD. In *Society in Question*, edited by R. Brym. Canada: Harcourt Brace & Company.

Basavarajappa, K.G., and S.S. Halli. 1997. A Comparative Study of Immigrant and Non-Immigrant Families in Canada with Special Reference to Income, 1986. *International Migration* 35 (2): 225-252.

Basran, Gurcharn, and Zong Li. 1998. Devaluation of Foreign Credentials as Perceived by Non-White Professional Immigrants. Paper presented in the regional workshop "Bridging the Gap," University of Regina, Saskatchewan, Canada, 29-31 October.

Bassler, Gerhard P. 1991. *The German Canadian Mosaic Today and Yesterday*. Ottawa: German-Canadian Congress.

Bell, Wendell. 1953. The Social Areas of the San Francisco Bay Region. *American Sociological Review* 18 (February): 39-47.

Berry, Reginald. 1987. Finding Identity: Separation, Integration, Assimilation, or Marginality? In *Ethnic Canada: Identities and Inequalities*, edited by L. Driedger. Canada: Copp Clark Pitman Ltd.

Blalock, Hubert M., Jr., and Paul H. Wilken. 1979. *Intergroup Processes: A Micro-Macro Perspective*. New York: The Free Press.

Blank, Rebecca M. 1994. The Employment Strategy: Public Policies to Increase Work and Earnings. In *Confronting Poverty: Prescriptions for Change*, edited by Danziger, Sandefur, and Weinberg. New York: Harvard University Press.

Bobo, Lawrence, and Camille L. Zubrinsky. 1996. Attitudes on Residential Integration: Perceived Status Differences, Mere in-group Preference, or Racial Prejudice? *Social Forces* 74 (3): 883-909.

Bolaria, Singh B., and Terry Wotherspoon. 1995. Income Inequality, Poverty and Hunger. In *Social Issues and Contradictions in Canadian Society, 2nd ed.*, edited by Singh Bolaria. Canada: Harcourt Brace & Company.

Brodbar-Nemzer, Jay, and Steven M. Cohen. 1993. An Overview of the Canadian Jewish Community. In *The Jews in Canada*, edited by R. Brym et al. Toronto: Oxford University Press.

Brooks-Gunn, Jeanne, Greg J. Duncan, and J. Lawrence Aber, eds. 1997. *Neighborhood Poverty*. New York: Russell Sage Foundation.

Burton, C. Emory. 1992. *The Poverty Debate: Politics and the Poor in America*. USA: Greenwood Press.

Cahoone, Lawrence E., ed. 1996. *From Modernism to Postmodernism: An Anthology*. USA: Blackwell Publishers.

Canadian Institute of Child Health. 1994. *The Health of Canada's Children: A Statistical Profile*. 2nd ed. Ottawa: Canadian Institute of Child Health.

Cheal, David. 1998. Culture and the Postmodern. In *New Society: Sociology for the 21st Century*, 2nd edition, edited by Robert Brym. Canada: Harcourt Brace.

Chekki, Dan A. 1995. Inequality and Poverty in Canadian Cities. *Research in Community Sociology* 5: 249-270.

Cheney, Peter. 1988. The Economic 'Underclass:' Left Behind by the Boom. *The Toronto Star*, June 9, pp.L1 and L4.

Choldin, Harvey M., and Claudine Hanson. 1982. Status Shifts within The City. *American Journal of Sociology* 47 (February): 129-141.

Clement, Wallace, and John Myles. 1994. *Relations of Ruling: Class and Gender in Postindustrial Societies*. Montreal: McGill-Queen's University Press.

Corak, Miles, and Andrew Heisz. 1996. *The Intergenerational Income Mobility of Canadian Men*. Statistics Canada, 11F0019MPE No.89.

Crane, Jonathan.1991. Effects of Neighborhoods on Dropping Out of School and Teenage Childbearing. In *The Urban Underclass*, edited by Jencks and Peterson. Washington, D.C.: The Brookings Institution.

Danziger, Sheldon H., and Daniel H. Weinberg. 1994. The Historical Record: Trends in Family Income, Inequality, and Poverty. In *Confronting Poverty: Prescriptions for Change*, edited by Danziger, Sandefur, and Weinberg. New York: Harvard University Press.

DeVoretz, Don J., ed. 1995. *Diminishing Returns: The Economics of Canada's Recent Immigration Policy*. Toronto: C.D. Howe Institute.

Driedger, L., ed. 1987. *Ethnic Canada: Identities and Inequalities*, Canada: Copp Clark Pitman Ltd.

–––. 1991. *The Urban Factor: Sociology of Canadian Cities.* Toronto: Oxford University Press.

Duffy, Ann, and Nancy Mandell. [1994] 1996. Poverty in Canada. In *Society in Question*, edited by Robert Brym. Canada: Harcourt Brace & Company.

Duffy, Ann, Nancy Mandell, and Norene Pupo, 1988. *Few Choices: Women, Work and Family.* Toronto: Garamond Press.

Duffy, Ann, and Norene Pupo. 1992. *Part-time Paradox: Connecting Gender, Work, and Family.* Toronto: McClelland & Stewart.

Duncan, Otis Dudley, and Beverly Duncan. 1955. A Methodological Analysis of Segregation Analysis. *American Sociological Review* 20 (2): 210-217.

Durkeim, Emile. [1857] 1951. *Suicide.* USA: Free Press.

Edwards, Richard C., Michael Reich, and David M. Gordon. 1973. *Labor Market Segmentation.* USA: D.C. Heath and Company.

Esping-Anderson, Gosta. 1990. *The Three Worlds of Welfare Capitalism.* New Jersey: The Princeton University Press.

Etzioni, Amitai. 1993. *The Spirit of Community: The Reinvention of American Society.* New York: Simon and Schuster.

Fassihian, Dokhi. 1998. CyberClash. http://www.iranian.com/Opinion/Dec98/Internet/index.html#clash. December (seen December 20, 1998).

Fellegi, Ivan P. 1996. On Poverty and Low Income. Http://www.statcan.ca/english/concepts/poverty/pauv.htm. Seen on January 27, 1998.

Fitchen, Janet M. 1995. Spatial Redistribution of Poverty through Migration of Poor People to Depressed Rural Communities. *Rural Sociology* 60 (2): 181-201.

Forest, Benjamin. 1995. West Hollywood as Symbol: The Significance of Place in the Construction of a Gay Identify. In *Undoing Place? A Geographical Reader*, edited by McDowell. US: John Wiley & Sons. Inc.

Gillespie, W. Irwin. 1997. The Deficit- and Debt-Reduction Challenge and the Distribution of Income in Canada. In *Equality and Prosperity: Finding Common Ground*, edited by Robson and Scarth. Toronto: C.D. Howe Institute.

Gillis, A.R. 1995. Urbanization. In *Sociology for the 21st Century*, edited by Robert Brym. Canada: Harcourt Brace & Company.

Glazer, Nathan. 1988. *The Limits of Social Policy.* USA: Harvard University Press.

Goar, Carol. 1993. Canada's Emerging 'Underclass.' *The Toronto Star*, April 10, p.D1.

Goldberg, Gertrude Schaffner. 1990. Canada: Bordering on the Feminization of Poverty. In *The Feminization of Poverty: Only in America?* edited by Goldberg and Kermen. New York: Praeger.

Gordon, Ian. 1995. The Impact of Economic Change on Minorities and Migrants in Western Europe. In *Poverty, Inequality, and the Future of Social Policy*, edited by McFate, Lawson, and Wilson. New York: Russell Sage Foundation.

Greenstone, J. David. 1991. Culture, Rationality, and the Underclass. In *The Urban Underclass*, edited by Jencks and Peterson. Washington, D.C.: The Brookings Institution.

Griffin, David R. 1988. *The Reenchantment of Science: Postmodern Proposals.* Albany: State University of New York Press.

Gross, Paul R., and Norman Levitt. 1994. *Higher Superstition: The Academic Left and Its Quarrels with Science.* Baltimore and London: The Johns Hopkins University Press.

Hajnal, Zoltan L. 1995. The Nature of Concentrated Urban Poverty in Canada and the United States. *Canadian Journal of Sociology* 20 (4): 497-528.

Halli, S.S. 1987. *How Minority Status Affects Fertility: Asian Groups in Canada.* New York: Greenwood Press.

Halli, S. S., and A. Kazemipur. 1998. Poverty and Intergenerational Mobility Among Immigrants in Canadian Cities. Paper presented in the regional workshop "Bridging the Gap," University of Regina, Saskatchewan, Canada, 29-31 October.

Harp, John, and John Hofley, eds. 1971. *Poverty in Canada.* Scarborough: Prentice-Hall of Canada.

Helling, Roudolph A. 1965. *The Position of Negroes, Chinese and Italians in the Social Structure of Windsor, Ontario.* Toronto: Ontario Human Rights Commission.

Hettne, Bjorn. 1995. *Development Theory and the Three Worlds,* 2nd ed. USA: Longman, Scientific & Technical.

Himelfarb, A., and C.J. Richardson. 1991. *Sociology for Canadians,* 2nd ed. Canada: McGraw-Hill Ryerson Limited.

Hofley, John R. 1971. Problems and Perspectives in the Study of Poverty. In *Poverty In Canada,* edited by Harp and Hofley. Scarborough: Prentice-Hall of Canada, Ltd.

Hou, Feng, and T.R. Balakrishnan. 1996. Immigration and the Changing Ethnic Mosaic of Canadian Cities. Paper presented for the "National Symposium on Immigration and Integration: New Challenges," Winnipeg, Canada, 25-27 October.

Huntington, Samuel P. 1996. *The Clash of Civilizations and the Remaking of the World Order.* New York: Simon & Schuster.

Iceland, John. 1995. Concentrated Poverty in U.S. Cities: A Look at Metropolitan-Level Causes, 1970-1980. *Research in Community Sociology* 5: 65-90.

Isajiw, Wsevolod W. 1999. *Understanding Diversity: Ethnicity and Race in the Canadian Context.* Toronto: Thompson Educational Publishing.

James, David R., and Karl E. Taeuber. 1985. Measures of Segregation. *Sociological Methodology:* 1-32.

Jargowsky, Christopher, and May Jo Bane. 1991. Ghetto Poverty in the United States, 1970-1980. In *The Urban Underclass,* edited by Jencks and Peterson. Washington, D.C.: The Brookings Institution.

Jencks, Christopher. 1992. *Rethinking Social Policy: Race, Poverty, and the Underclass.* Cambridge: Harvard University Press.

Jenkins, Margaret, and S.M. Miller. 1987. Upward Redistribution in the United States. In *Dynamics of Deprivation,* edited by Ferge and Miller. England: Gower Publishing Company.

Johnson, Leo A. 1974. *Poverty in Wealth.* Toronto: New Hogtown Press.

Johnson, Paul. 1997. *A History of the American People*. USA: HarperCollins Publishers.

Kazemipur, A., and S. S. Halli.1997. Plight of Immigrants: The Spatial Concentration of Poverty in Canada. *Canadian Journal of Regional Science* 20 (1,2): 11-28.

Kierans, Thomas E. 1996. Foreword. In *Are We Becoming Two Societies?* edited by Beach and Slotsve. Toronto: C.D. Howe Institute.

Krahn, Harvey. 1995. Social Stratification. In *New Society: Sociology for the 21st Century*, edited by Robert Brym. Canada: Harcourt Brace.

Krotki, Karol J. 1997. How the Proportion of Artificial Canadians Varied Among Regions of Canada and Ethnic Origins Between 1991 and 1996. *Canadian Journal of Regional Science* 20 (1,2): 169-180.

Lawson, Roger, and William J. Wilson. 1995. Poverty, Social Rights, and the Quality of Citizenship. In *Poverty, Inequality, and the Future of Social Policy*, edited by McFate, Lawson, and Wilson. New York: Russell Sage Foundation.

Lederer, K.M. 1972. *The Nature of Poverty: An Interpretative Review of Poverty Studies, With Special Reference to Canada*. Ottawa: Human Resources Research Council.

Lenkowsky, Leslie. 1986. *Politics, Economics, and Welfare Reform: The Failure of the Negative Income Tax in Britain and the United States*. Washington: American Enterprise Institute for Public Policy Research.

Lewis, Oscar. [1966] 1971. The Culture of Poverty. In *Poverty In Canada*, edited by Harp and Hofley. Scarborough: Prentice-Hall of Canada, Ltd.

Ley, David, and Heather Smith. 1997. Immigration and Poverty in Canadian Cities, 1971-1991. *Canadian Journal of Regional Science* 20 (1,2): 29-48.

Li, Peter. 1996. *The Making of Post-War Canada*. Toronto: Oxford University Press

———. 1998. Earnings of Immigrants. Paper presented in the regional workshop "Bridging the Gap," University of Regina, Saskatchewan, Canada, 29-31 October.

Lieberson, S. 1969. Measuring Population Diversity. *American Sociological Review* 34: 850-862.

———. 1981. An Asymmetrical Approach to Segregation. In *Ethnic Segregation in Cities*, edited by Peach et al. Athens: The University of Georgia Press.

Lindstrom-Best, Varpu. 1985. *The Finns in Canada*. Ottawa: Keystone Printing and Lithographing Ltd.

Logan, John R., Richard D. Alba, and Shu-Yin Leung. 1996. Minority Access to White Suburbs: A Multiregional Comparison. *Social Forces* 74 (3): 851-881.

Logan, John R., Richard D. Alba, Tom McNulty, and Brian Fisher. 1996. Making a Place in the Metropolis: Locational Attainment in Cities and Suburbs. *Demography* 33 (4): 443-453.

Logan, John R., and Mark Schneider. 1984. Racial Segregation and Racial Change in American Suburbs, 1970-1980. *American Journal of Sociology* 89 (4): 874-888.

MacLachlan, Ian, and Ryo Sawada. 1997. Measures of Income Inequality and Social Polarization in Canadian Metropolitan Areas. *The Canadian Geographer* 41 (4): 377-397.

Mahon, Rianne. 1991. From "Bringing" to "'Putting'": The State in Late Twentieth-Century Social Theory. *Canadian Journal of Sociology* 16 (2): 119-144.

Mann, W.E. 1970. *Poverty and Social Policy in Canada*. Toronto: The Copp Clark Publishing Company.

Marchak, M. Patricia. 1991. *The Integrated Circus*. Montreal and Kingston: McGill-Queen's University Press.

Marsh, I., ed. 1996. *Making Sense of Society*. London and New York: Longman.

Marx, Karl. [1939] 1973. *Grundrisse*. Britain: Penguin Books.

Massey, Douglas S. 1984. Ethnic Residential Segregation: A Theoretical Synthesis and Empirical Review. *Sociology and Social Research* 69 (3): 315-350.

Massey, Douglas S., Jaquin Arango, Graeme Hugo, Ali Kouaouci, Adela Pellegrino, and J. Edward Taylor. 1994. An Evaluation of International Migration Theory: The North American Case. *Population and Development Review* 20 (4): 699-751.

Massey, Douglas S., Gretchen A. Condran, and Nancy A. Denton. 1987. The Effects of Residential Segregation on Black Social and Economic Well-Being. *Social Forces* 66 (1): 29-56.

Massey, Douglas S., and Nancy A. Denton. 1988a. Suburbanization and Segregation in U.S. Metropolitan Areas. *American Journal of Sociology* 94 (3): 592-626.

–––. 1988b. The Dimensions of Residential Segregation. *Social Forces* 67 (2): 281-315.

–––. 1993. *American Apartheid: Segregation and the Making of the Underclass*. Cambridge: Harvard University Press.

Massey, Douglas S., and Mitchell L. Eggers. 1990. The Ecology of Inequality: Minorities and the Concentration of Poverty, 1970-1980. *American Journal of Sociology* 95 (5): 1153-88.

Massey, Douglas S., Andrew B. Gross, and Mitchell L. Eggers. 1991. Segregation, the Concentration of Poverty, and the Life Chances of Individuals. *Social Science Research* 20: 397-420.

Massey, Douglas S., Andrew B. Gross, and Kumiko Shibuya. 1994. Migration, Segregation, and the Geographic Concentration of Poverty. *American Sociological Review* 59 (June): 425-445.

Massey, Douglas S., and Shawn M. Kanaiaupuni. 1993. Public Housing and the Concentration of Poverty. *Social Science Quarterly* 74 (1): 109-122.

Mata, Fernando. 1997. *Intergenerational Transmission of Education and Socio-economic Status: A Look at Immigrants, Visible Minorities and Aboriginals*. Statistics Canada. Product registration number: 75F0002M.

McClelland, David C. 1972. *The Achieving Society*. New York: The Free Press.

McClelland, David C., and David G. Winter. 1969. *Motivating Economic Achievement*. New York: The Free Press.

McDowell, Linda. 1997. *Undoing Place? A Geographical Reader*. New York: John Wiley & Sons.

McFate, Katherine. 1995. Introduction: Western States in the New World Order. In *Poverty, Inequality, and the Future of Social Policy*, edited by McFate, Lawson, and Wilson. New York: Russell Sage Foundation.

McFate, Katherine, Timothy Smeeding, and Lee Rainwater. 1995. Markets and States: Poverty Trends and Transfer System Effectiveness in the 1980s. In *Poverty, Inequality, and the Future of Social Policy*, edited by McFate, Lawson, and Wilson. New York: Russell Sage Foundation.

McLaughlin, K.M. 1985. *The Germans in Canada.* Ottawa: Keystone Printing and Lithographing Ltd.

Mead, Lawrence M. 1986. *Beyond Entitlement: The Social Obligations of Citizenship.* USA: Free Press.

Merton, Robert K. 1968. *Social Theory and Social Structure.* New York: The Free Press.

Meyer, Susan E. 1991. How Much Does a High School's Racial and Socioeconomic Mix Affect Graduation and Teenage Fertility Rates? In *The Urban Underclass*, edited by Jencks and Peterson. Washington, D.C.: The Brookings Institution.

–––. 1995. A Comparison of Poverty and Living Conditions in the United States, Canada, Sweden, and Germany. In *Poverty, Inequality, and the Future of Social Policy*, edited by McFate, Lawson, and Wilson. New York: Russell Sage Foundation.

Morss, Elliot R. 1991. The New Global Players: How They Compete and Collaborate. *World Development* 19 (1): 55-64.

Murdie, Robert A. 1998. The Welfare State, Economic Restructuring and Immigrant Flows: Impacts of Socio-spatial Segregation in Greater Toronto. In *Urban Segregation and the Welfare State: Inequality and Exclusion in Western Cities*, edited by Musterd and Ostendorf. London and New York: Routledge.

Murray, Charles A. 1984. *Losing Ground: American Social Policy, 1950-80.* USA: Basic Books.

Musterd S., and W. Ostendorf. 1997. *Urban Segregation and the Welfare State: Inequality and Exclusion in Western Cities.* London and New York: Routledge

National Council of Welfare. 1992. *Poverty Profile: 1980-1990.* Canada: Minister of Supply and Services.

Nord, Mark, A.E. Luloff, and Leif Jensen. 1995. Migration and the Spatial Concentration of Poverty. *Rural Sociology* 60 (3): 399-415.

Olsen, Gregg M. 1996. Re-Modeling Sweden: The Rise and Demise of the Compromise in a Global Economy. *Social Problems* 43 (1): 1-20.

Oster, Sharon M., Elizabeth E. Lake, and Conchita Gene Oksman. 1978. *The Definition and Measurement of Poverty.* Vol. 1. Colorado: Westview Press.

Peach, Ceri, and Susan Smith. 1981. Introduction to *Ethnic Segregation in Cities*, edited by Peach, Robinson, and Smith. USA: The University of Georgia Press.

Peterson, Paul E. 1991. The Urban Underclass and the Poverty Paradox. In *The Urban Underclass*, edited by Jencks and Peterson. Washington, D.C.: The Brookings Institution.

Reid, Timothy E. 1972. *Canada's Poor: Are They Always to Be with Us?* Canada: Holt, Reinhart and Winston of Canada, Ltd.

Richardson, R. Jack. [1992] 1996. Canada and Free Trade: Why Did It Happen? In *Society in Question*, edited by Brym. Canada, Harcourt Brace & Company.

Rifkin, Jeremy. 1995. *The End of Work: The Decline of the Global Labor Force and the Dawn of the Post-Market Era.* New York: G.P. Putnam's Sons.

Robson, William B.P., and William Scarth. 1997. Equality and Prosperity: Some Facts and Alternative Interpretations. In *Equality and Prosperity: Finding Common Ground,* edited by Robson and Scarth. Toronto: C.D. Howe Institute.

Roelandt, T., and J. Veenman. 1992. An Emerging Ethnic Underclass in the Netherlands? *New Community* 19: 129-141.

Rosenau, Pauline M.1992a. Modern and Post-Modern Science: Some Contrasts. *Review* 25 (1): 49-89.

———. 1992b. *Post-modernism and the Social Sciences: Insights, Inroads, and Intrusions.* Princeton: Princeton University Press.

Ross, David P., E. Richard Shillington, and Clarence Lochhead. 1994. *The Canadian Fact Book on Poverty.* Ottawa: The Canadian Council on Social Development.

Ruggles, Patricia. 1990. *Drawing the Line: Alternative Poverty Measures and Their Implications for Public Policy.* Washington, D.C.: The Urban Institute Press.

Ruttan, Susan. 1992. Trustees Warned: Cuts Could Lead to 'Underclass'. *The Calgary Herald,* March 8. p.B1.

Sampson, Robert. 1997. What 'Community' Supplies. Proceedings of the National Community Development Policy Analysis Network Conference. USA: Brookings Institution.

Sarlo, Christopher A. 1992. *Poverty in Canada.* Vancouver: The Fraser Institute.

———. 1994. *Poverty in Canada,* 2nd ed. Vancouver: The Fraser Institute.

Satzewich, Vic. 1998. Race and Ethnic Relations. In *New Society: Sociology for the 21st Century,* edited by Brym. Toronto: Harcourt Brace Canada.

Scheler, Max. [1926] 1980. *Problems of a Sociology of Knowledge.* London: Routledge & Kegan Paul.

Schultz, Theodore W. 1993. *The Economics of Being Poor.* USA: Blackwell.

Sheffe, Norman. 1970. *Poverty.* Canada: McGraw-Hill.

Shevky, Eshref, and Wendell Bell. 1955. *Social Area Analysis: Theory, Illustrative Application, and Computational Procedures.* Westport, Conn.: Greenwood Press.

Shevky, Eshref, and Marilyn Williams. 1949. *The Social Areas of Los Angeles: Analysis and Typology.* Berkeley: University of California Press.

Shragge, Eric. 1993. *Community Economic Development: In Search of Empowerment and Alternatives.* Montreal: Black Rose Books.

Silver, Hilary. 1993. National Conceptions of the New Urban Poverty: Social Structural Change in Britain, France and the United States. *International Journal of Urban and Regional Research* 17: 336-354.

Simpson, George Eaton, and J. Milton Yinger. 1972. *Racial and Cultural Minorities,* 4th ed. New York: Plenum Press.

Teeple, Gary. 1995. *Globalization and the Decline of Social Reform.* Toronto: Garamond Press.

Tepperman, L. 1994. *Choices and Chances.* Toronto: Harcourt Brace Canada.

Tocqueville, Alexis de. [1856] 1955. *The Old Regime and the French Revolution.* USA: Doubleday Anchor Book.

Toffler, Alvin. 1980. *The Third Wave.* New York: Morrow.

Van Kempen, Eva T. 1994. The Dual City and the Poor: Social Polarisation, Social Segregation and Life Chances. *Urban Studies* 31: 995-1015.

Wallerstein, Immanuel. 1987. World-Systems Analysis. In *Social Theory Today*, edited by Giddens and Turner. Stanford: Stanford University Press.

Ward, Steven. 1995. The Revenge of the Humanities: Reality, Rhetoric, and the Politics of Postmodernism. *Sociological Perspective* 38 (2): 109-128.

Welsh, Larry. 1994. Canada's Social Safety Net Riddled with Holes: Creation of a Permanent 'Underclass' Feared. *The Halifax Chronicle Herald,* June 20, p.B8.

White, Michael J. 1983. The Measurement of Spatial Segregation. *American Journal of Sociology* 88: 1008-1018.

Whyte, Donald R. 1971. Sociological Aspects of Poverty: A Conceptual Analysis. In *Poverty In Canada*, edited by Harp and Hofley. Scarborough: Prentice-Hall of Canada, Ltd.

Wilson, Frank Harold. 1995. Concentrated Poverty, Housing Change, and Urban Redevelopment: Blacks in U.S. Cities, 1980-1990. *Research in Community Sociology* 5: 91-124.

Wilson, William J. 1987. *The Truly Disadvantaged: The Inner City, the Underclass, and Public Policy.* Chicago: The University of Chicago Press.

–––. 1996. *When Work Disappears: the World of the New Urban Poor.* New York: Vintage Books.

Winks, R.W. 1971. *The Blacks in Canada.* Montreal: McGill-Queen's University Press.

Winship, Christopher. 1977. A Reevaluation of Indexes of Residential Segregation. *Social Forces* 55 (4): 1058-1066.

# APPENDICES

**APPENDEIX 1**

## THE DISTRIBUTION OF CENSUS TRACTS (CTS) IN DIFFERENT POVERTY AREAS, 1986-1991

| | Poverty Rate of Census Tracts | | | | | | | | | | | | | | |
| | 0-9.99% | | | 10-19.99% | | | 20-29.99% | | | 30-39.99% | | | 40% + | | |
| City | 1986 | 1991 | 1986-91 Change | 1986 | 1991 | 1986-91 Change | 1986 | 1991 | 1986-91 Change | 1986 | 1991 | 1986-91 Change | 1986 | 1991 | 1986-91 Change |
|---|---|---|---|---|---|---|---|---|---|---|---|---|---|---|---|
| St. John's | 23.7 | 37.5 | 13.8 | 44.7 | 40.0 | -4.7 | 18.4 | 10.0 | -8.4 | 10.5 | 12.5 | 2.0 | 2.6 | 0.0 | -2.6 |
| Halifax | 51.4 | 54.7 | 3.3 | 33.8 | 30.7 | -3.1 | 10.8 | 12.0 | 1.2 | 4.1 | 1.3 | -2.8 | 0.0 | 1.3 | 1.3 |
| Moncton | 40.9 | 43.5 | 2.6 | 31.8 | 30.4 | -1.4 | 22.7 | 26.1 | 3.4 | 4.5 | 0.0 | -4.5 | 0.0 | 0.0 | 0.0 |
| Saint John | 16.7 | 27.9 | 11.2 | 31.0 | 34.9 | 3.9 | 28.6 | 23.3 | -5.3 | 16.7 | 7.0 | -9.7 | 7.1 | 7.0 | -0.1 |
| Chicoutimi-Jonquière | 3.1 | 28.6 | 25.5 | 59.4 | 45.7 | -13.7 | 21.9 | 17.1 | -4.8 | 15.6 | 8.6 | -7.0 | 0.0 | 0.0 | 0.0 |
| Quebec | 28.3 | 31.1 | 2.8 | 37.0 | 37.1 | 0.1 | 18.8 | 16.6 | -2.2 | 8.7 | 7.9 | -0.8 | 7.2 | 7.3 | 0.1 |
| Sherbrooke | 9.7 | 25.8 | 16.1 | 51.6 | 32.3 | -19.3 | 16.1 | 19.4 | 3.3 | 12.9 | 12.9 | 0.0 | 9.7 | 9.7 | 0.0 |
| Trois-Rivières | . | 11.8 | . | . | 55.9 | . | . | 14.7 | . | . | 8.8 | 0.0 | . | 8.8 | . |
| Montreal | 22.6 | 20.9 | -1.7 | 32.5 | 31.3 | -1.2 | 23.3 | 25.5 | 2.2 | 13.0 | 12.1 | -0.9 | 8.5 | 10.2 | 1.7 |
| Ottawa-Hull | 54.2 | 54.8 | 0.6 | 27.1 | 26.0 | -1.1 | 13.0 | 12.0 | -1.0 | 4.7 | 4.8 | 0.1 | 1.0 | 2.4 | 1.4 |
| Kingston | 57.1 | 64.7 | 7.6 | 31.4 | 23.5 | -7.9 | 8.6 | 8.8 | 0.2 | 2.9 | 2.9 | 0.0 | 0.0 | 0.0 | 0.0 |
| Peterborough | 60.9 | 56.5 | -4.4 | 26.1 | 34.8 | 8.7 | 8.7 | 4.3 | -4.4 | 4.3 | 4.3 | 0.0 | 0.0 | 0.0 | 0.0 |
| Oshawa | 72.7 | 69.4 | -3.3 | 22.7 | 20.4 | -2.3 | 2.3 | 10.2 | 7.9 | 2.3 | 0.0 | -2.3 | 0.0 | 0.0 | 0.0 |
| Toronto | 61.0 | 50.5 | -10.5 | 26.3 | 30.5 | 4.2 | 9.8 | 14.3 | 4.5 | 1.8 | 3.6 | 1.8 | 1.1 | 1.1 | 0.0 |
| Hamilton | 50.3 | 45.1 | -5.2 | 31.8 | 35.2 | 3.4 | 10.6 | 12.3 | 1.7 | 4.0 | 4.9 | 0.9 | 3.3 | 2.5 | -0.8 |
| St. Catharines-Niagara | 41.0 | 50.6 | 9.6 | 39.8 | 41.0 | 1.2 | 18.1 | 8.4 | -9.7 | 1.2 | 0.0 | -1.2 | 0.0 | 0.0 | 0.0 |
| Kitchener | 48.1 | 51.9 | 3.8 | 46.8 | 43.2 | -3.6 | 5.2 | 4.9 | -0.3 | 0.0 | 0.0 | 0.0 | 0.0 | 0.0 | 0.0 |
| Brantford | 42.9 | 52.4 | 9.5 | 38.1 | 38.1 | 0.0 | 14.3 | 9.5 | -4.8 | 4.8 | 0.0 | -4.8 | 0.0 | 0.0 | 0.0 |
| Guelph | 65.0 | 71.4 | 6.4 | 25.0 | 19.0 | -6.0 | 10.0 | 9.5 | -0.5 | 0.0 | 0.0 | 0.0 | 0.0 | 0.0 | 0.0 |
| London | 46.6 | 44.3 | -2.3 | 37.5 | 46.6 | 9.1 | 10.2 | 8.0 | -2.2 | 5.7 | 1.1 | -4.6 | 0.0 | 0.0 | 0.0 |
| Windsor | 43.1 | 44.1 | 1.0 | 32.8 | 30.5 | -2.3 | 20.7 | 18.6 | -2.1 | 1.7 | 6.8 | 5.1 | 1.7 | 0.0 | -1.7 |
| Sarnia-Clearwater | 54.2 | 62.5 | 8.3 | 41.7 | 29.2 | -12.5 | 4.2 | 4.2 | 0.0 | 0.0 | 4.2 | -4.2 | 0.0 | 0.0 | 0.0 |
| North Bay | 45.0 | 45.0 | 0.0 | 25.0 | 30.0 | 5.0 | 15.0 | 15.0 | 0.0 | 10.0 | 10.0 | 0.0 | 5.0 | 0.0 | -5.0 |
| Sudbury | 23.7 | 43.2 | 19.5 | 63.2 | 45.9 | -17.3 | 7.9 | 5.4 | -2.5 | 5.3 | 5.4 | 0.1 | 0.0 | 0.0 | 0.0 |
| Sault Ste. Marie | 39.1 | 40.9 | 1.8 | 47.8 | 40.9 | -6.9 | 4.3 | 13.6 | 9.3 | 8.7 | 4.5 | -4.2 | 0.0 | 0.0 | 0.0 |
| Thunder Bay | 53.3 | 53.3 | 0.0 | 36.7 | 40.0 | 3.3 | 10.0 | 3.3 | -6.7 | 0.0 | 3.3 | 3.3 | 0.0 | 0.0 | 0.0 |
| Winnipeg | 40.5 | 32.3 | -8.2 | 35.8 | 34.8 | -1.0 | 8.8 | 16.8 | 8.0 | 7.4 | 5.8 | -1.6 | 7.4 | 10.3 | 2.9 |
| Regina | 42.6 | 38.8 | -3.8 | 27.7 | 38.8 | 11.1 | 23.4 | 14.3 | -9.1 | 4.3 | 6.1 | 1.8 | 2.1 | 2.0 | -0.1 |
| Saskatoon | 18.2 | 33.3 | 15.1 | 59.1 | 41.7 | -17.4 | 11.4 | 16.7 | 5.3 | 9.1 | 6.3 | -2.8 | 2.3 | 2.1 | -0.2 |
| Lethbridge | 38.1 | 45.0 | 6.9 | 52.4 | 50.0 | -2.4 | 9.5 | 5.0 | -4.5 | 0.0 | 0.0 | 0.0 | 0.0 | 0.0 | 0.0 |
| Calgary | 38.5 | 35.9 | -2.6 | 42.7 | 40.5 | -2.2 | 15.4 | 16.3 | 0.9 | 2.8 | 6.5 | 3.7 | 0.7 | 0.7 | 0.0 |
| Red Deer | . | 37.5 | . | . | 37.5 | . | . | 12.5 | . | . | 12.5 | . | . | 0.0 | . |
| Edmonton | 38.5 | 32.3 | -6.2 | 41.2 | 35.5 | -5.7 | 16.0 | 21.5 | 5.5 | 3.2 | 8.1 | 4.9 | 1.1 | 2.7 | 1.6 |
| Kelowna | 20.0 | 53.8 | 33.8 | 76.0 | 34.6 | -41.4 | 0.0 | 11.5 | 11.5 | 4.0 | 0.0 | -4.0 | 0.0 | 0.0 | 0.0 |
| Kamloops | 31.8 | 40.9 | 9.1 | 50.0 | 40.9 | -9.1 | 9.1 | 18.2 | 9.1 | 9.1 | 0.0 | -9.1 | 0.0 | 0.0 | 0.0 |
| Matsqui | . | 55.2 | . | . | 34.5 | . | . | 10.3 | . | . | 0.0 | . | . | 0.0 | . |
| Vancouver | 32.8 | 36.2 | 3.4 | 43.1 | 46.0 | 2.9 | 17.9 | 14.1 | -3.8 | 3.6 | 2.0 | -1.6 | 2.6 | 1.7 | -0.9 |
| Victoria | 42.4 | 60.0 | 17.6 | 42.4 | 32.3 | -10.1 | 13.6 | 6.2 | -7.4 | 0.0 | 1.5 | 1.5 | 1.7 | 0.0 | -1.7 |
| Prince George | 39.1 | 43.5 | 4.4 | 52.2 | 47.8 | -4.4 | 4.3 | 4.3 | 0.0 | 4.3 | 4.3 | 0.0 | 0.0 | 0.0 | 0.0 |

**APPENDIX 2**

**THE POPULATION AND PROPORTION OF CITY'S POPULATION LIVING IN CTS WITH DIFFERENT POVERTY LEVELS, 1986**

| City | Poverty Level of Census Tract | | | | | | | | | |
|---|---|---|---|---|---|---|---|---|---|---|
| | 0-9.99% | | 10-19.99% | | 20-29.99% | | 30-39.99% | | 40% + | |
| | Popu-lation | % of City Popu-lation | Popu-lation | % of City Popu-lation | Popu-lation | % of City Popu-lation | Popu-lation | % of City Popu-lation | Popu-lation | % of City Popu-lation |
| St. John's | 31,130 | 20.0 | 79,825 | 51.4 | 24,310 | 15.6 | 17,870 | 11.5 | 2,310 | 1.5 |
| Halifax | 140,000 | 47.8 | 105,725 | 36.1 | 35,210 | 12.0 | 12,110 | 4.1 | 0 | 0.0 |
| Moncton | 42,290 | 42.1 | 30,605 | 30.4 | 22,355 | 22.2 | 5,285 | 5.3 | 0 | 0.0 |
| Saint John | 30,825 | 25.7 | 46,550 | 38.8 | 23,960 | 20.0 | 13,705 | 11.4 | 4,845 | 4.0 |
| Chicoutimi-Jonquière | 4,630 | 2.9 | 102,720 | 65.3 | 33,980 | 21.6 | 15,865 | 10.1 | 0 | 0.0 |
| Quebec | 163,935 | 27.5 | 263,800 | 44.3 | 111,315 | 18.7 | 36,625 | 6.1 | 20,315 | 3.4 |
| Sherbrooke | 11,025 | 8.6 | 78,860 | 61.7 | 15,375 | 12.0 | 13,530 | 10.6 | 9020 | 7.1 |
| Montreal | 679,175 | 23.5 | 1,127,470 | 39.0 | 637,240 | 22.1 | 275,100 | 9.5 | 168,835 | 5.8 |
| Ottawa-Hull | 447,950 | 55.2 | 220,845 | 27.2 | 102,490 | 12.6 | 33,150 | 4.1 | 6,890 | 0.8 |
| Kingston | 64,530 | 54.5 | 38,710 | 32.7 | 9,530 | 8.1 | 5,590 | 4.7 | 0 | 0.0 |
| Peterborough | 56,005 | 65.2 | 20,425 | 23.8 | 5,160 | 6.0 | 4,250 | 5.0 | 0 | 0.0 |
| Oshawa | 151,355 | 75.1 | 41,010 | 20.4 | 3,960 | 2.0 | 5,150 | 2.6 | 0 | 0.0 |
| Toronto | 2,033,030 | 59.8 | 912,640 | 26.8 | 338,405 | 10.0 | 79,460 | 2.3 | 35,705 | 1.1 |
| Hamilton | 283,425 | 51.4 | 169,635 | 30.8 | 59,110 | 10.7 | 24,985 | 4.5 | 14,395 | 2.6 |
| St. Catharines | 133,370 | 39.3 | 136,420 | 40.2 | 67,640 | 19.9 | 2,055 | 0.6 | 0 | 0.0 |
| Kitchener | 151,770 | 49.2 | 142,865 | 46.3 | 13,660 | 4.4 | 0 | 0.0 | 0 | 0.0 |
| Brantford | 37,375 | 42.0 | 38,290 | 43.0 | 12,165 | 13.7 | 1,165 | 1.3 | 0 | 0.0 |
| Guelph | 57,905 | 68.4 | 22,780 | 26.9 | 4,000 | 4.7 | 0 | 0.0 | 0 | 0.0 |
| London | 159,555 | 47.3 | 130,905 | 38.8 | 31,660 | 9.4 | 15,475 | 4.6 | 0 | 0.0 |
| Windsor | 120,840 | 48.1 | 73,660 | 29.3 | 50,620 | 20.2 | 1,675 | 0.7 | 4,275 | 1.7 |
| Sarnia-Clearwater | 44,225 | 52.0 | 37,370 | 44.0 | 3,405 | 4.0 | 0 | 0.0 | 0 | 0.0 |
| North Bay | 27,920 | 49.4 | 15,835 | 28.0 | 8,660 | 15.3 | 2,780 | 4.9 | 1,280 | 2.3 |
| Sudbury | 33,215 | 22.5 | 97,200 | 65.8 | 10,530 | 7.1 | 6,715 | 4.5 | 0 | 0.0 |
| Sault Ste. Marie | 26,865 | 32.0 | 48,080 | 57.2 | 3,330 | 4.0 | 5,755 | 6.8 | 0 | 0.0 |
| Thunder Bay | 64,610 | 53.6 | 48,865 | 40.5 | 7,090 | 5.9 | 0 | 0.0 | 0 | 0.0 |
| Winnipeg | 257,515 | 41.7 | 230,425 | 37.3 | 48,360 | 7.8 | 45,950 | 7.4 | 35,525 | 5.8 |
| Regina | 84,120 | 45.6 | 53,795 | 29.2 | 36,655 | 19.9 | 8,230 | 4.5 | 1,710 | 0.9 |
| Saskatoon | 42,375 | 21.4 | 115,330 | 58.1 | 23,325 | 11.8 | 15,475 | 7.8 | 1,865 | 0.9 |
| Lethbridge | 13,625 | 23.5 | 36,150 | 62.3 | 8,280 | 14.3 | 0 | 0.0 | 0 | 0.0 |
| Calgary | 259,735 | 39.0 | 290,720 | 43.7 | 96,895 | 14.6 | 15,455 | 2.3 | 3,000 | 0.5 |
| Edmonton | 289,895 | 37.3 | 322,640 | 41.5 | 125,860 | 16.2 | 28,480 | 3.7 | 10,930 | 1.4 |
| Kelowna | 17,370 | 19.6 | 67,170 | 75.6 | 0 | 0.0 | 4,280 | 4.8 | 0 | 0.0 |
| Kamloops | 11,575 | 19.0 | 39,245 | 64.3 | 3,540 | 5.8 | 6,665 | 10.9 | 0 | 0.0 |
| Vancouver | 412,555 | 30.3 | 607,925 | 44.6 | 261,725 | 19.2 | 40,315 | 3.0 | 39,920 | 2.9 |
| Victoria | 95,020 | 37.9 | 119,140 | 47.5 | 33,520 | 13.4 | 0 | 0.0 | 3,190 | 1.3 |
| Prince George | 20,030 | 29.8 | 37,755 | 56.1 | 4605 | 6.8 | 4,905 | 7.3 | 0 | 0.0 |
| **Average** | | **39.1** | | **43.0** | | **12.0** | | **4.6** | | **1.2** |

APPENDIX 2 (concluded)

THE PROPORTION OF CITY'S POPULATION LIVING IN CTS WITH DIFFERENT POVERTY LEVELS, **1986**

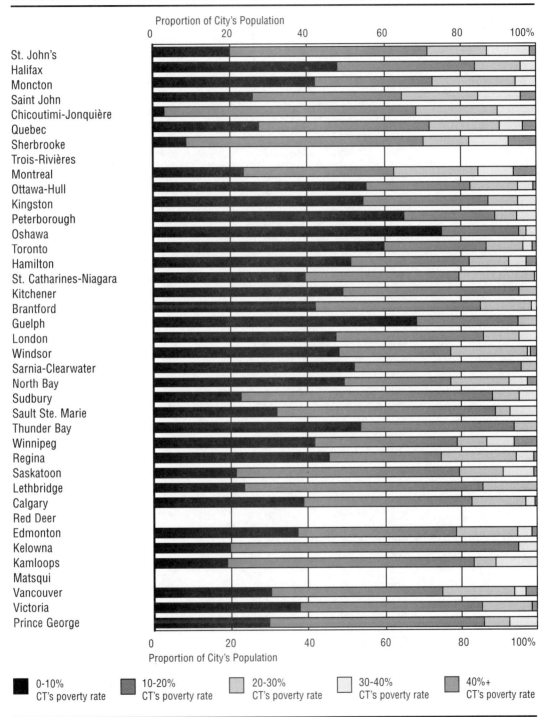

**APPENDIX 3**

**THE POPULATION AND PROPORTION OF CITY'S POPULATION LIVING IN CTS WITH DIFFERENT POVERTY LEVELS, 1991**

| | Poverty Rate of Census Tracts | | | | | | | | | |
|---|---|---|---|---|---|---|---|---|---|---|
| | 0-9.99% | | 10-19.99% | | 20-29.99% | | 30-39.99% | | 40% + | |
| City | Popu-lation | % of City Popu-lation | Popu-lation | % of City Popu-lation | Popu-lation | % of City Popu-lation | Popu-lation | % of City Popu-lation | Popu-lation | % of City Popu-lation |
| St. John's | 69,580 | 37.5 | 66,780 | 40.0 | 12,890 | 10.0 | 20,525 | 12.5 | 0 | 0.0 |
| Halifax | 175520 | 54.7 | 96,985 | 30.7 | 3,7650 | 12.0 | 1,865 | 1.3 | 5,560 | 1.3 |
| Moncton | 51,435 | 43.5 | 26,950 | 30.4 | 26,940 | 26.1 | 0 | 0.0 | 0 | 0.0 |
| Saint John | 53,605 | 27.9 | 39,835 | 34.9 | 18,355 | 23.3 | 6,325 | 7.0 | 5,440 | 7.0 |
| Chicoutimi-Jonquière | 50,000 | 28.6 | 74,850 | 45.7 | 24,725 | 17.1 | 9,980 | 8.6 | 0 | 0.0 |
| Quebec | 218,985 | 31.1 | 262,270 | 37.1 | 99,200 | 16.6 | 29,955 | 7.9 | 24,960 | 7.3 |
| Sherbrooke | 45,475 | 25.8 | 51,935 | 32.3 | 17,480 | 19.4 | 12,890 | 12.9 | 8,900 | 9.7 |
| Trois-Rivières | 13,900 | 11.8 | 86,380 | 55.9 | 19,305 | 14.7 | 8,715 | 8.8 | 6,565 | 8.8 |
| Montreal | 761,115 | 20.9 | 1,128,790 | 31.3 | 695,685 | 25.5 | 287,545 | 12.1 | 216,350 | 10.2 |
| Ottawa-Hull | 513,700 | 54.8 | 238,710 | 26.0 | 105,740 | 12.0 | 41,910 | 4.8 | 11,850 | 2.4 |
| Kingston | 88,010 | 64.7 | 29,250 | 23.5 | 8,270 | 8.8 | 6,395 | 2.9 | 0 | 0.0 |
| Peterborough | 55,255 | 56.5 | 34,725 | 34.8 | 2,490 | 4.3 | 4,085 | 4.3 | 0 | 0.0 |
| Oshawa | 174,155 | 69.4 | 46,840 | 20.4 | 17,000 | 10.2 | 0 | 0.0 | 0 | 0.0 |
| Toronto | 1,880,730 | 50.5 | 1,199,065 | 30.5 | 579,925 | 14.3 | 144,365 | 3.6 | 53,225 | 1.1 |
| Hamilton | 282,340 | 45.1 | 198,220 | 35.2 | 71,200 | 12.3 | 31,950 | 4.9 | 9,995 | 2.5 |
| St. Catharines-Niagara | 188,300 | 50.6 | 150,670 | 41.0 | 20950 | 8.4 | 0 | 0.0 | 0 | 0.0 |
| Kitchener | 187,670 | 51.9 | 151,615 | 43.2 | 13760 | 4.9 | 0 | 0.0 | 0 | 0.0 |
| Brantford | 46,855 | 52.4 | 41,340 | 38.1 | 7280 | 9.5 | 0 | 0.0 | 0 | 0.0 |
| Guelph | 74,420 | 71.4 | 17,690 | 19.0 | 4,040 | 9.5 | 0 | 0.0 | 0 | 0.0 |
| London | 173,330 | 44.3 | 177,085 | 46.6 | 23,345 | 8.0 | 2,920 | 1.1 | 0 | 0.0 |
| Windsor | 130,175 | 44.1 | 69,455 | 30.5 | 39,990 | 18.6 | 19,620 | 6.8 | 0 | 0.0 |
| Sarnia-Clearwater | 52,100 | 62.5 | 31,200 | 29.2 | 3,130 | 4.2 | 655 | 4.2 | 0 | 0.0 |
| North Bay | 29,830 | 45.0 | 23,760 | 30.0 | 7,090 | 15.0 | 1,620 | 10.0 | 0 | 0.0 |
| Sudbury | 67,300 | 43.2 | 73,600 | 45.9 | 7,950 | 5.4 | 7,240 | 5.4 | 0 | 0.0 |
| Sault Ste. Marie | 29,770 | 40.9 | 44,160 | 40.9 | 7,495 | 13.6 | 2,695 | 4.5 | 0 | 0.0 |
| Thunder Bay | 68,805 | 53.3 | 48,680 | 40.0 | 4,250 | 3.3 | 1,075 | 3.3 | 0 | 0.0 |
| Winnipeg | 21,8520 | 32.3 | 237,225 | 34.8 | 97,800 | 16.8 | 38,020 | 5.8 | 53,950 | 10.3 |
| Regina | 74,725 | 38.8 | 72,740 | 38.8 | 28,675 | 14.3 | 7,425 | 6.1 | 5,850 | 2.0 |
| Saskatoon | 64,160 | 33.3 | 91,795 | 41.7 | 40,330 | 16.7 | 9,865 | 6.3 | 1,625 | 2.1 |
| Lethbridge | 18,765 | 45.0 | 36,830 | 50.0 | 4,545 | 5.0 | 0 | 0.0 | 0 | 0.0 |
| Calgary | 266,685 | 35.9 | 312,250 | 40.5 | 116,410 | 16.3 | 49,370 | 6.5 | 3,390 | 0.7 |
| Red Deer | 18,900 | 37.5 | 23,280 | 37.5 | 9,075 | 12.5 | 5,415 | 12.5 | 0 | 0.0 |
| Edmonton | 290,165 | 32.3 | 278,405 | 35.5 | 172,175 | 21.5 | 69,000 | 8.1 | 22,215 | 2.7 |
| Kelowna | 63,670 | 53.8 | 37,430 | 34.6 | 9,610 | 11.5 | 0 | 0.0 | 0 | 0.0 |
| Kamloops | 22,060 | 40.9 | 33,820 | 40.9 | 11,235 | 18.2 | 0 | 0.0 | 0 | 0.0 |
| Matsqui | 54,125 | 55.2 | 48,415 | 34.5 | 8,815 | 10.3 | 0 | 0.0 | 0 | 0.0 |
| Vancouver | 547,145 | 36.2 | 739,040 | 46.0 | 229,970 | 14.1 | 38,105 | 2.0 | 29,615 | 1.7 |
| Victoria | 164,110 | 60.0 | 100,475 | 32.3 | 15,145 | 6.2 | 3,885 | 1.5 | 0 | 0.0 |
| Prince George | 24,485 | 43.5 | 39,640 | 47.8 | 4,915 | 4.3 | 265 | 4.3 | 0 | 0.0 |
| Average | | 44.3 | | 36.6 | | 12.7 | | 4.6 | | 1.8 |

APPENDIX **3** (concluded)

## THE PROPORTION OF CITY'S POPULATION LIVING IN CTS WITH DIFFERENT POVERTY LEVELS, **1991**

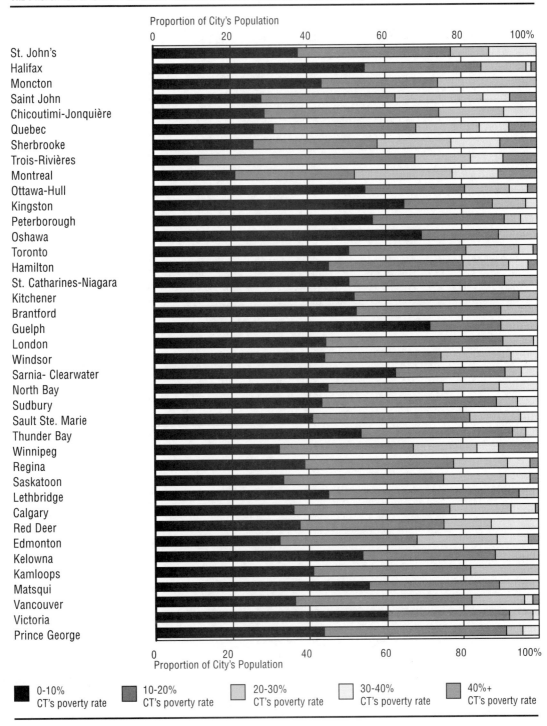

Proportion of City's Population

| | 0-10% CT's poverty rate | 10-20% CT's poverty rate | 20-30% CT's poverty rate | 30-40% CT's poverty rate | 40%+ CT's poverty rate |

**APPENDIX 4**

## THE CHANGES IN PROPORTION OF CITY'S POPULATION LIVING IN CTS WITH DIFFERENT POVERTY LEVELS, 1986-1991

| | Poverty Rate of Census Tracts | | | | | | | | | | Changes 1986-1991 | | | | |
| | 0-9.99% | | 10-19.99% | | 20-29.99% | | 30-39.99% | | 40% + | | Percent | | | | |
| | 1986 | 1991 | 1986 | 1991 | 1986 | 1991 | 1986 | 1991 | 1986 | 1991 | 0-9.99 | 10-19.99 | 20-29.99 | 30-39.99 | 40 + |
|---|---|---|---|---|---|---|---|---|---|---|---|---|---|---|---|
| St. John's | 20.0 | 37.5 | 51.4 | 40.0 | 15.6 | 10.0 | 11.5 | 12.5 | 1.5 | 0.0 | 17.5 | -11.4 | -5.6 | 1.0 | -1.5 |
| Halifax | 47.8 | 54.7 | 36.1 | 30.7 | 12.0 | 12.0 | 4.1 | 1.3 | 0.0 | 1.3 | 6.9 | -5.4 | 0.0 | -2.8 | 1.3 |
| Moncton | 42.1 | 43.5 | 30.4 | 30.4 | 22.2 | 26.1 | 5.3 | 0.0 | 0.0 | 0.0 | 1.4 | 0.0 | 3.9 | -5.3 | 0.0 |
| Saint John | 25.7 | 27.9 | 38.8 | 34.9 | 20.0 | 23.3 | 11.4 | 7.0 | 4.0 | 7.0 | 2.2 | -3.9 | 3.3 | -4.4 | 3.0 |
| Chicoutimi-Jonquière | 2.9 | 28.6 | 65.3 | 45.7 | 21.6 | 17.1 | 10.1 | 8.6 | 0.0 | 0.0 | 25.7 | -19.6 | -4.5 | -1.5 | 0.0 |
| Quebec | 27.5 | 31.1 | 44.3 | 37.1 | 18.7 | 16.6 | 6.1 | 7.9 | 3.4 | 7.3 | 3.6 | -7.2 | -2.1 | 1.8 | 3.9 |
| Sherbrooke | 8.6 | 25.8 | 61.7 | 32.3 | 12.0 | 19.4 | 10.6 | 12.9 | 7.1 | 9.7 | 17.2 | -29.4 | 7.4 | 2.3 | 2.6 |
| Trois-Rivières | | 11.8 | | 55.9 | | 14.7 | | 8.8 | | 8.8 | – | – | – | – | – |
| Montreal | 23.5 | 20.9 | 39.0 | 31.3 | 22.1 | 25.5 | 9.5 | 12.1 | 5.8 | 10.2 | -2.6 | -7.7 | 3.4 | 2.6 | 4.4 |
| Ottawa-Hull | 55.2 | 54.8 | 27.2 | 26.0 | 12.6 | 12.0 | 4.1 | 4.8 | 0.8 | 2.4 | -0.4 | -1.2 | -0.6 | 0.7 | 1.6 |
| Kingston | 54.5 | 64.7 | 32.7 | 23.5 | 8.1 | 8.8 | 4.7 | 2.9 | 0.0 | 0.0 | 10.2 | -9.2 | 0.7 | -1.8 | 0.0 |
| Peterborough | 65.2 | 56.5 | 23.8 | 34.8 | 6.0 | 4.3 | 5.0 | 4.3 | 0.0 | 0.0 | -8.7 | 11.0 | -1.7 | -0.7 | 0.0 |
| Oshawa | 75.1 | 69.4 | 20.4 | 20.4 | 2.0 | 10.2 | 2.6 | 0.0 | 0.0 | 0.0 | -5.7 | 0.0 | 8.2 | -2.6 | 0.0 |
| Toronto | 59.8 | 50.5 | 26.8 | 30.5 | 10.0 | 14.3 | 2.3 | 3.6 | 1.1 | 1.1 | -9.3 | 3.7 | 4.3 | 1.3 | 0.0 |
| Hamilton | 51.4 | 45.1 | 30.8 | 35.2 | 10.7 | 12.3 | 4.5 | 4.9 | 2.6 | 2.5 | -6.3 | 4.4 | 1.6 | 0.4 | -0.1 |
| St. Catharines-Niagara | 39.3 | 50.6 | 40.2 | 41.0 | 19.9 | 8.4 | 0.6 | 0.0 | 0.0 | 0.0 | 11.3 | 0.8 | -11.5 | -0.6 | 0.0 |
| Kitchener | 49.2 | 51.9 | 46.3 | 43.2 | 4.4 | 4.9 | 0.0 | 0.0 | 0.0 | 0.0 | 2.7 | -3.1 | 0.5 | 0.0 | 0.0 |
| Brantford | 42.0 | 52.4 | 43.0 | 38.1 | 13.7 | 9.5 | 1.3 | 0.0 | 0.0 | 0.0 | 10.4 | -4.9 | -4.2 | -1.3 | 0.0 |
| Guelph | 68.4 | 71.4 | 26.9 | 19.0 | 4.7 | 9.5 | 0.0 | 0.0 | 0.0 | 0.0 | 3.0 | -7.9 | 4.8 | 0.0 | 0.0 |
| London | 47.3 | 44.3 | 38.8 | 46.6 | 9.4 | 8.0 | 4.6 | 1.1 | 0.0 | 0.0 | -3.0 | 7.8 | -1.4 | -3.5 | 0.0 |
| Windsor | 48.1 | 44.1 | 29.3 | 30.5 | 20.2 | 18.6 | 0.7 | 6.8 | 1.7 | 0.0 | -4.0 | 1.2 | -1.6 | 6.1 | -1.7 |
| Sarnia-Clearwater | 52.0 | 62.5 | 44.0 | 29.2 | 4.0 | 4.2 | 0.0 | 4.2 | 0.0 | 0.0 | 10.5 | -14.8 | 0.2 | 4.2 | 0.0 |
| North Bay | 49.4 | 45.0 | 28.0 | 30.0 | 15.3 | 15.0 | 4.9 | 10.0 | 2.3 | 0.0 | -4.4 | 2.0 | -0.3 | 5.1 | -2.3 |
| Sudbury | 22.5 | 43.2 | 65.8 | 45.9 | 7.1 | 5.4 | 4.5 | 5.4 | 0.0 | 0.0 | 20.7 | -19.9 | -1.7 | 0.9 | 0.0 |
| Sault Ste. Marie | 32.0 | 40.9 | 57.2 | 40.9 | 4.0 | 13.6 | 6.8 | 4.5 | 0.0 | 0.0 | 8.9 | -16.3 | 9.6 | -2.3 | 0.0 |
| Thunder Bay | 53.6 | 53.3 | 40.5 | 40.0 | 5.9 | 3.3 | 0.0 | 3.3 | 0.0 | 0.0 | -0.3 | -0.5 | -2.6 | 3.3 | 0.0 |
| Winnipeg | 41.7 | 32.3 | 37.3 | 34.8 | 7.8 | 16.8 | 7.4 | 5.8 | 5.8 | 10.3 | -9.4 | -2.5 | 9.0 | -1.6 | 4.5 |
| Regina | 45.6 | 38.8 | 29.2 | 38.8 | 19.9 | 14.3 | 4.5 | 6.1 | 0.9 | 2.0 | -6.8 | 9.6 | -5.6 | 1.6 | 1.1 |
| Saskatoon | 21.4 | 33.3 | 58.1 | 41.7 | 11.8 | 16.7 | 7.8 | 6.3 | 0.9 | 2.1 | 11.9 | -16.4 | 4.9 | -1.5 | 1.2 |
| Lethbridge | 23.5 | 45.0 | 62.3 | 50.0 | 14.3 | 5.0 | 0.0 | 0.0 | 0.0 | 0.0 | 21.5 | -12.3 | -9.3 | 0.0 | 0.0 |
| Calgary | 39.0 | 35.9 | 43.7 | 40.5 | 14.6 | 16.3 | 2.3 | 6.5 | 0.5 | 0.7 | -3.1 | -3.2 | 1.7 | 4.2 | 0.2 |
| Red Deer | | 37.5 | | 37.5 | | 12.5 | | 12.5 | | 0.0 | – | – | – | – | – |
| Edmonton | 37.3 | 32.3 | 41.5 | 35.5 | 16.2 | 21.5 | 3.7 | 8.1 | 1.4 | 2.7 | -5.0 | -6.0 | 5.3 | 4.4 | 1.3 |
| Kelowna | 19.6 | 53.8 | 75.6 | 34.6 | 0.0 | 11.5 | 4.8 | 0.0 | 0.0 | 0.0 | 34.2 | -41.0 | 11.5 | -4.8 | 0.0 |
| Kamloops | 19.0 | 40.9 | 64.3 | 40.9 | 5.8 | 18.2 | 10.9 | 0.0 | 0.0 | 0.0 | 21.9 | -23.4 | 12.4 | -10.9 | 0.0 |
| Matsqui | | 55.2 | | 34.5 | | 10.3 | | 0.0 | | 0.0 | – | – | – | – | – |
| Vancouver | 30.3 | 36.2 | 44.6 | 46.0 | 19.2 | 14.1 | 3.0 | 2.0 | 2.9 | 1.7 | 5.9 | 1.4 | -5.1 | -1.0 | -1.2 |
| Victoria | 37.9 | 60.0 | 47.5 | 32.3 | 13.4 | 6.2 | 0.0 | 1.5 | 1.3 | 0.0 | 22.1 | -15.2 | -7.2 | 1.5 | -1.3 |
| Prince George | 29.8 | 43.5 | 56.1 | 47.8 | 6.8 | 4.3 | 7.3 | 4.3 | 0.0 | 0.0 | 13.7 | -8.3 | -2.5 | -3.0 | 0.0 |
| **Average** | **39.1** | **44.3** | **43.0** | **36.6** | **12.0** | **12.7** | **4.6** | **4.6** | **1.2** | **1.8** | **5.2** | **-6.4** | **0.7** | **0.0** | **0.6** |

**APPENDIX 5**

## THE AVERAGE YEARS OF EDUCATION FOR TWO GENERATIONS, ETHNIC GROUP BY CITY, 1991

| Ethnic Groups | Halifax | Quebec | Montreal | Sherbrooke and Trois-Rivières | Ottawa-Hull | Oshawa | Toronto | Hamilton | St. Catharines-Niagara | Kitchener | London | Windsor | Sudbury and Thunder Bay | Winnipeg | Regina | Edmonton | Calgary | Vancouver | Victoria |
|---|---|---|---|---|---|---|---|---|---|---|---|---|---|---|---|---|---|---|---|
| **1. British** | | | | | | | | | | | | | | | | | | | |
| Younger Generation (1-35 Years Old) | 7.268 | 7.972 | 7.401 | 7.691 | 7.701 | 7.156 | 7.547 | 7.303 | 7.175 | 7.219 | 7.379 | 7.334 | 7.115 | 7.037 | 7.183 | 7.417 | 7.108 | 7.381 | 7.198 |
| Older Generation (35+ Years Old) | 6.567 | 6.551 | 6.335 | 6.616 | 7.335 | 6.489 | 6.976 | 6.505 | 6.425 | 6.553 | 6.649 | 6.425 | 6.320 | 6.531 | 6.673 | 7.206 | 6.866 | 7.120 | 7.220 |
| **2. French origins** | | | | | | | | | | | | | | | | | | | |
| Younger Generation (1-35 Years Old) | 7.427 | 7.633 | 7.410 | 7.427 | 7.401 | 7.154 | 7.693 | 7.074 | 7.022 | 7.241 | 7.384 | 7.359 | 7.167 | 7.196 | 7.636 | 7.237 | 7.302 | 7.289 | 7.662 |
| Older Generation (35+ Years Old) | 6.174 | 6.340 | 6.027 | 5.935 | 6.281 | 5.610 | 6.601 | 5.960 | 5.126 | 5.459 | 6.446 | 5.833 | 5.324 | 5.931 | 6.199 | 6.649 | 6.288 | 6.456 | 7.261 |
| **3. Dutch (Netherlands)** | | | | | | | | | | | | | | | | | | | |
| Younger Generation (1-35 Years Old) | | | 7.500 | 6.600 | 8.156 | 7.736 | 8.119 | 7.595 | 7.810 | 7.812 | 7.800 | 8.286 | 7.333 | 7.244 | 7.143 | 7.820 | 7.543 | 7.222 | 7.735 |
| Older Generation (35+ Years Old) | | 6.667 | 7.544 | 7.000 | 7.881 | 6.379 | 7.130 | 6.498 | 5.840 | 7.398 | 6.531 | 7.103 | 6.429 | 6.137 | 6.216 | 7.326 | 6.661 | 6.685 | 7.303 |
| **4. German** | | | | | | | | | | | | | | | | | | | |
| Younger Generation (1-35 Years Old) | 7.667 | 6.667 | 7.786 | 8.143 | 8.377 | 8.256 | 8.269 | 7.862 | 7.574 | 7.315 | 7.694 | 7.809 | 7.527 | 7.309 | 7.174 | 7.659 | 7.501 | 7.674 | 7.364 |
| Older Generation (35+ Years Old) | 6.186 | 6.039 | 6.595 | 5.909 | 7.214 | 6.889 | 7.303 | 6.561 | 6.045 | 5.963 | 6.616 | 5.889 | 6.636 | 6.025 | 5.774 | 6.735 | 6.343 | 6.813 | 6.930 |
| **5. Other Western European Origin** | | | | | | | | | | | | | | | | | | | |
| Younger Generation (1-35 Years Old) | 8.333 | 8.047 | 7.750 | 8.250 | 8.250 | 6.500 | 8.254 | 8.100 | 8.000 | 6.200 | 7.600 | 7.667 | 7.667 | 7.852 | 7.286 | 7.895 | 8.727 | 7.769 | 8.000 |
| Older Generation (35+ Years Old) | 8.000 | 8.000 | 7.068 | 8.000 | 7.444 | 6.286 | 7.677 | 7.537 | 7.350 | 4.316 | 6.046 | 5.929 | 5.625 | 5.623 | 5.814 | 7.000 | 6.649 | 7.456 | 7.222 |
| **6. Hungarian (Magyar)** | | | | | | | | | | | | | | | | | | | |
| Younger Generation (1-35 Years Old) | | 8.500 | 7.675 | 9.000 | 8.440 | 7.714 | 8.081 | 7.839 | 7.148 | 7.400 | 7.955 | 7.571 | 7.889 | 7.292 | 6.750 | 7.574 | 7.750 | 7.667 | 8.000 |
| Older Generation (35+ Years Old) | | 8.667 | 6.897 | 5.333 | 8.333 | 6.714 | 7.357 | 6.087 | 6.114 | 7.108 | 6.727 | 6.233 | 7.059 | 6.057 | 5.449 | 6.739 | 6.322 | 6.729 | 7.000 |

**APPENDIX 5** (continued)

**THE AVERAGE YEARS OF EDUCATION FOR TWO GENERATIONS, ETHNIC GROUP BY CITY, 1991**

| Ethnic Groups | Halifax | Quebec | Mon-treal | Sher-brooke and Trois-Rivières | Ottawa-Hull | Oshawa | Toronto | Hamilton | St. Cath-arines-Niagara | Kitchener | London | Windsor | Sudbury and Thunder Bay | Winnipeg | Regina | Edmonton | Calgary | Vancouver | Victoria |
|---|---|---|---|---|---|---|---|---|---|---|---|---|---|---|---|---|---|---|---|
| **7. Polish** | | | | | | | | | | | | | | | | | | | |
| Younger Generation (1-35 Years Old) | | 8.143 | 7.522 | 9.000 | 8.269 | 7.833 | 7.956 | 7.886 | 7.346 | 7.389 | 7.597 | 8.375 | 7.786 | 7.496 | 7.688 | 8.000 | 7.900 | 7.800 | 8.182 |
| Older Generation (35+ Years Old) | | 8.375 | 6.527 | 7.000 | 7.630 | 6.225 | 7.009 | 6.341 | 5.838 | 6.463 | 6.745 | 6.700 | 5.161 | 5.811 | 5.976 | 6.657 | 6.490 | 6.828 | 6.821 |
| **8. Ukrainian** | | | | | | | | | | | | | | | | | | | |
| Younger Generation (1-35 Years Old) | | 7.667 | 7.836 | | 8.241 | 7.632 | 8.154 | 7.800 | 7.650 | 8.214 | 8.191 | 7.714 | 7.444 | 7.427 | 7.290 | 7.644 | 7.599 | 7.495 | 7.136 |
| Older Generation (35+ Years Old) | | 9.000 | 5.515 | | 7.515 | 5.692 | 6.418 | 5.821 | 5.812 | 6.256 | 6.333 | 5.977 | 5.646 | 5.759 | 6.218 | 6.705 | 6.182 | 6.416 | 6.458 |
| **9. Balkan origins:** Albanian; Bulgar, Croatian; Macedonian; Serb | | | | | | | | | | | | | | | | | | | |
| Younger Generation (1-35 Years Old) | | 9.000 | 7.611 | | 7.500 | 8.000 | 7.724 | 7.672 | 7.737 | 7.324 | 7.786 | 7.552 | 7.412 | 7.304 | 6.583 | 7.455 | 7.595 | 7.817 | 8.333 |
| Older Generation (35+ Years Old) | | 8.500 | 6.557 | 9.000 | 6.069 | 6.321 | 6.119 | 5.381 | 5.722 | 4.852 | 5.605 | 5.634 | 5.861 | 5.324 | 4.500 | 6.523 | 6.455 | 6.309 | 7.177 |
| **10. Greek** | | | | | | | | | | | | | | | | | | | |
| Younger Generation (1-35 Years Old) | | 8.250 | 7.306 | | 7.917 | 8.273 | 7.469 | 7.345 | 8.250 | 7.111 | 7.800 | 7.792 | 7.750 | 6.966 | 8.077 | 7.095 | 7.091 | 7.609 | 7.375 |
| Older Generation (35+ Years Old) | | 6.429 | 4.506 | 6.000 | 6.140 | 4.667 | 4.899 | 4.704 | 5.188 | 4.676 | 4.920 | 5.095 | 4.909 | 4.517 | 4.250 | 6.350 | 5.762 | 5.400 | 6.200 |
| **11. Italian** | | | | | | | | | | | | | | | | | | | |
| Younger Generation (1-35 Years Old) | | 8.611 | 7.550 | 7.000 | 8.124 | 7.939 | 7.670 | 7.868 | 7.745 | 7.640 | 7.932 | 7.989 | 7.786 | 7.544 | 7.727 | 7.766 | 7.642 | 7.687 | 7.667 |
| Older Generation (35+ Years Old) | | 6.875 | 4.299 | 7.154 | 5.314 | 5.038 | 4.528 | 4.750 | 4.952 | 4.931 | 5.319 | 4.946 | 4.936 | 4.849 | 7.143 | 5.487 | 5.151 | 5.237 | 5.177 |

# Appendix 5 (continued)

## The Average Years of Education for Two Generations, Ethnic Group by City, 1991

| Ethnic Groups | Halifax | Quebec | Mon-treal | Sher-brooke and Trois-Rivières | Ottawa-Hull | Oshawa | Toronto | Hamilton | St. Cath-arines-Niagara | Kitchener | London | Windsor | Sudbury and Thunder Bay | Winn-ipeg | Regina | Edmonton | Calgary | Vancouver | Victoria |
|---|---|---|---|---|---|---|---|---|---|---|---|---|---|---|---|---|---|---|---|
| **12. Portuguese** | | | | | | | | | | | | | | | | | | | |
| Younger Generation (1-35 Years Old) | | 7.167 | 5.884 | 9.000 | 6.960 | 6.636 | 6.225 | 6.204 | 8.000 | 6.186 | 6.726 | 5.889 | 7.188 | 5.989 | 5.400 | 6.350 | 6.463 | 7.160 | 6.833 |
| Older Generation (35+ Years Old) | | 6.250 | 3.820 | 4.857 | 4.118 | 5.000 | 3.783 | 3.467 | 8.000 | 3.704 | 3.969 | 4.786 | 4.615 | 3.784 | 3.125 | 6.350 | 3.684 | 4.641 | 5.000 |
| **13. Spanish** | | | | | | | | | | | | | | | | | | | |
| Younger Generation (1-35 Years Old) | | 8.083 | 6.854 | 9.000 | 7.857 | 7.000 | 7.164 | 6.862 | 5.727 | 7.429 | 6.600 | 7.546 | 7.000 | 6.577 | 7.000 | 6.813 | 6.806 | 6.878 | 7.833 |
| Older Generation (35+ Years Old) | | 7.417 | 6.158 | 5.400 | 6.259 | 7.000 | 6.575 | 5.600 | | 6.000 | 7.800 | 6.588 | 4.500 | 7.235 | 7.833 | 6.529 | 7.417 | 7.264 | 6.286 |
| **14. Jewish** | | | | | | | | | | | | | | | | | | | |
| Younger Generation (1-35 Years Old) | | | 8.074 | 9.000 | 7.930 | | 8.241 | 9.000 | 9.000 | 8.250 | 9.000 | 7.800 | 6.667 | 7.870 | 8.000 | 8.467 | 7.500 | 8.189 | 8.000 |
| Older Generation (35+ Years Old) | | 6.000 | 6.943 | 5.500 | 8.368 | 7.333 | 7.790 | 7.552 | 8.333 | 9.111 | 7.615 | 7.786 | 9.000 | 7.377 | 8.214 | 8.286 | 8.129 | 8.402 | 7.929 |
| **15. Other European origins** | | | | | | | | | | | | | | | | | | | |
| Younger Generation (1-35 Years Old) | | 7.778 | 8.421 | 5.667 | 8.377 | 7.200 | 7.967 | 7.761 | 7.840 | 7.354 | 7.500 | 7.372 | 7.219 | 7.471 | 7.297 | 7.745 | 7.859 | 7.646 | 7.583 |
| Older Generation (35+ Years Old) | | 8.286 | 7.323 | 8.667 | 8.236 | 6.172 | 7.170 | 6.694 | 6.086 | 6.695 | 7.183 | 5.981 | 5.471 | 6.429 | 6.292 | 6.862 | 6.771 | 6.755 | 7.159 |
| **16. Arab origins** | | | | | | | | | | | | | | | | | | | |
| Younger Generation (1-35 Years Old) | | 8.133 | 7.939 | 9.500 | 7.808 | 8.455 | 7.896 | 7.120 | 7.600 | 8.071 | 7.250 | 7.373 | 7.500 | 6.800 | | 5.794 | 6.421 | 7.824 | 9.000 |
| Older Generation (35+ Years Old) | | 8.063 | 7.255 | 7.500 | 6.061 | 6.667 | 7.127 | 6.129 | 6.700 | 8.000 | 5.621 | 6.220 | 9.000 | 5.769 | 7.250 | 5.707 | 5.405 | 6.886 | 7.200 |
| **17. West Asian origins** | | | | | | | | | | | | | | | | | | | |
| Younger Generation (1-35 Years Old) | | 5.000 | 7.601 | 7.000 | 8.067 | 8.000 | 7.651 | 7.313 | 7.818 | 7.846 | 6.333 | 7.286 | 7.500 | 8.357 | 8.600 | 7.571 | 7.563 | 7.663 | 8.667 |
| Older Generation (35+ Years Old) | | 8.250 | 6.486 | 9.500 | 7.375 | 7.800 | 7.343 | 6.429 | 5.546 | 5.667 | 5.600 | 7.692 | 2.000 | 8.167 | 6.500 | 8.667 | 8.375 | 7.705 | 9.000 |

**APPENDIX 5** (continued)

**THE AVERAGE YEARS OF EDUCATION FOR TWO GENERATIONS, ETHNIC GROUP BY CITY, 1991**

| Ethnic Groups | Halifax | Quebec | Montreal | Sherbrooke and Trois-Rivières | Ottawa-Hull | Oshawa | Toronto | Hamilton | St. Catharines-Niagara | Kitchener | London | Windsor | Sudbury and Thunder Bay | Winnipeg | Regina | Edmonton | Calgary | Vancouver | Victoria |
|---|---|---|---|---|---|---|---|---|---|---|---|---|---|---|---|---|---|---|---|
| **18. South Asian origins** | | | | | | | | | | | | | | | | | | | |
| Younger Generation (1-35 Years Old) | | 7.000 | 7.124 | 10.000 | 8.297 | 8.083 | 7.437 | 7.406 | 7.546 | 7.825 | 8.919 | 8.174 | 5.000 | 7.598 | 8.300 | 7.421 | 7.254 | 7.137 | 7.231 |
| Older Generation (35+ Years Old) | | 9.000 | 7.175 | 10.000 | 7.939 | 7.258 | 7.097 | 7.036 | 7.417 | 7.171 | 8.171 | 6.773 | 8.231 | 6.816 | 8.276 | 7.212 | 6.540 | 5.508 | 5.946 |
| **19. Chinese** | | | | | | | | | | | | | | | | | | | |
| Younger Generation (1-35 Years Old) | | 7.000 | 7.369 | 9.000 | 8.077 | 7.783 | 7.821 | 8.211 | 7.118 | 7.769 | 8.667 | 7.581 | 8.429 | 7.610 | 8.052 | 7.223 | 7.434 | 7.675 | 7.656 |
| Older Generation (35+ Years Old) | | 7.273 | 5.919 | 4.500 | 6.858 | 6.677 | 6.647 | 6.243 | 7.000 | 7.233 | 7.167 | 5.719 | 5.000 | 5.257 | 6.282 | 5.998 | 6.000 | 6.561 | 6.010 |
| **20. Filipino** | | | | | | | | | | | | | | | | | | | |
| Younger Generation (1-35 Years Old) | | 9.000 | 7.587 | | 7.435 | 9.000 | 7.866 | 8.160 | 7.100 | 7.250 | 7.333 | 7.357 | 7.500 | 6.867 | 7.357 | 7.687 | 7.900 | 7.759 | 7.615 |
| Older Generation (35+ Years Old) | | | 7.348 | | 7.767 | 8.000 | 7.977 | 7.921 | 8.000 | 8.750 | 6.600 | 8.350 | 10.000 | 6.269 | 7.400 | 7.884 | 7.678 | 7.952 | 6.917 |
| **21. Vietnamese** | | | | | | | | | | | | | | | | | | | |
| Younger Generation (1-35 Years Old) | | 7.700 | 7.303 | 8.500 | 7.583 | | 6.293 | 5.211 | 7.000 | 6.000 | 5.167 | 6.364 | 6.500 | 6.191 | 6.941 | 5.535 | 5.864 | 5.634 | 6.750 |
| Older Generation (35+ Years Old) | | 7.917 | 7.142 | 7.600 | 7.000 | | 5.962 | 5.667 | 7.000 | 4.000 | 5.000 | 7.400 | 9.500 | 6.222 | 4.429 | 6.085 | 5.630 | 5.224 | 6.000 |
| **22. Other East and South East Asian origins** | | | | | | | | | | | | | | | | | | | |
| Younger Generation (1-35 Years Old) | | 7.286 | 6.288 | 10.000 | 7.000 | 6.125 | 7.727 | 6.846 | 6.500 | 6.769 | 7.091 | 6.250 | 8.000 | 6.861 | 6.273 | 7.386 | 7.439 | 7.832 | 8.429 |
| Older Generation (35+ Years Old) | | 5.250 | 6.231 | 1.667 | 6.556 | 7.000 | 7.505 | 6.667 | 6.714 | 4.476 | 6.968 | 5.600 | 9.000 | 7.146 | 6.667 | 7.306 | 7.393 | 7.439 | 8.158 |
| **23. Latin, Central and South American origins** | | | | | | | | | | | | | | | | | | | |
| Younger Generation (1-35 Years Old) | | 6.769 | 6.951 | 5.000 | 7.032 | 7.400 | 7.144 | 6.875 | 4.500 | 6.310 | 6.611 | 6.200 | 10.000 | 6.867 | 6.313 | 6.688 | 6.800 | 6.976 | 5.667 |
| Older Generation (35+ Years Old) | | 8.231 | 6.665 | 7.000 | 6.931 | 9.500 | 6.959 | 7.462 | 10.000 | 7.500 | 6.333 | 7.250 | 8.000 | 6.920 | 6.000 | 7.405 | 8.000 | 7.702 | 7.400 |

# Appendix 5 (concluded)

## The Average Years of Education for Two Generations, Ethnic Group by City, 1991

| Ethnic Groups | Halifax | Quebec | Montreal | Sherbrooke and Trois-Rivières | Ottawa-Hull | Oshawa | Toronto | Hamilton | St. Catharines-Niagara | Kitchener | London | Windsor | Sudbury and Thunder Bay | Winnipeg | Regina | Edmonton | Calgary | Vancouver | Victoria |
|---|---|---|---|---|---|---|---|---|---|---|---|---|---|---|---|---|---|---|---|
| **24. Black/Caribbean origins** | | | | | | | | | | | | | | | | | | | |
| Younger Generation (1-35 Years Old) | 6.373 | 8.529 | 6.746 | 6.000 | 7.730 | 7.700 | 7.238 | 7.656 | 7.500 | 7.361 | 7.800 | 7.537 | 7.429 | 7.250 | 7.375 | 7.179 | 7.268 | 7.662 | 7.400 |
| Older Generation (35+ Years Old) | 5.256 | 8.615 | 6.425 | 9.625 | 7.320 | 6.930 | 6.807 | 7.274 | 6.389 | 7.371 | 7.100 | 6.857 | 4.875 | 7.413 | 7.727 | 7.578 | 7.531 | 7.351 | 7.667 |
| **25. Aboriginal** | | | | | | | | | | | | | | | | | | | |
| Younger Generation (1-35 Years Old) | 6.091 | 6.971 | 7.243 | 7.381 | 7.342 | 5.818 | 6.625 | 5.963 | 7.077 | 7.000 | 6.238 | 6.667 | 6.347 | 5.907 | 5.491 | 6.158 | 5.810 | 6.367 | 5.938 |
| Older Generation (35+ Years Old) | 9.000 | 6.333 | 5.320 | 5.636 | 5.610 | 9.000 | 5.946 | 5.938 | 5.381 | 6.000 | 5.357 | 5.000 | 5.093 | 4.811 | 5.431 | 6.283 | 5.367 | 5.955 | 6.087 |
| **26. Canadian** | | | | | | | | | | | | | | | | | | | |
| Younger Generation (1-35 Years Old) | 7.861 | 7.267 | 7.082 | 7.200 | 7.768 | 6.990 | 7.376 | 7.269 | 7.207 | 7.213 | 7.733 | 7.800 | 7.487 | 7.344 | 7.553 | 7.362 | 7.347 | 7.158 | 6.889 |
| Older Generation (35+ Years Old) | 5.731 | 7.444 | 5.396 | 6.111 | 7.295 | 6.634 | 6.936 | 6.699 | 6.402 | 6.427 | 6.532 | 6.483 | 6.977 | 6.991 | 6.927 | 7.266 | 7.077 | 6.948 | 7.080 |

Maximum Value = 10.000 Maximum Value = 5.9988
Minimum Value = 1.667 Minimum Value = 0.1667

**APPENDIX 6**

PROPORTION OF ETHNIC POPULATION BY GENERATION AND MAJOR SOURCE OF INCOME FOR TWO GENERATIONS, ETHNIC GROUPS BY CITY, 1991

(Percent)

| City | Major Source of Income | British Younger Generation | British Older Generation | French Younger Generation | French Older Generation | German Younger Generation | German Older Generation | Black / Caribbean Younger Generation | Black / Caribbean Older Generation |
|---|---|---|---|---|---|---|---|---|---|
| Halifax | Investment, Government Transfers, and No Income | 24.5 | 39.4 | 30.4 | 41.4 | 40.5 | 41.9 | 55.1 | 53.8 |
| | Wages, Salaries, and Self-Employment | 75.5 | 60.6 | 69.6 | 58.6 | 59.5 | 58.1 | 44.9 | 46.2 |
| Quebec | Investment, Government Transfers, and No Income | 26.1 | 43.3 | 20.0 | 41.1 | 21.4 | 56.5 | 52.8 | 58.3 |
| | Wages, Salaries, and Self-Employment | 73.9 | 56.7 | 80.0 | 58.9 | 78.6 | 43.5 | 47.2 | 41.7 |
| Montreal | Investment, Government Transfers, and No Income | 28.9 | 52.2 | 22.7 | 43.5 | 25.8 | 48.1 | 45.1 | 43.5 |
| | Wages, Salaries, and Self-Employment | 71.1 | 47.8 | 77.3 | 56.5 | 74.2 | 51.9 | 54.9 | 56.5 |
| Sherbrooke and Trois-Rivières | Investment, Government Transfers, and No Income | 25.8 | 56.0 | 24.9 | 46.7 | 14.3 | 54.5 | 75.0 | 37.5 |
| | Wages, Salaries, and Self-Employment | 74.2 | 44.0 | 75.1 | 53.3 | 85.7 | 45.5 | 25.0 | 62.5 |
| Ottawa-Hull | Investment, Government Transfers, and No Income | 26.2 | 43.7 | 21.8 | 40.5 | 27.2 | 37.0 | 36.9 | 32.8 |
| | Wages, Salaries, and Self-Employment | 73.8 | 56.3 | 78.2 | 59.5 | 72.8 | 63.0 | 63.1 | 67.2 |
| Oshawa | Investment, Government Transfers, and No Income | 18.2 | 41.7 | 23.2 | 22.5 | 27.8 | 24.6 | 12.7 | 16.7 |
| | Wages, Salaries, and Self-Employment | 81.8 | 58.3 | 76.8 | 77.5 | 72.2 | 75.4 | 87.3 | 83.3 |
| Toronto | Investment, Government Transfers, and No Income | 24.0 | 44.6 | 38.2 | 37.9 | 27.9 | 38.7 | 33.1 | 30.9 |
| | Wages, Salaries, and Self-Employment | 76.0 | 55.4 | 61.8 | 62.1 | 72.1 | 61.3 | 66.9 | 69.1 |
| Hamilton | Investment, Government Transfers, and No Income | 22.7 | 44.6 | 22.3 | 42.1 | 27.7 | 39.8 | 18.1 | 24.6 |
| | Wages, Salaries, and Self-Employment | 77.3 | 55.4 | 77.7 | 57.9 | 72.3 | 60.2 | 81.9 | 75.4 |
| St. Catharines-Niagara | Investment, Government Transfers, and No Income | 22.2 | 48.1 | 27.4 | 49.3 | 28.2 | 47.9 | 31.3 | 23.5 |
| | Wages, Salaries, and Self-Employment | 77.8 | 51.9 | 72.6 | 50.7 | 71.8 | 52.1 | 68.8 | 76.5 |
| Kitchener | Investment, Government Transfers, and No Income | 19.9 | 42.0 | 30.8 | 32.7 | 14.8 | 45.5 | 38.7 | 16.1 |
| | Wages, Salaries, and Self-Employment | 80.1 | 58.0 | 69.2 | 67.3 | 85.2 | 54.5 | 61.3 | 83.9 |
| London | Investment, Government Transfers, and No Income | 23.3 | 46.8 | 36.5 | 37.3 | 27.1 | 41.3 | 40.4 | 26.3 |
| | Wages, Salaries, and Self-Employment | 76.7 | 53.2 | 63.5 | 62.7 | 72.9 | 58.7 | 59.6 | 73.7 |
| Windsor | Investment, Government Transfers, and No Income | 23.2 | 50.8 | 20.8 | 42.1 | 32.8 | 52.4 | 55.0 | 52.4 |
| | Wages, Salaries, and Self-Employment | 76.8 | 49.2 | 79.2 | 57.9 | 67.2 | 47.6 | 45.0 | 47.6 |
| Sudbury and Thunder Bay | Investment, Government Transfers, and No Income | 25.6 | 48.4 | 24.8 | 40.4 | 29.2 | 43.0 | 30.0 | 37.5 |
| | Wages, Salaries, and Self-Employment | 74.4 | 51.6 | 75.2 | 59.6 | 70.8 | 57.0 | 70.0 | 62.5 |

**APPENDIX 6** (continued)

**PROPORTION OF ETHNIC POPULATION BY GENERATION AND MAJOR SOURCE OF INCOME FOR TWO GENERATIONS, ETHNIC GROUPS BY CITY, 1991**

| City / Major Source of Income | British | | French | | German | | Black / Caribbean | |
|---|---|---|---|---|---|---|---|---|
| | Younger Generation | Older Generation | Younger Generation | Older Generation | Younger Generation | Older Generation | Younger Generation | Older Generation |
| | | | | Percent | | | | |
| **Winnipeg** | | | | | | | | |
| Investment, Government Transfers, and No Income | 24.0 | 52.3 | 23.7 | 42.1 | 26.0 | 42.4 | 37.8 | 28.8 |
| Wages, Salaries, and Self-Employment | 76.0 | 47.7 | 76.3 | 57.9 | 74.0 | 57.6 | 62.2 | 71.2 |
| **Regina and Saskatoon** | | | | | | | | |
| Investment, Government Transfers, and No Income | 22.3 | 50.4 | 30.8 | 54.0 | 23.8 | 45.4 | 20.0 | |
| Wages, Salaries, and Self-Employment | 77.7 | 49.6 | 69.2 | 46.0 | 76.2 | 54.6 | 80.0 | 100.0 |
| **Calgary** | | | | | | | | |
| Investment, Government Transfers, and No Income | 24.6 | 41.4 | 34.0 | 31.6 | 32.3 | 39.4 | 40.7 | 33.3 |
| Wages, Salaries, and Self-Employment | 75.4 | 58.6 | 66.0 | 68.4 | 67.7 | 60.6 | 59.3 | 66.7 |
| **Edmonton** | | | | | | | | |
| Investment, Government Transfers, and No Income | 25.4 | 44.0 | 30.4 | 41.6 | 24.2 | 38.5 | 43.8 | 37.0 |
| Wages, Salaries, and Self-Employment | 74.6 | 56.0 | 69.6 | 58.4 | 75.8 | 61.5 | 56.3 | 63.0 |
| **Vancouver** | | | | | | | | |
| Investment, Government Transfers, and No Income | 25.8 | 51.1 | 38.8 | 47.0 | 31.4 | 44.3 | 40.5 | 36.0 |
| Wages, Salaries, and Self-Employment | 74.2 | 48.9 | 61.2 | 53.0 | 68.6 | 55.7 | 59.5 | 64.0 |
| **Victoria** | | | | | | | | |
| Investment, Government Transfers, and No Income | 29.2 | 60.2 | 34.7 | 55.7 | 45.7 | 59.1 | 66.7 | 16.7 |
| Wages, Salaries, and Self-Employment | 70.8 | 39.8 | 65.3 | 44.3 | 54.3 | 40.9 | 33.3 | 83.3 |

**APPENDIX 6** (continued)

**PROPORTION OF ETHNIC POPULATION BY GENERATION AND MAJOR SOURCE OF INCOME FOR TWO GENERATIONS, ETHNIC GROUPS BY CITY, 1991**

Percent

| City | Major Source of Income | Greek Younger Generation | Greek Older Generation | Italian Younger Generation | Italian Older Generation | Portuguese Younger Generation | Portuguese Older Generation | Spanish Younger Generation | Spanish Older Generation |
|---|---|---|---|---|---|---|---|---|---|
| **Halifax** | Investment, Government Transfers, and No Income | | | | | | | | |
| | Wages, Salaries, and Self-Employment | | | | | | | | |
| **Quebec** | Investment, Government Transfers, and No Income | 20.0 | 57.1 | 21.7 | 33.3 | 18.2 | 42.9 | 66.7 | 63.6 |
| | Wages, Salaries, and Self-Employment | 80.0 | 42.9 | 78.3 | 66.7 | 81.8 | 57.1 | 33.3 | 36.4 |
| **Montreal** | Investment, Government Transfers, and No Income | 17.4 | 33.9 | 14.4 | 35.4 | 17.9 | 27.8 | 41.5 | 36.0 |
| | Wages, Salaries, and Self-Employment | 82.6 | 66.1 | 85.6 | 64.6 | 82.1 | 72.2 | 58.5 | 64.0 |
| **Sherbrooke and Trois-Rivières** | Investment, Government Transfers, and No Income | 100.0 | | 44.4 | 38.5 | 50.0 | 28.6 | 25.0 | 100.0 |
| | Wages, Salaries, and Self-Employment | | 100.0 | 55.6 | 61.5 | 50.0 | 71.4 | 75.0 | |
| **Ottawa-Hull** | Investment, Government Transfers, and No Income | 27.6 | 31.7 | 17.2 | 38.3 | 19.3 | 22.6 | 65.1 | 34.6 |
| | Wages, Salaries, and Self-Employment | 72.4 | 68.3 | 82.8 | 61.7 | 80.7 | 77.4 | 34.9 | 65.4 |
| **Oshawa** | Investment, Government Transfers, and No Income | 11.1 | 38.5 | 7.4 | 26.3 | 15.4 | 12.5 | 14.3 | |
| | Wages, Salaries, and Self-Employment | 88.9 | 61.5 | 92.6 | 73.7 | 84.6 | 87.5 | 85.7 | 100.0 |
| **Toronto** | Investment, Government Transfers, and No Income | 14.2 | 28.5 | 11.4 | 28.2 | 13.0 | 25.5 | 31.9 | 29.8 |
| | Wages, Salaries, and Self-Employment | 85.8 | 71.5 | 88.6 | 71.8 | 87.0 | 74.5 | 68.1 | 70.2 |
| **Hamilton** | Investment, Government Transfers, and No Income | 12.5 | 42.3 | 11.5 | 38.2 | 14.0 | 32.0 | 22.0 | 25.0 |
| | Wages, Salaries, and Self-Employment | 87.5 | 57.7 | 88.5 | 61.8 | 86.0 | 68.0 | 78.0 | 75.0 |
| **St. Catharines-Niagara** | Investment, Government Transfers, and No Income | 8.3 | 33.3 | 15.0 | 37.5 | 50.0 | | 46.2 | |
| | Wages, Salaries, and Self-Employment | 91.7 | 66.7 | 85.0 | 62.5 | 50.0 | 100.0 | 53.8 | |
| **Kitchener** | Investment, Government Transfers, and No Income | 12.5 | 40.0 | 11.9 | 31.9 | 18.4 | 29.3 | 17.2 | 18.2 |
| | Wages, Salaries, and Self-Employment | 87.5 | 60.0 | 88.1 | 68.1 | 81.6 | 70.7 | 82.8 | 81.8 |
| **London** | Investment, Government Transfers, and No Income | 18.8 | 22.0 | 29.9 | 42.1 | 16.7 | 16.7 | 53.8 | 20.0 |
| | Wages, Salaries, and Self-Employment | 81.3 | 78.0 | 70.1 | 57.9 | 83.3 | 83.3 | 46.2 | 80.0 |
| **Windsor** | Investment, Government Transfers, and No Income | 12.1 | 35.0 | 9.6 | 37.9 | 14.3 | 25.0 | 44.4 | 37.5 |
| | Wages, Salaries, and Self-Employment | 87.9 | 65.0 | 90.4 | 62.1 | 85.7 | 75.0 | 55.6 | 62.5 |
| **Sudbury and Thunder Bay** | Investment, Government Transfers, and No Income | 30.0 | 45.5 | 13.8 | 44.6 | 19.0 | 18.2 | 42.9 | 100.0 |
| | Wages, Salaries, and Self-Employment | 70.0 | 54.5 | 86.2 | 55.4 | 81.0 | 81.8 | 57.1 | |

**APPENDIX 6** (continued)

**PROPORTION OF ETHNIC POPULATION BY GENERATION AND MAJOR SOURCE OF INCOME FOR TWO GENERATIONS, ETHNIC GROUPS BY CITY, 1991**

| City / Major Source of Income | Greek | | Italian | | Portuguese | | Spanish | |
|---|---|---|---|---|---|---|---|---|
| | Younger Generation | Older Generation | Younger Generation | Older Generation | Younger Generation | Older Generation | Younger Generation | Older Generation |
| | | | | | Percent | | | |
| **Winnipeg** | | | | | | | | |
| Investment, Government Transfers, and No Income | 13.2 | 39.3 | 18.4 | 38.6 | 11.3 | 20.2 | 25.6 | 23.5 |
| Wages, Salaries, and Self-Employment | 86.8 | 60.7 | 81.6 | 61.4 | 88.7 | 79.8 | 74.4 | 76.5 |
| **Regina and Saskatoon** | | | | | | | | |
| Investment, Government Transfers, and No Income | 12.5 | 16.7 | 12.5 | 14.3 | 11.1 | 50.0 | 18.2 | 83.3 |
| Wages, Salaries, and Self-Employment | 87.5 | 83.3 | 87.5 | 85.7 | 88.9 | 50.0 | 81.8 | 16.7 |
| **Calgary** | | | | | | | | |
| Investment, Government Transfers, and No Income | 20.0 | 25.0 | 18.7 | 32.6 | 27.6 | 10.5 | 36.1 | 37.5 |
| Wages, Salaries, and Self-Employment | 80.0 | 75.0 | 81.3 | 67.4 | 72.4 | 89.5 | 63.9 | 62.5 |
| **Edmonton** | | | | | | | | |
| Investment, Government Transfers, and No Income | 46.7 | 35.0 | 15.1 | 34.0 | 28.6 | 22.6 | 29.7 | 40.9 |
| Wages, Salaries, and Self-Employment | 53.3 | 65.0 | 84.9 | 66.0 | 71.4 | 77.4 | 70.3 | 59.1 |
| **Vancouver** | | | | | | | | |
| Investment, Government Transfers, and No Income | 19.6 | 33.7 | 21.2 | 39.5 | 19.5 | 24.5 | 53.2 | 43.1 |
| Wages, Salaries, and Self-Employment | 80.4 | 66.3 | 78.8 | 60.5 | 80.5 | 75.5 | 46.8 | 56.9 |
| **Victoria** | | | | | | | | |
| Investment, Government Transfers, and No Income | 25.0 | 50.0 | 33.3 | 40.6 | 26.1 | 30.0 | 20.0 | 28.6 |
| Wages, Salaries, and Self-Employment | 75.0 | 50.0 | 66.7 | 59.4 | 73.9 | 70.0 | 80.0 | 71.4 |

APPENDIX 6 (continued)

PROPORTION OF ETHNIC POPULATION BY GENERATION AND MAJOR SOURCE OF INCOME FOR TWO GENERATIONS, ETHNIC GROUPS BY CITY, 1991

| City | Major Source of Income | Jewish | | Other European | | Arab origins | | West Asian origins | |
|---|---|---|---|---|---|---|---|---|---|
| | | Younger Generation | Older Generation | Younger Generation | Older Generation | Younger Generation | Older Generation | Younger Generation | Older Generation |
| | | | | | Percent | | | | |
| **Halifax** | Investment, Government Transfers, and No Income | | | | | | | | |
| | Wages, Salaries, and Self-Employment | | | | | | | | |
| **Quebec** | Investment, Government Transfers, and No Income | | 50.0 | 23.1 | 30.8 | 75.9 | 38.5 | 75.0 | 25.0 |
| | Wages, Salaries, and Self-Employment | | 50.0 | 76.9 | 69.2 | 24.1 | 61.5 | 25.0 | 75.0 |
| **Montreal** | Investment, Government Transfers, and No Income | 21.8 | 50.3 | 34.9 | 51.1 | 45.0 | 41.3 | 35.3 | 41.1 |
| | Wages, Salaries, and Self-Employment | 78.2 | 49.7 | 65.1 | 48.9 | 55.0 | 58.7 | 64.7 | 58.9 |
| **Sherbrooke and Trois-Rivières** | Investmen, Government Transfers, and No Income | 50.0 | | | 22.2 | 20.0 | 44.4 | | |
| | Wages, Salaries, and Self-Employment | 50.0 | 100.0 | 100.0 | 77.8 | 80.0 | 55.6 | 100.0 | 100.0 |
| **Ottawa-Hull** | Investment, Government Transfers, and No Income | 22.0 | 40.2 | 32.0 | 38.5 | 33.2 | 36.8 | 49.3 | 26.3 |
| | Wages, Salaries, and Self-Employment | 78.0 | 59.8 | 68.0 | 61.5 | 66.8 | 63.2 | 50.7 | 73.7 |
| **Oshawa** | Investment, Government Transfers, and No Income | | | 25.9 | 42.1 | | | 42.9 | 60.0 |
| | Wages, Salaries, and Self-Employment | | 100.0 | 74.1 | 57.9 | | 100.0 | 57.1 | 40.0 |
| **Toronto** | Investment, Government Transfers, and No Income | 17.7 | 41.9 | 22.1 | 43.0 | 29.1 | 32.0 | 44.2 | 40.4 |
| | Wages, Salaries, and Self-Employment | 82.3 | 58.1 | 77.9 | 57.0 | 70.9 | 68.0 | 55.8 | 59.6 |
| **Hamilton** | Investment, Government Transfers, and No Income | 9.8 | 39.3 | 32.4 | 56.5 | 46.8 | 51.7 | 38.5 | 31.6 |
| | Wages, Salaries, and Self-Employment | 90.2 | 60.7 | 67.6 | 43.5 | 53.2 | 48.3 | 61.5 | 68.4 |
| **St. Catharines-Niagara** | Investment, Government Transfers, and No Income | 57.1 | 44.4 | 20.6 | 48.8 | 25.0 | 50.0 | 14.3 | 27.3 |
| | Wages, Salaries, and Self-Employment | 42.9 | 55.6 | 79.4 | 51.2 | 75.0 | 50.0 | 85.7 | 72.7 |
| **Kitchener** | Investment, Government Transfers, and No Income | 75.0 | 33.3 | 23.9 | 37.2 | 55.0 | 42.9 | 23.8 | 55.6 |
| | Wages, Salaries, and Self-Employment | 25.0 | 66.7 | 76.1 | 62.8 | 45.0 | 57.1 | 76.2 | 44.4 |
| **London** | Investment, Government Transfers, and No Income | 27.3 | 53.8 | 30.0 | 38.9 | 45.9 | 44.8 | 44.4 | 20.0 |
| | Wages, Salaries, and Self-Employment | 72.7 | 46.2 | 70.0 | 61.1 | 54.1 | 55.2 | 55.6 | 80.0 |
| **Windsor** | Investment, Government Transfers, and No Income | 31.3 | 42.9 | 22.4 | 58.4 | 50.0 | 51.3 | 33.3 | 27.3 |
| | Wages, Salaries, and Self-Employment | 68.8 | 57.1 | 77.6 | 41.6 | 50.0 | 48.7 | 66.7 | 72.7 |
| **Sudbury and Thunder Bay** | Investment, Government Transfers, and No Income | 25.0 | | 21.3 | 55.2 | | | 40.0 | |
| | Wages, Salaries, and Self-Employment | 75.0 | 100.0 | 78.7 | 44.8 | | 100.0 | 60.0 | 100.0 |

APPENDIX 6 (continued)

PROPORTION OF ETHNIC POPULATION BY GENERATION AND MAJOR SOURCE OF INCOME FOR TWO GENERATIONS, ETHNIC GROUPS BY CITY, 1991

| City / Major Source of Income | Jewish Younger Generation | Jewish Older Generation | Other European Younger Generation | Other European Older Generation | Arab origins Younger Generation | Arab origins Older Generation | West Asian origins Younger Generation | West Asian origins Older Generation |
|---|---|---|---|---|---|---|---|---|
| | | | | | Percent | | | |
| **Winnipeg** | | | | | | | | |
| Investment, Government Transfers, and No Income | 11.6 | 50.5 | 25.0 | 53.8 | 7.7 | 33.3 | 47.6 | 27.3 |
| Wages, Salaries, and Self-Employment | 88.4 | 49.5 | 75.0 | 46.2 | 92.3 | 66.7 | 52.4 | 72.7 |
| **Regina and Saskatoon** | | | | | | | | |
| Investment, Government Transfers, and No Income | 33.3 | 42.9 | 25.6 | 52.5 | | 37.5 | 33.3 | 100.0 |
| Wages, Salaries, and Self-Employment | 66.7 | 57.1 | 74.4 | 47.5 | 100.0 | 62.5 | 66.7 | |
| **Calgary** | | | | | | | | |
| Investment, Government Transfers, and No Income | 16.1 | 50.9 | 31.1 | 47.6 | 40.6 | 36.8 | 51.9 | 38.9 |
| Wages, Salaries, and Self-Employment | 83.9 | 49.1 | 68.9 | 52.4 | 59.4 | 63.2 | 48.1 | 61.1 |
| **Edmonton** | | | | | | | | |
| Investment, Government Transfers, and No Income | 23.4 | 41.0 | 24.2 | 42.7 | 34.3 | 34.6 | 35.7 | 14.3 |
| Wages, Salaries, and Self-Employment | 76.6 | 59.0 | 75.8 | 57.3 | 65.7 | 65.4 | 64.3 | 85.7 |
| **Vancouver** | | | | | | | | |
| Investment, Government Transfers, and No Income | 25.2 | 46.9 | 25.3 | 52.0 | 46.7 | 28.6 | 45.5 | 54.5 |
| Wages, Salaries, and Self-Employment | 74.8 | 53.1 | 74.7 | 48.0 | 53.3 | 71.4 | 54.5 | 45.5 |
| **Victoria** | | | | | | | | |
| Investment, Government Transfers, and No Income | 33.3 | 57.1 | 40.0 | 55.7 | 100.0 | 60.0 | 20.0 | 20.0 |
| Wages, Salaries, and Self-Employment | 66.7 | 42.9 | 60.0 | 44.3 | | 40.0 | 80.0 | 80.0 |

APPENDIX 6 (continued)

PROPORTION OF ETHNIC POPULATION BY GENERATION AND MAJOR SOURCE OF INCOME FOR TWO GENERATIONS, ETHNIC GROUPS BY CITY, 1991

(Percent)

| City | Major Source of Income | South Asian origins — Younger Generation | South Asian origins — Older Generation | Chinese — Younger Generation | Chinese — Older Generation | Filipino — Younger Generation | Filipino — Older Generation | Vietnamese — Younger Generation | Vietnamese — Older Generation |
|---|---|---|---|---|---|---|---|---|---|
| **Halifax** | Investment, Government Transfers, and No Income | | | | | | | | |
| | Wages, Salaries, and Self-Employment | | | | | | | | |
| **Quebec** | Investment, Government Transfers, and No Income | 50.0 | 50.0 | 45.5 | 100.0 | 100.0 | | 41.2 | 36.4 |
| | Wages, Salaries, and Self-Employment | 50.0 | 50.0 | 54.5 | | | | 58.8 | 63.6 |
| **Montreal** | Investment, Government Transfers, and No Income | 38.0 | 36.4 | 31.7 | 39.1 | 44.1 | 52.2 | 31.1 | 40.6 |
| | Wages, Salaries, and Self-Employment | 62.0 | 63.6 | 68.3 | 60.9 | 55.9 | 47.8 | 68.9 | 59.4 |
| **Sherbrooke and Trois-Rivières** | Investment, Government Transfers, and No Income | 100.0 | 100.0 | 50.0 | 75.0 | | | 33.3 | 60.0 |
| | Wages, Salaries, and Self-Employment | | | 50.0 | 25.0 | | | 66.7 | 40.0 |
| **Ottawa-Hull** | Investment, Government Transfers, and No Income | 17.6 | 12.8 | 29.7 | 29.7 | 31.3 | 24.1 | 47.6 | 31.4 |
| | Wages, Salaries, and Self-Employment | 82.4 | 87.2 | 70.3 | 70.3 | 68.8 | 75.9 | 52.4 | 68.6 |
| **Oshawa** | Investment, Government Transfers, and No Income | 3.6 | 28.6 | 16.2 | 20.0 | 12.5 | 22.2 | | |
| | Wages, Salaries, and Self-Employment | 96.4 | 71.4 | 83.8 | 80.0 | 87.5 | 77.8 | | |
| **Toronto** | Investment, Government Transfers, and No Income | 21.5 | 26.1 | 25.5 | 33.1 | 29.3 | 30.7 | 48.5 | 42.2 |
| | Wages, Salaries, and Self-Employment | 78.5 | 73.9 | 74.5 | 66.9 | 70.7 | 69.3 | 51.5 | 57.8 |
| **Hamilton** | Investment, Government Transfers, and No Income | 12.5 | 18.2 | 23.2 | 26.9 | 34.2 | 39.5 | 58.5 | 50.0 |
| | Wages, Salaries, and Self-Employment | 87.5 | 81.8 | 76.8 | 73.1 | 65.8 | 60.5 | 41.5 | 50.0 |
| **St. Catharines-Niagara** | Investment, Government Transfers, and No Income | 26.7 | 33.3 | 15.4 | 15.4 | 22.2 | 23.1 | 100.0 | 100.0 |
| | Wages, Salaries, and Self-Employment | 73.3 | 66.7 | 84.6 | 84.6 | 77.8 | 76.9 | | |
| **Kitchener** | Investment, Government Transfers, and No Income | 19.4 | 23.3 | 34.8 | 20.7 | 14.3 | 12.5 | 35.7 | 55.6 |
| | Wages, Salaries, and Self-Employment | 80.6 | 76.7 | 65.2 | 79.3 | 85.7 | 87.5 | 64.3 | 44.4 |
| **London** | Investment, Government Transfers, and No Income | 27.4 | 22.0 | 28.6 | 14.3 | 30.0 | 20.0 | 57.9 | 25.0 |
| | Wages, Salaries, and Self-Employment | 72.6 | 78.0 | 71.4 | 85.7 | 70.0 | 80.0 | 42.1 | 75.0 |
| **Windsor** | Investment, Government Transfers, and No Income | 38.9 | 55.0 | 39.0 | 33.3 | 28.0 | 36.8 | 13.0 | 100.0 |
| | Wages, Salaries, and Self-Employment | 61.1 | 45.0 | 61.0 | 66.7 | 72.0 | 63.2 | 87.0 | |
| **Sudbury and Thunder Bay** | Investment, Government Transfers, and No Income | 11.1 | 15.4 | 14.3 | 31.3 | 100.0 | 100.0 | 87.5 | 50.0 |
| | Wages, Salaries, and Self-Employment | 88.9 | 84.6 | 85.7 | 68.8 | | | 12.5 | 50.0 |

**APPENDIX 6** (continued)

**PROPORTION OF ETHNIC POPULATION BY GENERATION AND MAJOR SOURCE OF INCOME FOR TWO GENERATIONS, ETHNIC GROUPS BY CITY, 1991**

Percent

| City / Major Source of Income | South Asian origins Younger Generation | South Asian origins Older Generation | Chinese Younger Generation | Chinese Older Generation | Filipino Younger Generation | Filipino Older Generation | Vietnamese Younger Generation | Vietnamese Older Generation |
|---|---|---|---|---|---|---|---|---|
| **Winnipeg** | | | | | | | | |
| Investment, Government Transfers, and No Income | 17.0 | 28.4 | 30.7 | 33.7 | 18.1 | 23.6 | 40.3 | 26.1 |
| Wages, Salaries, and Self-Employment | 83.0 | 71.6 | 69.3 | 66.3 | 81.9 | 76.4 | 59.7 | 73.9 |
| **Regina and Saskatoon** | | | | | | | | |
| Investment, Government Transfers, and No Income | 35.5 | 28.6 | 28.7 | 41.9 | 23.8 | 26.7 | 15.2 | 42.9 |
| Wages, Salaries, and Self-Employment | 64.5 | 71.4 | 71.3 | 58.1 | 76.2 | 73.3 | 84.8 | 57.1 |
| **Calgary** | | | | | | | | |
| Investment, Government Transfers, and No Income | 19.1 | 24.5 | 22.7 | 34.5 | 24.8 | 31.4 | 32.1 | 32.1 |
| Wages, Salaries, and Self-Employment | 80.9 | 75.5 | 77.3 | 65.5 | 75.2 | 68.6 | 67.9 | 67.9 |
| **Edmonton** | | | | | | | | |
| Investment, Government Transfers, and No Income | 19.3 | 30.7 | 24.3 | 33.1 | 25.8 | 34.5 | 45.1 | 40.0 |
| Wages, Salaries, and Self-Employment | 80.7 | 69.3 | 75.7 | 66.9 | 74.2 | 65.5 | 54.9 | 60.0 |
| **Vancouver** | | | | | | | | |
| Investment, Government Transfers, and No Income | 15.7 | 30.2 | 26.5 | 36.9 | 29.3 | 29.8 | 46.1 | 55.9 |
| Wages, Salaries, and Self-Employment | 84.3 | 69.8 | 73.5 | 63.1 | 70.7 | 70.2 | 53.9 | 44.1 |
| **Victoria** | | | | | | | | |
| Investment, Government Transfers, and No Income | 18.5 | 33.3 | 20.4 | 44.6 | 26.3 | 40.0 | 37.5 | |
| Wages, Salaries, and Self-Employment | 81.5 | 66.7 | 79.6 | 55.4 | 73.7 | 60.0 | 62.5 | 100.0 |

**APPENDIX 6** (concluded)

**PROPORTION OF ETHNIC POPULATION BY GENERATION AND MAJOR SOURCE OF INCOME FOR TWO GENERATIONS, ETHNIC GROUPS BY CITY, 1991**

Percent

| City | Major Source of Income | Other East and South East Asian origins | | Latin, Central and South American origins | | Other single origins | |
|---|---|---|---|---|---|---|---|
| | | Younger Generation | Older Generation | Younger Generation | Older Generation | Younger Generation | Older Generation |
| Halifax | Investment, Government Transfers, and No Income | | | | | | |
| | Wages, Salaries, and Self-Employment | | | | | | |
| Quebec | Investment, Government Transfers, and No Income | 23.5 | 50.0 | 42.9 | 33.3 | 33.3 | 66.7 |
| | Wages, Salaries, and Self-Employment | 76.5 | 50.0 | 57.1 | 66.7 | 66.7 | 33.3 |
| Montreal | Investment, Government Transfers, and No Income | 30.7 | 38.4 | 48.0 | 45.0 | 53.2 | 52.9 |
| | Wages, Salaries, and Self-Employment | 69.3 | 61.6 | 52.0 | 55.0 | 46.8 | 47.1 |
| Sherbrooke and Trois-Rivières | Investment, Government Transfers, and No Income | 57.1 | 100.0 | 16.7 | 100.0 | 100.0 | 100.0 |
| | Wages, Salaries, and Self-Employment | 42.9 | | 83.3 | | | |
| Ottawa-Hull | Investment, Government Transfers, and No Income | 52.2 | 36.1 | 39.7 | 40.0 | 78.9 | 59.4 |
| | Wages, Salaries, and Self-Employment | 47.8 | 63.9 | 60.3 | 60.0 | 21.1 | 40.6 |
| Oshawa | Investment, Government Transfers, and No Income | 7.7 | 16.7 | 22.2 | 50.0 | 12.5 | 40.0 |
| | Wages, Salaries, and Self-Employment | 92.3 | 83.3 | 77.8 | 50.0 | 87.5 | 60.0 |
| Toronto | Investment, Government Transfers, and No Income | 25.5 | 34.3 | 35.7 | 33.6 | 54.5 | 42.0 |
| | Wages, Salaries, and Self-Employment | 74.5 | 65.7 | 64.3 | 66.4 | 45.5 | 58.0 |
| Hamilton | Investment, Government Transfers, and No Income | 43.9 | 55.3 | 41.2 | 27.3 | 60.0 | 100.0 |
| | Wages, Salaries, and Self-Employment | 56.1 | 44.7 | 58.8 | 72.7 | 40.0 | |
| St. Catharines-Niagara | Investment, Government Transfers, and No Income | 28.6 | 35.7 | | | 30.0 | 14.3 |
| | Wages, Salaries, and Self-Employment | 71.4 | 64.3 | 100.0 | | 70.0 | 85.7 |
| Kitchener | Investment, Government Transfers, and No Income | 28.2 | 23.5 | 51.9 | 20.0 | 20.0 | 66.7 |
| | Wages, Salaries, and Self-Employment | 71.8 | 76.5 | 48.1 | 80.0 | 80.0 | 33.3 |
| London | Investment, Government Transfers, and No Income | 15.6 | 48.4 | 38.5 | 28.6 | 60.0 | 50.0 |
| | Wages, Salaries, and Self-Employment | 84.4 | 51.6 | 61.5 | 71.4 | 40.0 | 50.0 |
| Windsor | Investment, Government Transfers, and No Income | 41.7 | 40.0 | 20.0 | 66.7 | 50.0 | 66.7 |
| | Wages, Salaries, and Self-Employment | 58.3 | 60.0 | 80.0 | 33.3 | 50.0 | 33.3 |
| Sudbury and Thunder Bay | Investment, Government Transfers, and No Income | 100.0 | 20.0 | 100.0 | 100.0 | 100.0 | 100.0 |
| | Wages, Salaries, and Self-Employment | | 80.0 | | | | |

**APPENDIX 6** (concluded)

**PROPORTION OF ETHNIC POPULATION BY GENERATION AND MAJOR SOURCE OF INCOME FOR TWO GENERATIONS, ETHNIC GROUPS BY CITY, 1991**

| City | Major Source of Income | Other East and South East Asian origins | | Latin, Central and South American origins | | Other single origins | |
|------|------------------------|:---:|:---:|:---:|:---:|:---:|:---:|
| | | Younger Generation | Older Generation | Younger Generation | Older Generation | Younger Generation | Older Generation |
| | | | | Percent | | | |
| **Winnipeg** | Investment, Government Transfers, and No Income | 23.1 | 45.0 | 38.3 | 28.0 | 63.6 | 62.5 |
| | Wages, Salaries, and Self-Employment | 76.9 | 55.0 | 61.7 | 72.0 | 36.4 | 37.5 |
| **Regina and Saskatoon** | Investment, Government Transfers, and No Income | 22.2 | | 28.0 | | 29.4 | 40.0 |
| | Wages, Salaries, and Self-Employment | 77.8 | 100.0 | 72.0 | 100.0 | 70.6 | 60.0 |
| **Calgary** | Investment, Government Transfers, and No Income | 36.4 | 31.4 | 19.6 | 24.3 | 38.6 | 48.5 |
| | Wages, Salaries, and Self-Employment | 63.6 | 68.6 | 80.4 | 75.7 | 61.4 | 51.5 |
| **Edmonton** | Investment, Government Transfers, and No Income | 29.4 | 26.4 | 33.9 | 21.4 | 34.0 | 45.2 |
| | Wages, Salaries, and Self-Employment | 70.6 | 73.6 | 66.1 | 78.6 | 66.0 | 54.8 |
| **Vancouver** | Investment, Government Transfers, and No Income | 28.8 | 30.9 | 43.5 | 29.7 | 25.7 | 33.3 |
| | Wages, Salaries, and Self-Employment | 71.2 | 69.1 | 56.5 | 70.3 | 74.3 | 66.7 |
| **Victoria** | Investment, Government Transfers, and No Income | 52.9 | 44.4 | 16.7 | 40.0 | 40.0 | 33.3 |
| | Wages, Salaries, and Self-Employment | 47.1 | 55.6 | 83.3 | 60.0 | 60.0 | 66.7 |